What people are

God Bless the Broken Bones

God Bless the Broken Bones won't tickle your ears with pleasant words. Instead what you'll find is a year of one man's seemingly uncensored thoughts, fears, frustrations, longings, gratitude, and self-exhortations. Raw yet eloquent, William Ferraiolo's musings reveal the daily challenges to living a life of equanimity and honor—and why there's no worthier goal. At times this book might offend you. It will certainly challenge you. And if you're willing, it might change you. I recommend you see for yourself. **Seth J. Gillihan, PhD**, clinical psychologist and author of *The CBT Deck, Cognitive Behavioral Therapy Made Simple* and *Retrain Your Brain: Cognitive Behavioral Therapy in 7 Weeks*

What emerges from *God Bless the Broken Bones* is a very human portrait of a single year, each page the intellectual record of one day. Trained philosopher Ferraiolo pivots from quotidian events to universal concepts nimbly, but this book is not for academics. It's for everyone who ever felt like life is a conversation between different parts of themselves. *God Bless the Broken Bones* puts one man's version of this dialogue on display. It offers answers then challenges those answers a few pages later. Ferraiolo is less concerned with the product of thought than its processes. His writing calls readers to examine their lives the same way. **David Stevens**, Associate Professor, Department of English, University of Richmond, author of *The Word Rides Again: Rereading the Frontier in American Fiction*

Equal parts bracing, discomfiting, and illuminating. A ringside seat to the author's worthy struggles to live the best of the Stoic and Cynic traditions in the modern world. If you're looking for feel-good platitudes, move along, but if ancient wisdom delivered with the immediacy of a palm heel strike sounds refreshing, this is what you've been looking for.

Robert Glenn, father, pilot, Navy veteran

Ferraiolo's book, *God Bless the Broken Bones*, is a welcome punch to the face, akin to that one from a friend who's willing to punch you in the face when you most deserve it, and we would do well to appreciate it each morning, yet even this is less than nothing compared to those who face genuine suffering every day of their lives. Highly recommended.

Brint Montgomery, PhD, professor at Southern Nazarene University, coauthor of *Relational Theology*

God Bless the Broken Bones

Meditations over One Botched,
Bungled, and Beautiful Year

God Bless
the Broken Bones

Meditations over One Botched, Bungled, and Beautiful Year

William Ferraiolo

BOOKS

Winchester, UK
Washington, USA

JOHN HUNT PUBLISHING

First published by O-Books, 2020
O-Books is an imprint of John Hunt Publishing Ltd., 3 East St., Alresford,
Hampshire SO24 9EE, UK
office@jhpbooks.com
www.johnhuntpublishing.com
www.o-books.com

For distributor details and how to order please visit the 'Ordering' section on our website.

ISBN: 978 1 78904 484 3
978 1 78904 485 0 (ebook)
Library of Congress Control Number: 2019949662

A CIP catalogue record for this book is available from the British Library.

Design: Stuart Davies

UK: Printed and bound by CPI Group (UK) Ltd, Croydon, CR0 4YY
US: Printed and bound by Thomson-Shore, 7300 West Joy Road, Dexter, MI 48130

We operate a distinctive and ethical publishing philosophy in
all areas of our business, from our global network of authors to
production and worldwide distribution.

Contents

Introduction   1

January   6
February   37
March   65
April   96
May   126
June   157
July   187
August   218
September   249
October   279
November   310
December   340

Other Books by this Author   371

In memory of Diogenes the Cynic—and his search for an honest man

There are people to thank, but most of them would probably prefer not to be associated with this book. Thanks again to the crew at John Hunt Publishing. Sorry about that, but you cannot escape responsibility. The book cover is a dead giveaway.

Introduction

If you find that you agree with all or most of the thoughts and opinions expressed in this book, please seek psychiatric care or neurological testing *immediately*, as there must be something very, *very* wrong with you. Even *the author* of this book regards many of the views presented herein to be shocking, repugnant, and unworthy of open utterance. So, the author *wrote them down* in order to avoid *saying them out loud*. You are holding a compendium of one year's worth of musings, deliberations, and ruminations emanating from a somewhat dysfunctional mind. Many of the reflections you will read here are manifestations of a dark and troubled psyche. The author *needs help*. Thus, the person responsible for the words you are reading composed this collection of meditations for much the same reason that a person suffering from constipation might take a laxative. There is, perhaps, no need to pursue the metaphor further.

Paying attention persistently, you can learn a lot about yourself over the course of a year. The world and your presence in it offer limitless possibilities for experience and for the enhancement of your understanding. Do not be surprised if some of that experience is a little, or *more* than a little, unpleasant or worrisome. It is entirely possible that you will break some bones (perhaps your own, perhaps not). Do not be surprised if you encounter a great deal of botched and bungled humanity (perhaps your own, perhaps not). All the while, be sure that you remain attentive to the opportunity to encounter the beautiful. The botched, the bungled, and the beautiful are just some of the ingredients that make up your life, or even just one year of it. You may decide that you wish to write down some of your observations along the way. It can be a very interesting and edifying project. This book is one person's attempt to sift through a year of meditating upon reality and a very small role in it.

There are other benefits to paying careful attention as well. You can, for example, learn how to identify deceit and dissimulation when politicians, advertisers, attorneys, and other professional prevaricators hurl it your way. You will notice *a lot* of that kind of thing. Paying attention to your life is not always so simple, nor is it always particularly pleasant. Distractions and challenges present themselves relentlessly, and some of what you encounter is bound to be unsettling. Indeed, the stumbling blocks and dangers to your character pop up many times per day. In addition to your own foibles and peccadilloes, you will encounter a ceaseless avalanche of human suffering and inadequacy everywhere you go. If you let it, the world, and all of the problems conjured into being by its populace, will get under your skin and annoy the hell out of you. The whole thing can drive you clear around the bend. Evidently, the human struggle never ends—except, maybe, when you *die*. After a lifetime of toil and trouble, you get to drop dead. There it is. All *true* stories end that way. *Death.* Perhaps there is life *after* death, but there clearly *is* bodily death. You have *seen* dead bodies, have you not? At the moment, however, you are alive. Do you know how much time you have left? That information is difficult to come by. If you are ever informed about how much time you have left by, for example, a physician, it is probably because the end is nigh. So, in *your* case, *how* nigh is it? You probably have no idea. So? What are you going to do about *that*? You *are* here, breathing in and out, and reading these words right now. Your past is gone. You can do nothing about what you have done or what you have left irreparably undone. Obsessing about the past, or about how things might have gone, is fairly pointless unless you can apply some of the lessons you have learned to *future* events. Are you willing to do what is necessary to improve yourself and make progress? Do you have the capacity to be mercilessly honest about who and what you are, what your circumstances may be, and what limitations are inherent and ineradicable elements of the human condition as you exemplify it? In other words, are you prepared to stop bullshitting yourself? Are you prepared to call out the pretense and nonsense that saturates your culture? Are you prepared for the *truth* whatever the truth may be? If not, put this book back where you found it. Go back to your life of comforting lies and illusions. The author did not write this book for liars, pathetic weaklings, or perpetual adolescents who masquerade as adults. What you read here may serve, metaphorically, as a backhand to your face, or a body shot to your liver or solar plexus. If you really think that you do not *need* a rhetorical beat down, you are free to pick up a romance novel or watch a game show. Go smoke a joint. If, on the other hand, you are prepared for some rigorous *mental exercise*, then keep reading.

Your life *has* a purpose. It may not be evident to you at the moment, but that purpose awaits your discovery. You can embrace that purpose, pursue it as best you are able, and die knowing that you have done your *best*, or you can allow yourself to drift aimlessly through a life that seems meaningless and empty. What is your preference? Choose purpose or choose the abyss of purposelessness. If you prefer the former, this book should suit you. If you prefer the latter, perhaps this book may amuse a cynical or nihilistic streak in you, or it might provide you with a bit of pointless diversion. That *is* pathetic, but maybe that is also the best you can manage. This book is the best that the author could manage. Perhaps the *author* is pathetic. This *has* been suggested on more than one occasion. In any event, read on. Give it a try. The author hopes that doing so will prove worthy of your time and effort. There are, of course, no *guarantees* about that. There are no guarantees that you will live long enough to *complete* the book. That is just one disquieting facet of the human condition. Tomorrow is promised to *no one*. Death stalks you as it stalks us all. Perhaps that realization may lend a bit of urgency to your search for purpose, meaning, and the possibility of a flourishing life. Perhaps it will not. You have choices lying before you. Perhaps you ultimately *are* the choices that you make. This *could* be interesting. The author wishes you good luck. That, and a few dollars, will get you a cappuccino at Starbucks. The author has only *words* to offer you. Keep reading.

One Year

January 1

Do not indulge in the ridiculous practice of making New Year's resolutions. You either have the willpower to resolve that you must change some behavior or you do not. Attaching your decision to the entirely arbitrary construct of the "new year" will *not* endow you with heretofore-unrealized fortitude. Perhaps the calendar's most consistent value is reminding you of the tiny bits of artificial nonsense to which you tacitly accede each day. There is precisely *nothing* in the natural world that requires the "first day of the year" to occur on any particular day. One revolution around the sun, oversimplified as that description may be, is indicative of the position of this planet relative to the nearest star and, apart from astronomical considerations, or correlation with the "four seasons" (another construct — why not *six*?), it is not entirely clear what is crucial about moving from "here" to "there" one more time (especially given that the entire solar system is hurtling through space). Indeed, this planet is *nowhere near* where it was at this time last year. Our sun is traveling at terrific speed and pulling the rest of the solar system along with it. On this day, the "first day of the year," however, it is evidently crucial that a lot of people need to be nursing hangovers and failing to adhere to their "resolutions." Happy New Year! Bah. Do not participate in some sham holiday just because it is common practice among the masses. Do you feel compelled to think like everyone around you? That is, at best, a recipe for mediocrity and a life so very *ordinary*. Are you aiming to be ordinary? Celebrate your fortitude on *every* day, or on *none* of them. A day is a day is a day.

January 2

How often do you find yourself consciously *performing* rather than simply conducting yourself in accordance with your natural proclivities and your honest inclinations? You are a *person*, but you sometimes notice yourself becoming a *persona* or playing a character—perhaps a *caricature* of yourself. In other words, you sometimes catch yourself being full of shit. Is that a crass way to put it? Do you deserve better? When you feel compelled to behave as someone else *expects* you to behave, or as you want someone to *perceive* you as behaving, then you are *pretending* to live *your* life, but you are *actually* living like a character in a script that you did *not* author. You are doing so without even having had the opportunity to *read the script*. Come to think of it, are you *not*, in fact, a character in a play written by *God*, or by *no one*, and are you *not*, in fact, trying to figure out how to play the role you have been assigned as best you are able? You did not create this world, you did not organize the environment on this planet, and you did not get to decide the time, place, or circumstances of your birth. Of course, *no one* gets to do *any* of that. Like everyone else, you just "showed up" at some point, and now you have to figure out what to do. At the very least, try to avoid becoming a bullshit artist. The world has more than enough pretenders, more than enough charlatans, and many more liars than it could ever have needed. The least you could do is to avoid becoming precisely the kind of person that you despise. Is *that* so much to ask? Start by being honest about your own *ignorance*.

January 3

Resist the tendency to allow your person to atrophy physically, morally, and intellectually. You have seen the consequences of sloth and lassitude in these areas. You are intimately aware of the tragedy of bodies, minds, and characters that have become weak, pathetic, and embarrassing due to disuse. How many friends, associates, and family members have you observed as they declined and became something less than shadows of the selves they had once been? You have watched an absolute *bull* of a man deteriorate to the point that he needed help getting out of a chair and could not use the restroom without assistance. You have known pillars of the community who became criminals, vagrants, or burdens to the surrounding society. You have interacted with persons bordering upon genius that allowed their minds to decline into irrationality, disinterest and, at least arguably, madness. Any talent that you fail to use, fail to exercise, or fail to acknowledge, can become an instrument of your undoing. How dare you waste your gifts? Vigilance! If you are not a tough and rigorous taskmaster where *your own* conduct and *your own* character are concerned, then you certainly have no business offering advice, counsel, or criticism where anyone *else* is concerned. Perhaps you have no business offering counsel in *any* case, but you certainly ought to get your own house in order before you even *contemplate* criticism of others. Yes, the temptation *is* greater in some cases than in others.

January 4

Contempt is sometimes warranted, frequently hard to resist, and often quite understandable. It is, however, far less than ideal to adopt a generally contemptuous cast of character, or an outlook that lends itself too readily or too easily to directing your contempt outward at your fellow talking apes. Remind yourself every so often that you are as much a primate as anyone else, and many of the other apes have regarded *you* with contempt— and not *always* without just cause. The disdainful attitude is not conducive to very much in the way of accomplishment or progress. It tends to motivate negative or counterproductive behavior in *most* cases or, worse yet, it lends itself to lethargy, resignation, or despair. If you allow yourself to fall into despair and inactivity due to the behavior, beliefs, or values of other persons, then you are allowing them to control you. Is it not pathetic to subject your mental states to control by those for whom you have contempt? The world is filled with people and organizations that are quite adept at manipulating the public, especially those who allow themselves to be susceptible to the overly easy slide into contempt, disdain, or despair. Be careful not to make yourself a "soft target" for those who hope to shove *their* thoughts, values, and worldview into *your* head. Keep your guard up and protect yourself at all times. The bell is about to ring.

January 5

Fighters are instructed to protect themselves at all times, and there are good reasons for this advice. As it turns out, this is wise counsel *outside* of the ring and the cage as well, and it would serve you to "keep your hands up" (so to speak) any time any potential conflict presents itself. There is no shortage of backstabbers in *any* walk of life. Sometimes a scoundrel wants your money, sometimes a criminal wants your life, sometimes a degenerate wants your children, sometimes a miscreant wants to deprive you of your peace of mind, and sometimes a piece of human debris wants to drag you down to his level, because idiocy loves company. The degenerate resents anyone who lives a decent life or pursues virtue. Scoundrels hate to admit that not everyone is as repugnant and deviant as they know themselves to be. It is wise to be on your guard when those who seek to undermine your virtue, such as it is, come creeping in your direction. A creep does not approach for noble purposes. Protect yourself at all times. Indeed. Your body, your mind, and your character are in almost constant danger from attack, subversion, and atrophy. If you fail to safeguard those aspects of your life that matter most, and that lie within *your* direct control, you invite terrible consequences. Do not invite a vampire into your home. Also, look both ways before you cross the street.

January 6

A bad temper is a dangerous inclination, and you would do well to get yours under control or, better yet, to extirpate the inclination entirely. When have you made a good decision under the influence of anger or rage, and when have you been pleased by your behavior after your fit of temper has subsided? On the other hand, you have had many, *many* occasions to regret what you have said and what you have done in those circumstances in which anger has guided your hands, your mouth, and your feet. How many easily avoidable confrontations has your bad temper led you to instigate, and how much damage has been done to your friends, your colleagues, and your character, because you declined to devote the necessary effort to rectify your temperament and your behavioral tendencies? In fact, have your problems and challenges not been overwhelmingly attributable to your own failures of self-discipline? Have you not suffered enough due to your disorderliness? Rage is not a good look. Anger is *weakness*. You need not rouse yourself to a condition of rage in order to respond to *any* challenge, *any* problem, or *any* attack that may be directed your way. Indeed, you are *far* more likely to respond in a wise and virtuous fashion, and you are *far* more likely to function efficiently, if you keep your head and mind your temper. This is *not* always easy. Do it anyway.

January 7

Of all the drugs with which people manage to ruin their lives, as well as the lives of their friends, family, and other loved ones, is any more frequently abused, and is any more societally detrimental than alcohol? Surely, *one* drink is not as devastating in its effects as is *one* dose of heroin, or *one* intake of methamphetamine, but the problem drinker rarely ingests just one shot of the preferred poison. Like potato chips, it is very difficult to have just one. There is almost always something enticing, it seems, about the *next* drink. There is something seductive about this particular form of dissolution. The self-destructive urge manifests in more forms than anyone can count, and it conceals itself in more ways than virtually any other threat, but it is never far removed from *you*, is it? To be sure, you cannot help but wonder if it is ever very far removed from *any* of us. Self-hatred is just about *everywhere*, afflicting just about *everyone*. What does that tell you about your species? Raise a glass to the talking primates. You can toast the jabbering apes as they fling their feces, climb trees, groom each other, and you *should* remember that *you* are a member of this species, and you share its evolutionary history. Indeed, you can understand the desire to remain drunk or under the influence of some drug or other upon consideration of certain immutable facts about you, and about many of the other psychotic mandrills with the opposable thumbs. What, after all, is more fun than a barrel of drunken monkeys?

January 8

Moral conundrums have a way of leading to decision paralysis, do they not? Often, it is better to do the *wrong* thing decisively than it is to do the right thing only after protracted procrastination. Also, the wrong decision is often preferable to *no* decision at all. Then again, the wrong act and the wrong decision are both, at their very root and marrow... *wrong*. So, how are you to make a decision when reason, the available evidence, and your focused intellectual efforts are simply insufficient to identify an answer with which you may move forward with confidence and moral clarity? Reason, after all, should not be expected to settle *every* outstanding issue. Reason is, presumably, an evolutionary adaptation (of sorts), and it certainly has its invaluable functions, but no single capacity ought to be expected to cull and separate *all* data and *all* possible responses to the observable evidence, or all imaginable experience. It is no sin to allow your "gut," your a-rational inclinations, to choose — when reason is simply not up to the task. It is unwise to refrain from doing *anything* unless and until you are quite confident that you know *everything*. You ought not to allow yourself to become *nothing more* than a "gut player," but it does not follow from this that you are duty-bound to ignore your "gut," your instincts, or your native inclinations entirely. There is probably a healthy balance to be found here. You do not, of course, know that you will, in fact, find it. You *can*, however, try.

January 9

Events transpire as they will, and they pay no heed to *your* will or your pre-reflective whims and interests. For this reason, you would do well to restrict your interest to the *very* small sphere of phenomena that are determined by *your* deliberations and *your* choices without the mediation or collaboration of anything external to your will. Even your *own body* is not yours to control. Did you *choose* the aging body you now inhabit? Are you in charge of the functioning of your brain and its governance of the rest of your body and its massively complex and interrelated systems? Can you *decide* that you will not fall prey to viral or bacterial infection? Is your genetic endowment subject to manipulation by your mental states? Did you get to decide how the environment impacted the development of your brain? The questions could continue, but the point is made. You are in control of *nothing* beyond *your* psychological states—if *even those* are truly within your power. Focus on what you *can* control. Do your best to compel, purely by force of your own decisions that "it shall be so," and demand no alteration of the fixed past or the laws of nature governing the multifarious connections linking past, present, and future. Good luck with trying to control *that*. *Decide* that the next stranger you encounter shall regard you as a wonderful human being, worthy of emulation. Does your *decision* determine that stranger's assessment of you? It does *not*. Decide that you will *not launch into a song* at this moment. Do you see how easy that was?

January 10

If a friend intentionally behaves in a manner that is contrary to your interests and does so, moreover, to benefit himself, then he reveals that you should never have regarded him as a *friend* in the first place. You must, therefore, blame *yourself* if something of this nature occurs. Was it not *you* that misjudged this person, and was it not *you* that misunderstood the true nature of the relationship? Do not expect a scoundrel to *introduce* himself as one. It is *your* responsibility to choose your friends and associates wisely. Take the time, and make the effort to get to know the true character of those with whom you consider friendship, business relations, or any other for long-term association. Pay careful attention to how persons with whom you come into contact conduct themselves in their dealings with others. Almost anyone can *pretend* to be virtuous for a short time. *Very* few can maintain this pretense for an extended period. Have patience and keep your eyes open. Your choice of companionship is not a matter to be taken lightly. If you associate with scoundrels, charlatans, imbeciles, or miscreants, then you will find it very difficult to maintain your pursuit of wisdom and virtue, and you will find it very difficult to convince anyone else that you genuinely value such pursuits. The path to wisdom should not wend through the garden of idiocy any more often than is absolutely necessary.

January 11

The expression, "It's not the end of the world," is almost always asinine. First, only the *literal* end of the world is, in fact, the end of the world. So, the assertion is trivial and gratuitous. Second, the expression almost always constitutes a trivialization of some event that has caused someone some degree of suffering, anxiety, or disquiet. To be sure, a lot of this worry is readily avoidable through rational self-discipline, but the goal of encouraging rational self-governance is hardly advanced by spouting truisms and platitudes at people who are worried or angry. Indeed, the facile resort to platitudes in lieu of close, careful analysis of the issue at hand is likely to inculcate a general lassitude where reason and critical thinking are called for. Consider *your* response to someone saying, "It's not the end of the world," at the moment you most require counsel or a bit of comforting interaction. Would you value that input? Would you be ennobled or edified by such a fatuous utterance? Consider the kind of advice, or the type of comfort that you *would* value when circumstances are most trying, and do your best to offer such counsel when another party comes to you for it. If you are unable or unwilling to offer valuable and relevant input, then it is inadvisable to spout platitudes just for the sake of having something to say, or just for the sake of making noise with your face. Silence would be preferable.

January 12

Never assume that the people you encounter are going to share your beliefs, your values, or your worldview. Some of them may do so, but most of them will not, and many of those with whom you differ are liable to react to your disagreement in something less than perfectly rational fashion. Indeed, *you* have been known to respond to circumstances in less than ideal fashion, have you not? Disagreements are nothing more than a series of noises emanating from mouths, or a series of pixels on a few computer screens. What do you care about stray noises uttered or stray marks made in this or that medium? If such things are sufficient to undercut your serenity, then your self-discipline is lacking, indeed. Do not blame the rest of the world for *your* failure to control yourself and your patterns of thought. No one is obligated to agree with you about anything, or "see things your way." It is also worth noting that the "way you see things" is as apt to depart from the way that things *actually are* as is anyone else's worldview. The fact that you *believe* something to be a fact is not, in and of itself, evidence that your belief actually *corresponds* to the *genuine* facts. Your beliefs are, to some degree at least, up to you. The objective facts, however, do *not* depend upon you or require your permission in order that they obtain. Only a fool insists that the world *must* dance to *his* tune.

January 13

Charm is not properly regarded as an intrinsic character trait. Charm is an activity in which people engage for purposes of manipulating others. Never trust a "charming" person. It is especially dangerous and unwise to spend time in the company of inveterately, habitually charming persons. Those are the ones that always have something "up their sleeves," always a hidden agenda. Manipulation and deception are their primary modes of interaction and their favorite methods for satisfying their desires. A sociopath is, almost invariably, a talented "charmer." The victims typically succumb to the wiles conjured by the "charming" criminal after he maneuvers his prey into a position of helplessness or willful ignorance of his designs. You know that the most successful politicians have mastered the art of charming the masses. How many have done so for noble or altruistic purposes? Do you need *even* the fingers of *one* hand for the counting? The charmer *is* the snake. Do not become the charmer's victim. When you realize that you are hearing the sweet sounds of flattery, or that you are experiencing the soothing effects of being told precisely what you antecedently *wanted* to be told, this is the moment that it is most crucial to take a step back, raise your guard, and ask whether you are being persuaded by evidence, or whether you are falling into the deadly trap of forming beliefs on the basis of desire and aversion, rather than following the evidence wherever it may lead. Wishful thinking is for children.

January 14

Never cheat in any contest, any game, or as part of any relationship in which you are a participant. The cheat can *never* again be trusted by anyone that he has cheated, and he *should* never be trusted by *anyone* else either. If you cheat, you reveal a weakness of character and a form of cowardice as well. If you win some contest due to cheating, your victory is worse than meaningless. The term "victory" is not properly applicable to the outcome in any case in which rules have been violated or the competitor has attained an outcome via dishonest methods. You have no business participating in any practice that is contrary to virtue, and you have no business tolerating any associate of any type who seeks advantage through scurrilous means. Losing a competition with your decency intact is infinitely preferable to prevailing at the *expense* of your decency. A cheat is a repugnant creature. What are you implicitly saying about yourself, your abilities, and your character, when you resort to con artistry rather than legitimate competition? Surely, this is *not* the behavior of a confident or competent participant in the contest at hand. If you are so pathetic that you need or want to resort to deception rather than rely on your skill and wits, then what conclusion should anyone, yourself included, draw about the quality of your wits and skill? Do *not* disgrace yourself. Avoid the vice of chicanery at all costs.

January 15

Diogenes of Sinope was the first person, as far as we know, to call himself a "cosmopolitan" (Citizen of the Cosmos). Contrary to popular contemporary misinterpretation, the Cynic philosopher did *not* mean that he regarded all people as equally worthwhile "citizens of the world." He meant that he was subject *only* to *natural law* (Laws of the Cosmos), and that all social constructs and *civil* laws were properly regarded as nonsense with no binding compulsion. "Laws" passed by men meant *nothing* to Diogenes. They are subject to change, often motivated by corruption, weakness, or stupidity, and they could be violated upon any agent's whim. Surely, consequences for breaking man-made "laws" may ensue, but that fact does not endow them with moral legitimacy. It was, at one time, perfectly legal to own slaves. People and governments pass foolish laws on a regular basis. You need not take foolishness seriously. Was not slavery perfectly legal just a couple centuries ago? Were women not legally debarred from casting a vote in federal elections even more recently? Does the law in many places *still* not prohibit slaughtering a healthy, unborn human being in the womb, even when there is no danger to the mother's life and no fetal malformation? The fact that the law *allows* a particular form of behavior is scant evidence that the behavior in question constitutes *decency*. A decent person will violate an indecent law without compunction.

January 16

Do not indulge in resentment when persons, or other entities that do not merit your approval, manage to succeed and triumph in some arena over which your will has no purchase. Whether the arena is politics, sports, business, or even warfare, it is incumbent upon you to recognize that you have been granted *no* assurance that victory must always go to the most noble, or to the party with which you share the greatest affinity. If you are rooting for any particular outcome, you thereby invite the possibility, indeed the *probability*, of frustrated desire and incurred aversion. Emotional attachment to such matters virtually guarantees utterly needless and easily avoidable suffering. Why allow your contentment to depend upon events that take no heed of your desires? This is *masochism*. Restrict your concern to *your* mind and the proper, rational governance thereof. Mind *your own* business. Perhaps it is better to put the point this way: Your mind *is* your own business. Even better: Your mind is your *only* business. Let the world hurl its supposed benefits and detriments your way, or let the world take no interest in your affairs whatsoever. None of that is any of your concern. Who told you that you are *entitled* to this or that share of the world's various dispensations? Where did you get the idea that an injustice transpires merely because another person is endowed with some advantage that you lack? What you have is *more* than enough, if you just use it wisely.

January 17

The "signal to noise" ratio in contemporary socio-political discourse is, to put it charitably, somewhat less than ideal. Screed and screeching seem to get much more attention than closely reasoned argument or civil discourse. When is the last time you saw or heard a politician or commentator praised for a display of intellectual prowess, or admired for careful analysis of a complex issue? It seems that the content of speech, and other forms of expression, is generally ignored in favor of the race, sex, religious beliefs, ethnicity, or sexual orientation of the person or persons engaged in the speech act at hand. Political dialogue has degenerated into a series of ad hominem attacks, straw man fallacies, disingenuous slippery slope assertions, and various appeals to force and pity. The fallacy appears to have become the preferred mechanism of attempts at persuasion. Furthermore, it would seem that this mechanism is deployed fairly successfully in many cases. Much of the public is incapable of distinguishing between legitimate argumentation and expressions of abject irrationality. A significant proportion of the public vote for the candidate that looks better on television. Is *that* indicative of a citizenry to be taken seriously? Hardly. Perhaps you can raise one and a half cheers for democracy. Perhaps that is more than democracy deserves.

January 18

Have you "made something of yourself," as you have been regularly advised, both directly and indirectly, that you are obligated to do? The question is sincere. What is your life that anyone ought to take notice of it or congratulate you for any part of it? Brandish your greatest accomplishment and let the entire world to cast judgment upon it. What have you got? What have you done with your opportunity to draw breath, live a human life, and engage with your fellow talking apes? You have done precious little to alter or impact the course of history. You have discovered no heretofore hidden principles of the natural order. You have produced no masterpiece to inspire others to heights that they would have otherwise failed to attain. Your contributions to the world's collected wisdom are paltry at best, and you may actually have done more harm than good. It is possible, and this is not a possibility over which you ought to pass lightly, that you have actually impeded the path to wisdom and understanding for more persons than you have aided in enlightening. It is not *impossible* that your contribution to the lives of those with whom you have associated has been, all things considered, more impairment than benefit. Do you *know* that the reverse is the case? You will not, by all current appearances, leave the world a better place than you found it. So, what *have* you done with your life? Satisfied?

January 19

Indifference, provided that it is rationally grounded and genuine, is one of the most powerful psychological bulwarks against the inevitable "slings and arrows" of unruly Fate and Fortune. What terrors are to be deployed against a rational agent that is sincerely indifferent to events that lie beyond the agent's control? Perhaps the specter of death may be held out as a terror of universal proportion. It is both inevitable and, as far as you can tell, final and irreversible. Does it not send a chill up your spine? For the uninstructed, death may, indeed, serve as a constant source of disquiet and persistent anxiety. What are pre-reflective proclivities to *you*? Have you not received instruction from Epictetus, Socrates, Epicurus, the Buddha, Jesus, and many others who have seen through the imaginary terrors of mortality? The body dies and the self either becomes extinct, or it persists, or it is revealed to have been an illusion all along. In any event, a source of distress disappears. Are you concerned about material wealth or the lack thereof? Suppose that you were to be granted enough money to be confident that neither you nor your family would ever have to worry about financial circumstances again. Would you have no remaining concerns? Would you not still wonder if you are living a *virtuous* life? Would you not still wish to pass the perennial values along to the next generation? Perhaps your material holdings are inadequate *given your desires*. If so, the *holdings* are certainly *not* the problem.

January 20

Avoid allowing fear to dictate your actions or your aspirations. Failure is nothing to be taken seriously unless the failure in question is a matter of your will, your courage, or your moral purpose. All else that goes by the name "failure" in common parlance is properly regarded with detached indifference. Did some award go to someone other than you? What of it? If the recipient is, in fact, better qualified for the award than you are, then you are entitled to no complaint whatsoever. Congratulate the victor and wish the best to all concerned. If the recipient of the award is *not* more deserving than you, then perhaps someone has made a mistake. Why should you concern yourself with someone else falling into some error in judgment? Have you been granted a guarantee that all persons in positions of power must always agree with *your* assessments of the relative merits of all competitors for various honors? No? Tend to your own business then. Your business is improving *your* character, detaching your interest from anyone's *assessment* of your character, and developing rational indifference to the dispensations of all of those elements of the world over which your will has no purchase. When someone is awarded with this or that honor, go ahead and applaud along in a polite show of respect and congratulations. There is no benefit in a petulant refusal to acknowledge the occasion or the chosen recipient. Honors of this type come and they go. Who told you to care for such "honors" anyway? You should only care for *honor*.

January 21

You have been told that it is inappropriate to exploit the weak and the stupid. You are also aware that you have often experienced the urge to do so and, right or wrong, you know that you have, in fact, exploited those who are easy prey on more than one occasion. If you are brutally honest, you must confess that you have enjoyed doing so, and you must also admit that you have made short shrift of the weak and the stupid without any subsequent compunction, regret, or remorse on more than one occasion. Is this a character flaw on your part, or is it perfectly natural and entirely justifiable for a wolf to feed upon sheep? Why should weakness and stupidity *not* incur a price commensurate with the inadequacies in question? Imbeciles may not *deserve* to suffer because of the stupidity under which they labor, but is their suffering not *inevitable*? When you see a flock of sheep, and you notice some wolves circling and prowling around them, ask if there is any reason that you should "root for" the sheep to survive. If the sheep survive, does that not mean that the wolves drift a bit closer to starvation? It is not as if the wolves can adopt a vegetarian diet, or obtain their sustenance without eating some form of prey or another. Wolves eat sheep because it is not in their nature to prefer the welfare of the sheep to their own. Wolves eat sheep because they *must*. You are not obligated to suffer fools gently. Sheep do not matter.

January 22

You struggle to maintain rational indifference as you watch Western culture committing suicide by allowing millions of people from utterly incompatible cultures, who have no interest whatsoever in assimilation, and no respect whatsoever for Western cultural traditions, to flood into Western nations. The stupidity is staggering. The impending collapse of the West is blindingly obvious. The denial of this obvious impending collapse is shockingly disingenuous. Everyone who claims not to perceive the coming collapse of the West is either lying, poorly informed, or indulging in willful ignorance of a state of affairs that they find too terrifying to acknowledge. Just observe the socio-cultural and economic developments in Britain, France, Germany, Italy, Canada, and the United States of America. These nations become increasingly unrecognizable, or barely recognizable, as the societies into which the older native residents were born during the middle decades of the 20th Century. The people of the West look around them and wonder what happened to the cultures that they knew, and that seemed so stable just a few decades ago. Either that or *you* are mistaken in your assessment of current conditions and the likely broad consequences thereof. You would not mind being mistaken in this matter. In any event, you can do nothing to forestall whatever future awaits the West. Indeed, the West may have precious little future left. You must, therefore, learn to retain equanimity nonetheless.

January 23

What, if anything, are you called upon to do with your life? You need not conceive of this as a divine calling or as a mission assigned to you by God (although you are certainly free to consider the possibility), but you ought to think about what it is, if anything, that you are trying accomplish with the totality of your life here on this planet. Are you not better off living a life with some overarching purpose, as opposed to wandering through your days with no particular aim and no particular conception of principles to guide your conduct, and by reference to which you fix your values? In other words, are you not better off living a life of purpose rather than a life devoid of purpose? A purposeless life is all well and good for a dog, a cat, or an imbecile. It is advisable for you to aspire to a higher calling than the typical designs of dogs, cats, or imbeciles. Those creatures cannot help but act in accordance with their fixed and limited natural inclinations. They do what they do irrespective of the wisdom or foolishness of their pursuits and interests. They are destined to live and die without ever attaining any appreciable understanding of the possibilities available to those beings that can conceive of overarching plans, principles, and the natural laws constraining the unfolding of events. You, however, are endowed with the capacity to *reason*. *You* have the capacity to conceive of foundational principles that govern your life's work. Purpose or aimlessness — choose. *Everything* rides on that choice.

January 24

The condition of loneliness is not determined by external states of affairs or by proximity to other persons. You can experience abject loneliness in a crowd, surrounded by family and friends, or in the middle of a conversation with a colleague or associate. You can also live in complete isolation for years at a time, indeed for the entirety of your adult life, without experiencing loneliness for a single moment. Loneliness is largely a matter of your attitude regarding your current circumstances and your need for interpersonal relations. If you experience no psychological or emotional need for company or companionship, the absence of company is not oppressive or unpleasant in the least. Indeed, if you are compelled to keep company with other persons when you would prefer to be alone with your thoughts, the feeling of companionship is unlikely to ensue. In other words, it is often somewhat oppressive and uncomfortable *not* to be left alone. There are times, and those periods of time may be quite extended, during which you crave the absence of company, and you long for the peace and quiet required to organize your thoughts, construct a conception of the kind of future you wish to manifest, and consider the degree to which you are currently living in conformity with your most fundamental values and interests. Sometimes a period of isolation is precisely what you need. Even in a crowd, you can retreat into your own thoughts. Wherever you go, remember to take your *mind* with you.

January 25

You face something of a Hobson's choice today, or so it seems. You can opt for a state of affairs that is far less than optimal, but that provides at least *some* benefit, or you can choose to end up with precisely *no* benefit whatsoever. Should this not be a fairly straightforward matter? Given any cost-benefit analysis or any reasonable assessment of relative utility, something has got to be better than *nothing*—provided, of course, that the "something" in question is something *good*, and given that acquisition of this benefit does not require the sacrifice of anything that is of greater value (e.g. your decency or your peace of mind). Why, then, do you struggle with the choice in question? Are you allowing foolish pride to get the better of your reason? Is ego serving as a stumbling block in this matter? Do you believe that you are entitled to better options? Do not be a fool. You are *entitled* to precisely nothing. You did not *earn* the right to optimal states of affairs. You did not *earn* a choice in this matter or, as far as that goes, you did not *earn* any choice in any set of conditions. At the most fundamental level of consideration, you really ought to recognize that you did not even *earn* this life that you are living. No one *earns* birth into a human life. Be grateful that you have *any* choice at all.

January 26

The story of the Tower of Babel is a biblical allegory about the danger and impropriety of human hubris. The attempt to build a tower to the heavens is indicative of a desire to occupy a realm reserved for beings with which humans are not fit to consort. What compels so many people to pursue aims that are clearly loftier than talking apes deserve? The quest for immortality, for example, seems to be gaining purchase in the public's imagination. What is a desire for immortality if not a manifestation of petulant ingratitude for human life as it stands? If a standard, mortal human life, complete with its inevitable terminus, is not sufficient for you, then *yours* is not the sort of human life that ought to be extended *at all*—much less endowed with an eternal elongation so that your dissatisfaction can go on *forever*. What kind of dissatisfied dimwit longs for his discontent to adopt endless proportions? Your duty is to learn how to remain serene and satisfied no matter what circumstances may arise. Do not indulge in the irrational and quixotic quest to construct some form of utopia, or to attain existence on an elevated plane. If the world as it stands is insufficiently gratifying for your tastes, then your *tastes* are the problem. Who told you that *nothing* is off limits to you and to your like? Who do you think you are? There may well be corners "where angels fear to tread." Do not be the fool that insists upon rushing into such places.

January 27

In the absence of "rough men willing to do violence" in defense of their people, no society can long endure. For this reason, you must respect the military, the police, and all of those willing to place their lives on the line if doing so is necessary to preserve their families, their culture, and all of those persons who are unwilling or unable to defend themselves against the wolves that prowl constantly at the gates. There are, to be sure, some miscreants among even those cohorts that are, at large, most deserving of your respect and admiration. Those who befoul the institutions representing the defenders of that which you hold dear, and those who sully the institutions without which your loved ones would live in constant danger, those miscreants deserve your contempt and punishment commensurate with their crimes. If a military man is found guilty of raping a woman in some nation during a conflict, then let that bastard hang. If not, then send him to Leavenworth, Kansas so that he may suffer incarceration for the rest of his filthy life. The others, however, have earned your admiration, your respect, and your unyielding loyalty. Without the men and women of the military, the life that you enjoy would be unthinkable. God bless those who stand ready to fight. God bless the warriors! God bless the troops that place their lives on the line so that *you* do not have to risk *your* life. Anyone who does not respect the troops is, thereby, unworthy of *your* respect.

January 28

There is nothing admirable about drunkenness or functioning under the influence of mind-altering narcotics. What a shame that so many people, in particular, so many adolescent and young adult males, have convinced themselves that being drunk or "high" is, somehow, a condition about which bragging is justified. How many assaults, how many instances of domestic violence, and how many cases of driving under the influence, including cases in which innocent persons died, would never have occurred had alcohol and narcotics been ingested in reasonable amounts, or in *no* amounts whatsoever? What *is* the attraction of inebriation? Why are so many people willing to sacrifice their sanity and their self-control for the sake of imbibing one's drink of choice or one's drug of choice? You must *never* allow your character and your behavior to be determined by the introduction of narcotics or excessive alcohol into your bloodstream. Have you *not* seen the consequences of this lifestyle, of this character flaw, of this maladaptive habit, up close and in person? Are you incapable of drawing the obvious inferences about drunkenness and the disaster that follows in its wake? You have *no right* to allow yourself to be enslaved to a mere substance. You certainly have no right to cause *others* to suffer because of your moral and intellectual dissolution. Govern *yourself!*

January 29

Pretense may be necessary to keep a culture intact, but that does not make it any less pretentious or odious. Evidently, we must pretend a good deal if we are to avoid a war of all against all. You can only infer that this fact, if it *is* a fact, is indicative of some fairly deep-seated perversion in the fabric of humankind. We cannot be entirely honest about what we believe, what we value, and what we hope to achieve. We cannot be honest about who we are and what we want, because we fear the judgment and disapprobation of our fellow talking primates, for whom we have, at best, a grudging and inconstant tolerance. Perhaps we need to hide our true selves if we are to get along with the other selves that we encounter on a regular basis. So, we *pretend*. Actually, you do not particularly care about what anyone else is compelled to do, but *you* have been driven to pretense on more than one occasion. Each time, you have felt diminished by the affectation. Each time, you have regretted the posturing, and you have, in retrospect, imagined a method of avoiding the pretense in question. Perhaps pretense is a *necessary* evil, but that does not make it any less an *evil*. Indeed, if pretense is necessary to keep a society functioning, it is worth considering whether, all things considered, it would not be preferable to allow the society in question to dissolve. In that event, you could at least *stop* pretending. Surely, *that* would be an improvement.

January 30

You intentionally insulted and belittled a man today. Having had time to consider the matter, you realize that the insult was unnecessary, but you can find no hint of remorse for it. Is this because you believe the man *deserved* to be insulted, or is it because you regard him as such an inferior specimen that you simply cannot muster regret for the remark? Given your current cognitive distance from the event, is it not at least a little surprising that you still do not know why your conscience is not particularly troubling you? Perhaps it is the reaction from those onlookers present that stands athwart the psychological mechanisms of guilt. Everyone who saw and heard the exchange appeared to be "on your side" and pleased by your remark. Can it be that something so flimsy as the appearance of *approval* from others is sufficient to dull your conscience? This is curious business indeed. In retrospect, you still feel *nothing* about passing this insult. Actually, in recalling the event, you are pleased that you chose to do so. Even in retrospect, you derive at least a bit of pleasure from putting that idiot in his place. What does it mean? Does this make you petty or small of spirit? Perhaps it does. Perhaps that is a character flaw. At the moment, even *that* possibility does not particularly bother you. The fact is, you have a bit of a mean streak in you and you are not in any great hurry to extirpate that element of your character. Sometimes, cruelty comes in handy. The world is a rough place. Learn when you need to be rough. Do not fear those moments.

January 31

The stupidity is thick, pervasive, and relentless today. Perhaps this is so *every* day, but today you are especially *aware* of the idiocy that seems to hound you at every turn and impose itself upon you without pausing to take a breath—or allowing *you* to take one. *Why* has it become so fashionable for nitwits to *pretend* to understand matters about which they have not the *faintest* idea, and to *pretend* to have accomplished feats that they are manifestly incapable of even approaching? More importantly, however, *why* is this bothering you so much *today*? Liars and charlatans pop off regularly, and expose themselves as frauds *many* times per day. Why have you allowed this to get the better of you on *this* particular day? Did you fail to get a good night's sleep? You *have* struggled with that difficulty for *many* years. Perhaps you have been subconsciously triggered by something that recalled some previous irritant. Your experience with idiocy, including *your own*, is tragically extensive, and the consequences of stupidity have been brought home to you more times than you can count, and certainly on more occasions than you care to remember. Perhaps some of the memories of these occasions have been repressed or reinterpreted in retrospect, but you can feel the cognitive and emotional weight of the frustrations with which stupidity is associated in your mind. It can be enervating indeed. The struggle surfaces now and again. Maybe the stupid just *smolders* a bit more than usual today.

February 1

When you successfully resist an unwholesome, unwise, or ignoble temptation, it is permissible to note your success, and to encourage yourself to sustain and enhance your resistance to untoward urges. You are even permitted to congratulate yourself, and to indulge in a brief and rationally restrained episode of *pride*. This is not the sort of pride that is, with just cause, listed as one of the Seven Deadly Sins. *That* particular vice should never be borne lightly or rationalized as "only" a brief indulgence. In fact, it may be that "pride" is not quite the optimal term for what you may legitimately experience when you do the right thing and avoid doing something that ought not to be done. Perhaps "satisfaction" is closer to the condition that you are permitted to enjoy. There is a wholesome form of satisfaction to be had from virtuous action. This is as it should be. Virtue is its own reward, and satisfaction ensues. If more people understood and experienced the joy of virtuous behavior, and if more people were, perhaps, compelled to experience the intrinsic dissatisfaction and shame of perpetrating vice, then you can only expect that this would lead to many more spontaneous acts of honor and decency, and far fewer ill-conceived indulgences in vice. Your character cannot escape being tainted by vicious behavior, and your character is automatically improved every time that you do the right thing for the right reason. It is good to experience the immediate, internal consequences of your actions. It is good to understand that they are unavoidable.

February 2

If you are fortunate enough to experience a few solid moments of genuine silence, do not forget to *enjoy* that brief respite from the nearly relentless clamor that seems to follow you in each waking hour of every day of your life. Silence is, indeed, golden— and it is far more *rare* than gold has ever been. The constant background buzzing and chattering of the contemporary world is almost a form of oppression, and it is an oppression that appears to be embraced eagerly and reinforced by most of your fellow denizens of the modern world. Is it possible that the majority actually enjoys incessant blather and ubiquitous prattle? They both produce and consume an awful lot of the stuff, and they seem to be willing to pay fairly handsomely for the privilege. Consider the number of televisions, laptop computers, tablets, automobile entertainment systems, and all of the other noisemaking apparatus, and it is difficult to convince yourself that the masses value silence or that they dislike incessant noise, blather, and poor substitutes for "entertainment" masquerading as some form of "art" or other. In any event, try not to contribute any more to the cacophony than is absolutely necessary. In other words, shut up once in a while. Most of what you have to say is, frankly, somewhat less than indispensable to the world at large. Everyone can make do without your input. Let them try to do so once in awhile.

February 3

You have always been drawn to the higher places in the natural world. Life in the valley is fine enough, but it entails a sense of *enclosure* and a vague hint of something like claustrophobia. Traveling through the foothills, however, you experience a sense of release, and you come in touch with an unfettered sensation. Gazing *down* at a mountain lake provides an experience that outstrips even your encounters with the vast stretches of oceans or deserts expanding beyond your horizon. A mountain lends itself to, at the very least, the *illusion* of peaceful, serene distance from the places that humans congregate, as well as a feeling of being *above* all of the nonsense generated by people desperately trying to impress one another. That kind of silliness happens "down there" among the huddled masses. It is no accident that we use phrases such as "rising above" the ordinary. If you do not experience yourself as standing at something of an elevation, then your mind is likely to be dragged down to the common places, down to the realm of the quotidian and the mundane. What, after all, is special or fascinating about flatlands, valleys, and places where gutters and sewers are constant elements of the landscape? No, you are not meant to pass your entire life in the lowlands. Your place is on higher ground. Serenity is higher than a parking lot in front of a valley strip mall. Peace is *up*, if you are willing to tilt your gaze to look for it.

February 4

You should be grateful for the fact that you seem to have no appreciable talent for making music, singing, or otherwise entertaining crowds of people with an instrument. It is also worth noting that you appear to have no talent for acting and no desire to pursue the Hollywood dreams that have ruined so many promising lives. Had you been endowed with any marketable ability in this arena, you would, almost certainly, have pursued a career as a musician or an actor and, judging by the base rate alone, you would have struggled, failed, and wasted a lot of time, as well as those *very* meager talents with which you are *actually* endowed. The same is true of athletic talent. You should thank God that you were never quite large enough, fast enough, or skilled enough to make a go of it as a boxer, cage fighter, or professional football player. You *do* have something of an aptitude for and, for as long as you can remember, an overwhelming fascination with combat and collision sports. Had mixed martial arts been an option in your adolescence, it is not at all clear that you could have been dissuaded from pursuing a career in the cage. This would have been, quite probably, catastrophic in your case. Consider the damage you would have sustained, over and above the damage you have *actually* endured, had you been just a *little* closer to the kind of suspicion that you could have made a run at professional athletics. Thank God that you are *not* particularly physically gifted. Had you been born with *talent*, it might have *ruined your life*.

February 5

Yeats tells us that "the center cannot hold," and warns that mere anarchy prepares to descend upon the world. Have you not felt an approaching darkness for some extended time now? Perhaps this is merely a manifestation of the darkness inside of *you*, and perhaps you project your pessimism onto the world in which you find yourself embedded, but that hypothesis has never had the "ring of truth" from your perspective. Is it the perspective that is flawed, or is it the hypothesis that fails to map onto reality? The veneer of civilization is thin indeed, and various forces, it seems, are bending their efforts upon the project of tearing it away. Is it the prospect of nuclear war that you sense as the instigation of the anarchy that Yeats perceived just past his horizon? He may have been contemplating warfare and its possible consequences, but he could not have envisioned the instantaneous destructive force of nuclear warheads that are now possessed by many of the world's most powerful nations and their leaders. Everything that you call "society" can be shattered, scattered, and replaced by chaos at any moment. Can you maintain rational detachment from *that* prospect? Diogenes could have managed it. He would have made do with his tub, a simple cloak, and his cupped hands for drinking water from ponds and streams. *Perhaps*, he would have made do. Today, *giardia* seems to be present in nearly every body of fresh water. Have humans managed to produce an environment in which even Diogenes *the Dog* could not live naturally? Sad.

February 6

You cannot help but note your good fortune and experience overwhelming gratitude when you see the news of the day from around the world. Your nation and its culture have problems, to be sure, and there is a great deal of pathology that goes by the name of "culture" in your society, but there is precious little, in the contemporary era, by way of genocide, malaria, or citizens being slaughtered *en masse* by your nation's government. You have, for the time being, ready access to potable water, ample supplies of nutritious food, and nearly every form of modern medical care and technology. You need to travel from your king-sized bed to your plush living room sofa if you want to watch streaming entertainment on your large-screen plasma television. If you want to find out a bit of information or engage in a few rounds of research, you are required to open your laptop and press a series of buttons. Will the main course be steak, chicken, or salmon tonight? You can easily have any of them. The next time you feel the inclination to complain about *anything at all*, you need only contemplate what it is like for most of the population of the planet, even in the contemporary world (to say nothing of those who occupied the ancient, pre-scientific world), to recognize the ingratitude and petulance of that frame of mind. Given your circumstances, you really ought to thank God, or your lucky stars, and hold your cantankerous tongue.

February 7

It is very difficult to resist the urge to take pleasure in the failure and humiliation of persons whom you dislike. *Schadenfreude* may not be an admirable tendency, but you *must* admit that its temptation draws on you heavily when your detractors fall flat on their faces. In all honesty, this is a tendency that you are disinclined to resist with every fiber of your being or every iota of resolve that you can muster. There are people who richly deserve to be humiliated in public, are there not? Is it really one of the most scarlet sins to enjoy watching a corrupt, self-important, criminal being dragged away, in handcuffs, to a place that he will find *very* inhospitable? You did not weep when you read that Jeffrey Dahmer was beaten to death in prison and, to this day, you see no reason to have done so, nor any reason to bemoan his passing now. There *are* people who *deserve* to suffer. Do not deny that you derive pleasure from watching them do so. Perhaps you should resist this cast of character and seek to extirpate it from your personality, but you know that you have exerted *very* little effort to rid yourself of it. What does this tell you about yourself? There *is* pettiness within you, there *is* a character flaw, and you have not, *thus far*, exerted much effort to do anything about it. Should this not trouble you? It does *not* trouble you enough to do a great deal about the "problem." Perhaps you do not *really* believe that it is such a *problem* after all. Interesting, is it not?

February 8

Anyone who has the legal right to carry a gun, or any other weapon, and chooses to walk around unarmed and, therefore, *defenseless* against *armed* assailants, multiple attackers, or aggressors more skilled in unarmed combat is *begging* to be victimized. This is not the same thing as claiming that such persons *deserve* to be victimized. So long as the persons in question are innocent, they deserve no such thing, and it would be wildly inappropriate for you to wish any such fate upon them. There are, nonetheless, fairly obvious regularities and probabilities of which it is advisable to take note. Violent criminals, *shockingly*, do *not* respect the law and do not respect the rights or liberties of other persons. Violent criminals also *prefer unarmed victims* to those who carry a gun or knife. These are *not* controversial observations. It is foolish enough to take a knife to a gunfight, but it is even more asinine to carry no weapon into a potential fight for which there are *no* rules, no referees, no observers, and no mercy to be expected from one's potential opponents. It is pathetic enough to be unarmed in defense of yourself, but it is nothing short of shameful and irresponsible to be incapable of defending your loved ones in the event that they are in your company when the assailants strike. There are people depending upon *you* for their protection and safety. Do *everything* you can to discharge your duty toward these people.

February 9

Identify *anything* that any other person or any external power can take from you, and you have thereby identified something that is not *really* yours and that never was really yours to control. Your house can be taken from you through various legal (or illegal) machinations. Your home, therefore, is only "yours" in the sense that a hotel room is "yours." You are to take care of it, as best you can, for as long as it may remain in your care. Your family members can be taken from you by accident, disease, murder, and other events beyond your control. Even *your family* is, therefore, not really *yours* (in the sense in which your *will* is yours). God, or nature, or various contingencies, can destroy any human being at any moment. Your obligation is to love and care for your family to the very best of your ability, for as long as you are both alive and capable of defending them and their interests. Even your will, your mind, and your consciousness can be ripped away by death or brain damage. How many perfectly healthy, well-functioning brains have been addled, or even crippled, by Alzheimer's or dementia? Even within your own family, you have seen what neurological deterioration can do to the brain and, more importantly, to its higher cognitive functions over time. *Govern your mind* while you can. It is, ultimately, *all* you have.

February 10

If you are ever tempted to lie or to conceal information in the process of making your case, defending your position, or engaging in any debate either directly or obliquely, you are to resist this temptation, and you are to tell the truth, expose all relevant data, and explain both your position *and* your opponent's position in the most honest and charitable fashion of which you are capable. *Never* indulge in dishonesty as part of *any* debate concerning *any* matter—great or small. If you are incapable of defending your position with open honesty, then you are either on the wrong side of the debate, or you are intellectually deficient or craven. Do not turn yourself into a coward, a liar, or a casuist for the sake of "coming out on top" in some battle of wits. Though you may fool your opponent or the audience, *you* will know what you have done. You will also know that you have degraded yourself by behaving as a charlatan, and "winning" by way of *cheating*. Persons in possession of a true proposition and the wherewithal to express, explain, and defend that true proposition, simply have *no reason* to dissemble or conceal *anything*. If you are both right and bright, then you need not fear any opponent or any audience. Do not concern yourself with convincing *anyone* of *anything*. Concern yourself *only* with getting at the truth. The truth may or may not "set you free," but the pursuit of it is far nobler than is convincing idiots to nod in unison.

February 11

Some traditions are noble and worthy of preservation. Other traditions have either outlived their usefulness, or they were never useful or worthy of preservation in *any* case. Your first responsibility in matters pertaining to tradition is to learn how to distinguish between the noble and the ignoble, the worthy and the unworthy, the virtuous and the mere products of cultural inertia. Once you identify a noble tradition that enhances your culture and maintains societal dignity, you are obligated to do everything within your power to maintain the honorable and ennobling tradition. Make the attempt to convince your fellow citizens to adopt and treasure the traditions that you find to be admirable. Present a rational argument, provide all available evidence, and patiently explain it to those who need a bit more time to digest the relevant information. Try your best to make the most compelling case that you can. Do not, however, insist that everyone else or, indeed, *anyone* else must agree with you, or share your values, or adopt your worldview. Some noble traditions, it seems, are destined for extinction. Like the dinosaurs, their strengths may fail to conform to a changing environment. When nobility dies, you may mourn for *a moment*. No more than that is permitted. Extended, impotent mourning is *ignoble*. Surely, one does not respond to the death of nobility by indulging in ignoble behavior. Then again, what else is left?

February 12

Once more around the sun, and everyone says, "Happy Birthday!" Inevitably, there will be cake, gifts, singing, and other assortments of stylized nonsense. Bah. This ritual commemorates nothing unique or significant, and you have always struggled to avoid disappointing those who seem compelled to make a big deal of such occasions. You do not wish to throw cold water on anyone's celebration, and you do not want to be a killjoy, but this particular caprice has become a bit more difficult to stomach with each passing year. You are not a child, and your desperate need for attention is not an inclination you wish to reinforce through this annual rite of self-indulgence. You know that any request that others ignore your birthday, refrain from wasting money on presents you do not need, and just treat this like any other passing day, will be met with consternation. Custom, it seems, outstrips reason where ritual is concerned. So, "Happy Birthday!" it is. You are now fifty years old. Half a century down, and you know not how much time remains. You will continue to get a bit older each day… until you drop dead. Scripture enjoins you to "put away childish things." You know the translation. The world is going to knock you down, kick your teeth in, provide you with many opportunities to despair, but you are not permitted to give up. Getting knocked down just means you get the opportunity to get up again. Do whatever it takes. *Embrace the suck.*

February 13

A nothing of a day confronts you, but you know that the character of the day *itself* is not the issue. The condition of the world or the weather is not within your control, is it? Your mind and your attitude *are*, however, within your control. Is it not *you* living the day, and are *you* not responsible for your own assessments of your present experience? The sky is overcast. So? This has no power to determine a darkening of your mood. Can you not think your own thoughts and color them as brightly as you please, irrespective of the weather? Surely, it is within your power to focus your attention and your energy on maintaining some thought more ennobling than, "blah," or some attitude more respectable than, "I am bored." How pathetic is *boredom* as a state of being? You have no excuse for being bored. Marshal your inner resources and make something out of this day that lies before you. Perhaps it is a nothing of a *self* that actually confronts you, and troubles you. Perhaps weakness and lethargy are the real enemies here. Do not blame the sky! Do not blame the circumstances in which you find yourself embedded. Blame no one and nothing other than your own weakness of character. Once you have properly placed the blame, get about the business of working to extirpate every weakness, every flaw, and every gap in your armor that you find. There is no time to rest, and certainly no time for self-pity or another lapse of courage. Overcome your inclination to sloth, and get something done.

February 14

Valentine's Day is a great, steaming pile of cultural degeneracy, as well as corporate greed and manipulation, wrapped in garish paper and tied up with a gigantic red bow. Apart from selling overpriced chocolates, moribund flowers, and tragically unromantic and vapid greeting cards, the point of this holiday escapes you. Was Saint Valentine of Rome obsessed with cardboard cutouts of "hearts" that do not remotely resemble an actual human heart? Did he really like roses? If so, why exactly are you supposed to care about that, and what warrants a ritual devoted to such a weirdo? Do not, however, just for the reason that it is silly, fail to enjoy this odd holiday with the one that you love most of all. Play along with the charade, but do not succumb to its sentimentality, or to any of the attendant fairy tales. Take the opportunity to do something special for the one person who, more than anyone else on this planet, helps make your life feel like it is actually worth living. Why *not* today (as well as other days)? Why *not* express your love and adoration to your spouse? Turn the disingenuous façade of this ridiculous holiday into something sincere. That may be the best revenge against the purveyors of the great fraud. Take their attempt to monetize affection and strip it of its pecuniary accretions. There may be only a subtle distinction that turns this charade on its head, but it is a distinction nonetheless. It is bit like the distinction between pretending to be polite and being polite with sincerity.

February 15

There is something vaguely Kafkaesque about your experience of this day, is there not? It feels more like *The Trial* than *The Metamorphosis*, but something disorienting hangs over you, or so it seems. Where is the progress? Does *anything* feel as if it is moving the direction you would choose? Many projects and various corresponding aspirations presented themselves this morning, but none came fully to fruition in anything approaching a satisfying fashion. Is this because your aspirations were unrealistic, or because your efforts were inadequate—or was it merely a chance product of concatenated happenstance over which you had no control? More importantly, how should a rational adult respond to a day filled with one fairly mild frustration after another? Should you chalk it up as "one of those days," or should you take some time to reevaluate your goals, your interests and your standard methods of accomplishing quotidian tasks? It would be something indeed if you were to realize, as a result of fairly mundane experience, that you have been governing your entire life poorly. There are lessons even in the smaller challenges. Have you not, for example, learned how to navigate safely through your home in the dark because you suffered a stubbed toe somewhere along the route? Try to learn *something* from everything you encounter.

February 16

Playing tug-o-war with the dog today, you managed, somehow, to injure your right shoulder, and you noticed that you were slightly short of breath by the end of the playful struggle. The dog did not appear to be nearly as fatigued and exhibited no sign of injury. The dog is far less than half your size. Are you really *that* out of shape? If so, you had better get back to regularly working on your cardiovascular conditioning, and you had better do something about your diet, if that is part of your poor functionality. You know that you are afforded only a finite number of breaths in this lifetime, but surely that number can be increased, and your time can be, at least in principle, extended somewhat through an assiduous program of exercise. There are people who *need* you, and there are obligations outstanding that will require a fair number of years from you still. Do not facilitate your demise through lassitude or sloth. Of course, there are no guarantees in this arena, but you still have a duty to *try* to persist for as long as fate and circumstance allow you to remain useful to your project or to other people. How many times have you silently criticized other middle-aged persons who have allowed themselves to become soft, lazy, and weak? Do not allow *yourself* to become a hypocrite. Do *not* become what you behold with contempt. Get back to diligent conditioning. Train for optimal functionality. This is not a matter of aesthetics or a project to undertake "for show." You never know when you will need to be sharp.

February 17

You allowed yourself to experience a pang of disappointment this morning as you listened to members of the political commentariat lying, dissembling, and doing their best to mislead and misinform the viewing public. How is it possible that you *still* experience any such psychological state as you watch and listen to well-established charlatans, liars, and partisan "spin doctors," degrading themselves even further? These people are professional prevaricators. Experiencing frustration as they ply their trade is like allowing yourself to be disillusioned when a snake oil salesman's product fails to "cure what ails you." What did you expect? Waiting for a miracle, were you? Anyone dumb enough to buy snake oil is too intellectually defective to be entrusted with money. Have you not been buying snake oil for many, many years now? Every time you turn on a television "news" program, you are swilling snake oil, or bathing in it, or using it for eye drops. What does it say about your intellect that you keep watching and listening to people who get *paid* to lie? Perhaps you are simply gullible. Perhaps you prefer lies to which you are accustomed rather than truths with which you are not so well acquainted. Find something better to do with your time and your mind. Drugs and alcohol are not the only things that corrode your brain.

February 18

When you woke this morning, you were startled, you felt cold, and your heart was pounding as if you had been having a nightmare. Oddly, you could recall *nothing* of the dream that you had been experiencing, apart from an intense feeling of acute frustration. There was something, in the context of the dream, that you *had* to accomplish, or some horrifying consequence (you have no recollection of the nature of the consequence) would ensue, and you awoke knowing that you had failed, and that disaster struck. This was, of course, only a dream, but you find yourself wondering, during your waking hours, if this dream is not some kind of subconscious allegory of your real life and your unvarnished assessments of your accomplishments and failures. Is there not something terrifying nagging at the periphery of your experience? Something is coming. It feels dark and foreboding. Perhaps it is already too late. Perhaps you still have time. You had better hope there is time yet. Perhaps the dream, like nearly all of your other dreams, will turn out to be *nothing more* than a dream. Somehow, this particular frustration dream is indicative of a lurking thing just beneath the surface level of your consciousness. Perhaps the darkness is *within you*, and you are just inclined to project it onto the outside world, and to imagine that you are endowed with some type of vague clairvoyance. The "allegory" hypothesis is more than just a little pretentious, is it not?

February 19

It is surprisingly common for people to behave as if you need their good will, their approval, or their respect. You are not conscious of any such necessity, but so many people seem to regard themselves as utterly indispensable to your well-being. This is most curious, is it not? This one informs you that he is unimpressed with your work, and behaves as if he just *knows* that this news has ruined your day and left you crestfallen. That one tells you that she thinks you look old and tired, and she does so with a disingenuously apologetic, sarcastic flair that indicates how deeply she believes she has just thrust in the dagger. Like children calling each other "stupid head!" they relish the damage they imagine they have done to your fragile psyche. You *are* a child, are you not? No? You are *not* a child? Ah, therein lies your invulnerability. You simply need not care about what anyone else thinks about anything, including what anyone thinks about *you*. What, exactly, would make *you*, or anything *about* you, a worthy topic of conversation. All you need to do is recognize that the same is true of everyone else. Nothing about *them* is worthy of your concern, and certainly nothing that the unworthy think about you, a number among their rank, is worthy of any particular worry. Learn to care as little about what others think of you, as you worry about them and their lives of not-so-quiet desperation. Done.

February 20

What is going on with people who do not love dogs? No, really. Sure, you are willing to give a pass to people who have been badly bitten, or people who come from environments in which dogs are essentially wild predators that periodically kill the children. That kind of thing tends to sow enmity between the species in question. People who encounter the same (mostly) docile, fun-loving, people-loving, goofy dogs that *you* regularly encounter, however, are simply a different and somewhat baffling story. Here is a creature that loves you and worships at your feet as long as you feed it, do not torture it, and play with it every so often (an intrinsically enjoyable experience for *you*), and there are people who "do not like" that? How is this possible? How does anyone take the experience of petting a puppy and turn it into an unpleasantness? It is not as if it is a matter of not liking *cats*. Everyone can understand *that*. Even "cat people" understand that a lot of people hate cats, or regard them as little nuisances over which they trip and stumble. But, dogs? Puppies? Wonderful bundles of fur, tongue, and nearly unconditional love are objects of distaste for some people? How? Why? It is a bit like hating the concept of motherhood, or wine, or chocolate! There can be *no* common ground with these loonies. One imagines *terrorists* rejecting the company of dog haters! They are *deranged*, it seems. Baffling.

February 21

You slept, but you feel as if you have been awake for a week. Evidently, there is some distinction between *real* sleep and whatever you awoke from after this ersatz "slumber" that you experienced last night. This is becoming a more common occurrence than you can explain by reference to sinus problems, muscle spasms, or even the sleep apnea that you are fairly confident you do not have. It is not cramps in your legs that cause this daylong haze. The prospect of a dietary issue is not impossible, but there is no particular reason to cling to that hypothesis. Something else seems to be afoot. It *feels* (for lack of a better term) like something on the *inside* is fatigued. Your *mind* is tired today. Your character is not performing at optimal efficiency. That is, clearly, an infelicitous way to describe whatever this condition is that hovers like a cloud around your soul. No, that way of putting it is not really any better, is it? Is there a neurological issue at the root of this difficulty? Is it, perhaps, a biochemical imbalance (and is there a "proper balance" in this area?)? Go see a physician if you believe that doing so might help. Apart from that, stop marinating in self-pity already. Are you unable to "handle" your current condition? Really? Consider military personnel who have had to survive for months on less than one hour of sleep each night, and have had to be prepared to kill or be killed at any moment along the way. They lived through *that*, and you complain about *your* circumstances? Stop. Man up and take care of the business at hand.

February 22

This morning you woke with the near certainty that you have contracted a cold, the flu, or some other upper respiratory infection. Ah, what a wonderful excuse for lethargy, sloth, complaint, and a generally listless waste of the day. You briefly considered calling in sick to work. That is to say, you considered abrogating a professional obligation, one that you clearly had insufficient cause for shirking, and you nearly became precisely the type of colleague that you despise as lazy and pathetic. You contemplated turning yourself into *that* over a dry throat and some sniffles? For this, you really ought to hang your head in shame. Perhaps there is some solace to be taken in recognizing that you declined to shirk your professional responsibilities, but *how* did you allow yourself even to contemplate such a disgraceful possibility? Considering an act of weakness and cowardice is the first step toward a life of sloth, dissolution, and vapidity. What is this pathetic weakness that nips at your heels all too often? Men have sallied forth into battle with missing limbs, blindness in one eye, and bodily trauma the likes of which you have never experienced. You *dare* to allow a *cold* to present itself as an excuse? You actually entertained *that* thought? Weakling. Where is your fortitude? Hang your head in dishonor, and do not entertain such thoughts again. Okay, you are being at least a tad melodramatic about this. Dial it back, get washed up, grab a bag of lozenges, and get to work.

February 23

The disingenuous, duplicitous, lying frauds got on your nerves again today. Oddly enough, they said things that they clearly did not believe to be true, and they did so in a cynical attempt to benefit themselves. Somehow, you managed to become irritated by this behavior. Whose fault is that? Surely, you know that many people whom you will encounter each day are liars and charlatans. Many people are incompetent and are also desperate to conceal their incompetence. Some people are criminals and have developed skills appropriate to confidence scams and other forms of corruption. Sometimes, you wonder if these types do not hold the *majority* among the populace at large. How many times can you allow the same sort of malefactor to get under your skin via the same kind of childish, underhanded misbehavior? Indeed, *who* is behaving like the child in the interactions in question? You must learn to be better prepared to turn away from dissembling dimwits, and to do so without frustration, anger, or despair for the future of Western Culture. These people are the equivalent of hyenas or skunks. Avoid their company when possible, and regard them with the contempt you generally reserve for lower animals when their presence must be endured. It is not surprising that a skunk emits an unpleasant odor. What kind of dunderhead gets upset when imbeciles act like imbeciles? Expect no better. Manage your expectations, and respond to stupidity with *reason*. Problem solved.

February 24

Your particular narrative has progressed well beyond its midpoint, has it not? You are, in other words, more than halfway dead. Surely, you do not expect to live to one hundred years of age. If not, you are more than halfway through with your journey through this "vale of tears," and it might behoove you to take stock of your accomplishments, or lack thereof, to this point. It is worth your while to acknowledge the time that has elapsed, and the comparative dearth of time that remains. Of course, you may have *far* less time remaining than statistical averages would indicate. At this point, you have already lived longer than did Alexander the Great, Jesus Christ, or John Lennon. Where do you get the sense of entitlement to more life than you have already lived? John F. Kennedy did not live as long as *you* have lived. Of course, Kennedy was also something of a corrupt, lying charlatan, but that may be the subject of a separate meditation. For all the time you have been allotted, can you produce the product of your labors, or the culmination of your efforts that ought to impress anyone—including yourself? What lands have you conquered, what lives have you saved, what masses have you inspired, what works of genius have you offered your fellow human beings? Apart from eating, drinking, and complaining, what other accomplishments can you present? Lay your cards on the table. Read 'em and weep.

February 25

Some people seem to derive pleasure, or some type of perverse satisfaction, from pushing their luck, and pushing to see just how far their malevolence will be tolerated. Adolescence persists a bit longer than nature intended in some cases. It is no sin to bring closure to such investigations of the limitations you may impose upon the poorly behaved, and the consequences of pushing a bit further than is advisable. Perhaps you do them a *favor* by illustrating the results of pressing too hard upon those unwilling to bear too much pressing. It is one thing for an adolescent jackass with more testosterone than brains to learn a lesson at the mere expense of a few scars, or a broken bone and a helping of wounded ego. You can still provide lessons of this variety when called upon to do so, or when it just seems well deserved. It is something else entirely for the troublemakers to learn the relevant lesson as the last act in a lifetime of childishness. It is better that you embarrass an imbecile in public, than it is that the imbecile expires in a private backroom of some club, barroom, or in a dark corner of some penitentiary—in a pool of his own blood and vomit. Better a backhand than a blade, a barrel, or punches and kicks delivered by a throng of frenzied convicts. Not every lesson needs to culminate in death or permanent disability. Some, however, tend to issue in horrors. At least you will not do *that*—probably.

February 26

A new challenge presents itself today. This time it is not a matter of physical pain, irritating colleagues, lying politicians, or the impending collapse of Western Civilization, although those phenomena are always present as "background radiation," but in this instance the issue is a contractual matter. The latest contract you have been offered, and that you accepted, is something of a disappointment. It differs from previous contracts in a manner that is financially disadvantageous to you, and no justification for the alteration has been presented. The offer was, more or less, of the "take it or leave it" variety. You opted to take it. Never lose sight of the fact that no one *compelled* you to do so. Do not tell yourself that you had no viable alternatives, or that financial exigencies served as coercive circumstances about which you could do nothing. Declining the offer and "walking away" would have been no great difficulty. If you are an adult in possession of your faculties, you are obligated to kindle no resentment regarding the new terms. No one forced your hand in this matter. There was neither a knife to your throat, nor a gun to your head—and, had there been, you *could* still have chosen death rather than the alternative. Do not harbor ill will regarding a mere contract. Forces beyond your control largely dictate most of this business. You could have signed, or you could have refrained from signing. You signed. That ends it. Waste no further thought on this.

February 27

A scheduled event failed to come to fruition today. Perhaps the Fates intervened to prevent it, or maybe it was nothing more than a matter of conflicting schedules and insufficient opportunity to correct a bit of confusion or some misunderstanding. Either way, this is, at worst, a fairly trivial inconvenience and, at best, an opportunity to explore alternatives to the planned event. Indeed, the event in question was not one to which you looked forward with any particular relish. You were hardly champing at the bit to get to it, after all. More importantly, you have before you a chance to enhance your patience, and to expand your emotional forbearance in the face of contingencies unrealized or a disruption of your schedule. This has actually been something of a difficulty for you. Though you did not realize this about yourself until recently, you crave structure, and you tend to get upset when your routine is disrupted or your expectations for the flow of the day's events prove to be inaccurate. This is *not* a healthy habit of thought. So what if external events did not coincide with your expectations? Surely, you recognize that the world and its inhabitants are under no obligation to satisfy your desires or produce the occurrences that you happen to expect. Learn to *restrain* your expectations and desires. Restrict them to the things that cannot be disrupted by the external world. Thus, you will have nothing to fear from the Fates.

February 28

Facts are, indeed, stubborn things, and they do not, for the most part, lend themselves easily to felicitous alteration. Events transpire, consequences ensue, and you can do little or nothing about the vast majority of all events in the universe. Even occurrences involving other persons lie almost entirely beyond your control. People mostly do as they wish, think what they can, or what they cannot help but think, and they say, more or less, whatever happens to pop out of their mouths whether any of it is coherent or sensible or not. One unpleasant fact is that the "culture war" is over, and the "opposing side" has clearly been victorious. The culture has gone, almost entirely, "the wrong way." What, however, is the real "problem" with this state of affairs? Is it not that you allowed yourself to identify with one side as opposed to the other in a culture war? You allowed your desires to attach to conditions beyond your control. The culture and its evolution are *not* yours to control, *never* will be up to you, and *never* have been impacted in any significant measure by your efforts. Why waste your efforts and incur emotional distress about something like that? You have no business allowing your hopes to attach to cultural phenomena of *any* type at all. Do not stamp your feet like a petulant child and throw a fit because you find popular culture to be ignoble and filthy. Turn away from the spectacle. Go fishing. Take a hike and notice the beauty of nature. Stand in the light, soak up some sun, and remember that no culture can deprive you of *that*.

March 1

The world is filled to overflowing with people who have no interest in *learning* anything, and who are passionately committed to believing comforting nonsense irrespective of evidence to the contrary. The capacity of the average person to believe what he *wants* to believe, rather than observing the *facts*, is absolutely astonishing. Do these people *actually* believe the patent nonsense that they spout so relentlessly, or are they merely putting on a show and pretending to embrace childish idiocy? It is often difficult to distinguish between stupidity and dishonesty. Presumably, the citizens of this world are something of a mixed bag. You have encountered a miniscule percentage of those who populate, and have populated, this planet. Some are probably genuine "true believers" in flat-earth style nonsense. Others are, no doubt, merely disingenuous trolls who take pleasure in contrarianism for its own sake. Still others are, almost certainly, of the *willfully* ignorant variety. They make it their business to refrain from knowing things that would cause them discomfort or emotional distress. They do not *wish* to know the truth unless it happens to provide comfort or moral cover. As for *you*, there is simply insufficient evidence for taxonomy. Surely, you are as susceptible to false belief as is anyone else. Are your errors in earnest, or do *you* also manage not to know propositions that you prefer not to acknowledge.

March 2

Today, you became aware that you had spent a significant amount of time operating in something of a cognitive fog. You were on something like autopilot for a good long while earlier in the day. You had accomplished a number of fairly quotidian tasks, you had read a few articles, and you had eaten breakfast, but a bit later, you could not have recounted much of what you had done. Subsequently, upon "waking up," you could not help but consider how much of your adult life had passed in a similar type of mental state. How much of your *waking* life have you spent in a less than fully wakeful condition? Put it all together, and you cannot help but suspect that years of your life have passed by without your quite perceiving it. This matter is not, of course, readily quantifiable, but it is fairly clear that a *lot* of your life has gone by and you have failed to *notice* it. There is a sense in which you have *not been there* for much of your life. You have been absent, perhaps, as frequently as you have been present for *your own* experiences. This has to be at least a little disturbing, does it not? As far as you know, you get only *one* life, and you are at least halfway through it. Only now are you realizing that you have been functioning as little more than a zombie from your cradle to the present day. Do *not* waste any more time sleepwalking your way to your own death. You have been granted this life, and you really ought to pay attention.

March 3

Your body is not what it once was. There seems to be somewhat *more of it* than you recall observing in the mirror when you were younger. The additional mass also seems not to have distributed itself in the most felicitous fashion that you might have imagined. You are becoming a little thicker in the middle, are you not? This becomes more glaringly obvious with a somewhat startling regularity. You have actually wondered, not entirely in ironic or impish fashion, if your current mirror is, somehow, telling a less than exact tale. You look and you think, "Is *that* accurate?" This is absurd, of course, but such is the degree of physical transformation your physique has undergone. This deterioration has occurred in spite of a fairly regular and robust practice of physical exercise. You have been working out diligently since you were twelve years old! Imagine what you would look like at this point, and imagine how degraded your physical capacity would be by now, if you had not developed an interest in physical fitness from a fairly young age. How on earth do so many people manage to exercise so little without turning into something like bread pudding? In any event, do not become lax in this area. Drop and give yourself twenty push-ups. Turn over and churn out twenty sit-ups. That is, of course, barely a beginning. Keep working at it, or suffer the consequences of allowing your body to become a shambling mound.

March 4

What is all this nonsense you hear these days about the nature of "the narrative," emanating from the media, the halls of government, and the populace at large? What is "the narrative" of the day, and for whom is this story being constructed? You do not recall anyone demanding the construction of a yarn. The intended audience, presumably, has not *requested* a bedtime story. What, therefore, is this jabbering about the telling of tales? The public is a beast, and the beast does not seem to know what it wants, or even what it needs, but you do not perceive this alleged demand for campfire stories. In the absence of clearly expressed desires, you can expect the merchants of mendacity, and the purveyors of prevarication to step in and start *informing* the public of what they are *obligated* to desire, and what those worthy of the culture's embrace must say and must do. If you want to be accepted, the elite class will inform you, it is necessary to want the "right things," to value the "right things," and even to ask for what you are instructed to request. The public will be *made* to care about what the elites *command* them to value. The public will be *compelled* to embrace the cultural suck, even when the public knows that they are being improperly used. *You* will do nothing of the kind. Stand athwart the tide if you must, but do so with the understanding that the tide *will* win. You know that the tide takes no notice of *you*.

March 5

Today, you "rendered unto Caesar" a tax payment that was, at first blush, a bit beyond your expectations. Indeed, even upon retrospective consideration, it still seems like you paid an awful lot more than you should have been compelled to pay. Of course, since tax laws are readily available for your perusal, and given that you were perfectly capable of having calculated, at the very least, a rough estimate of your probable liability, any surprise about the total bill is entirely *your* fault, is it not? Due diligence tends to obviate shock around tax time. It also tends to help in other areas, does it not? Either perform the requisite due diligence, or learn to become accustomed to surprise, disquiet, and needless emotional distress. Better still, learn to stop attaching any significance to pecuniary phenomena, and allow all attendant disquiet to dissipate as a result of your disinterest. What *is* so fascinating about money, anyway? It is a social construct for expediting exchanges of various markers allegedly signifying legitimate claims to dispense with resources. It is a construct to replace bartering in chickens, beef, and various forms of grain. In other words, money is an *invention*. It is made up. Try eating it. See what you can do with it apart from handing it over to another person. Do not lose sight of the intrinsic nature of the thing for which so many are willing to kill, to commit crime, and to debase their character. Do not degrade yourself for a toy.

March 6

When you witness the depravity and the general moral decrepitude of the age, you struggle to avoid despair, and you have to stretch to find a reason to embrace hope about *any* potential future just over the horizon. Despair, however, is not particularly useful, and it is not particularly adaptive, is it? Hope, of course, is not always particularly well justified, nor is *it* always a generally adaptive strategy. Indeed, you are not certain that *any* general cast of mind, or *any* general approach to the events and the culture that surround you, is likely to prove to be especially adaptive. The only sensible course of action, and the only strategy that holds out any hope of success, is directing your efforts at self-rectification and self-improvement. Do not concern yourself with humanity at large, or with the general downward gradient of your nation, its culture, and the attendant decline of things that you once valued, and phenomena that you once regarded as paramount concerns. Many things that you once loved, or *thought* that you once loved, are now irreparably damaged or lost forever. Despair is always irrational, but it is not always easy to resist. Do not allow your mental states to depend upon anything that lies beyond your control, and you will experience despair less frequently. Thus, desolation is dispatched and serenity is recaptured. Captain *your* soul. The rest is so much detritus.

March 7

Uncomfortable truths are no less true than are those from which you derive consolation or succor. All too often you have seen the public "avert its eyes" *en masse* rather than acknowledge facts that are both awkward and incontrovertible. It is never difficult to find masses that are willing to deny the undeniable, defend the indefensible, and submit their credulity to the kind of strain that ought to result in an audible, resounding *snap*! How often have you heard admonitions that you "must" embrace ludicrous and obvious mischaracterizations of reality, accompanied by thinly veiled threats of reprisal or ostracism if you *dare* to challenge the prevailing absurd orthodoxies of the day? Let the powers that be ostracize you to their hearts' content, and you are well aware that they derive *enormous* pleasure from casting out the heretics. What form of reprisal do you need to fear? Perhaps you will be deprived of the financial means of sustaining yourself and your family. There are plenty of ways to make money, are there not? Perhaps someone, or some mob of people, will beat you to death in a dark alley somewhere. That is certainly a possibility. Did you believe yourself to be immortal in the absence of a beating unto death? Everybody gets to die from something or other. Do you prefer *cancer* to a beating? Do not trouble yourself about the inevitable. The crowd cannot *make* you a coward. Only *you* can defile yourself. Decline to do so.

March 8

Your patience was tested today, and you did not exactly pass that particular test with flying colors, did you? Anyone who claims that "there are no stupid questions" has spent precious little time interacting with the talking primates. Either that, or the claim is just one more bit of disingenuous "political correctness," intended to make the speaker appear charitable and gentle. The amount of bullshit shoveled for the sake of making people appear to be more admirable or virtuous than they really are is simply staggering. In any event, the world positively *abounds* with moronic inquiries, and the more asinine the question, the louder and more relentlessly it is likely to be asked. Indeed, there appears to be something of an inverse proportionality between wisdom and volume. Those least endowed with the former are nearly always inclined to accentuate the latter. In the case of a moronic or disingenuous question, *any* response serves only to extend and exacerbate the torturous exchange. Imbeciles are seldom satisfied with replies, and attempts at evasion always seem to slip by unnoticed. The disingenuous pseudo-question masking a criticism or an adolescent attempt to garner attention for the inquirer will never warrant a response—nor will any response suffice. Perhaps silence is a viable option in some cases, but it must be accompanied by distance from the interlocutor. Morons cannot *bear* silence. There *are* reasons that people get punched in the face.

March 9

So many people are desperate to believe themselves to be different, they crave to be unique and interesting, and they work to prove their uniqueness with such common ferocity, that they become disturbingly similar to all the other desperate people that brandish their inimitability like so many switchblades and blackjacks. There is a surprising number, and a seemingly *growing* number, of the disingenuously weird. Indeed, as far as you can tell, weirdness is cultivated at least as often as it is innate, or as often as it is thrust upon the weirdo by fate, trauma, or biochemistry. The sincerely weird certainly exist, and many of them are worth the trouble required to learn how to communicate with them. As for these ersatz weirdoes, the same simply cannot be said. The phony weirdo is one of the most boring creatures on the face of the planet. What is this bizarre inclination to *appear* to be bizarre? Perhaps it is a cry for help, but why should anyone wish to be of assistance to the strange alien residing among the honest peasants populating the quiet countryside—living out their pathetic lives of not-always-especially-quiet desperation? Let the freaks live as they choose, and let them die of their idiotic choices, if that is to be the way of things. You need not pretend to empathize with pretenders. Indeed, a case can be made that you are obligated to be more sincere and authentic than that.

March 10

Sometimes a miserable job has to be done, and sometimes that miserable job legitimately falls to *you*, and your responsibility is not abrogated merely because it is affixed to a bit of misery for you. It is precisely in the face of the prospect of misery or tedium that it is *most* important that you do *not* shirk your obligations. When your task is terrible, but necessary, you must embrace the suck, and you *must* do whatever is required to discharge your assignments as efficiently and as diligently as you are able. Do not complain when it is your turn to take up the next phase of a tedious task. Remember that you are not the first, and will not be the last, to bear this type of onus. Do not whine, even within the confines of your own consciousness, about the "terrible burdens" of your fate. It is, almost certainly, not unique to you, and things could absolutely have been far, far worse for you. Chart a course through the dismal days to come, and do not veer from that course when the inevitable challenges arise. Do not even *consider* quitting. Do not allow yourself even to contemplate this option. *Never* surrender. It will be far too tempting to allow such considerations to take hold of your mind and to allow despair or disgust to take root. Press forward with diligence, resilience, and singularity of purpose. Going through hell may be unavoidable. If so, you *keep going*. The alternative is, or ought to be, unthinkable.

March 11

You encountered yet another complaint today, and yet another claim that some pathetic weakling was "offended" by something you said. You gave the matter the fairest consideration of which you were capable, you tried to empathize with the complainant, and did your level best to see your detractor's side of the issue. You tried, in other words, to put yourself in the other person's shoes. All of these efforts uncovered precisely *nothing* that warranted "offense" or umbrage. Indeed, you could not even understand how it would be *possible* to become outraged in the circumstance in question. What conclusion can you, in your most charitable and most convivial attitude, possibly reach regarding this latest gripe? What is *really* going on here? Honesty bids the assessment that this is yet another episode of utterly phony, entirely manufactured "outrage," and nothing more than an attempt by yet another useless, disingenuous cry-bully to intimidate you into silence through an implied threat of disapprobation, reinforced with some potential institutional sanction. Well, when did you declare your intention to placate hypersensitive imbeciles? When did you sign an accord that prohibits speech and behavior that is not approved by charlatans, weaklings, and bureaucrats? Never? Ah, then there is no more to be said about the matter. Let them weep, wail, and gnash their teeth.

March 12

You received positive news today, but your enjoyment of this news has been dampened somewhat by the necessity of accepting an unexpected, significant delay in gratification. The expected benefit will not be available to you until approximately one year has elapsed. You had expected to enjoy the benefit in question within roughly half the time. You found this vaguely upsetting. A question, therefore, presents itself. What kind of pathetic adolescent *are* you? Can you not embrace a year's worth of waiting to "get the goodies"? A child manages to wait this long between birthdays, and even the most impatient persons understand that Christmas comes only once a year. Yet, here you are, more than halfway through your journey on this planet, and your initial response to the news that you will have to wait a little longer for a reward that, in all honesty, you are not quite certain that you have *earned* is an internal hissy fit. What is your excuse for allowing the experience of good news to be tempered by a mere delay on the way to its fruition? If you have no more command over your emotions than does an impetuous youngster, perhaps you do not deserve to enjoy the satisfaction of your desires. Perhaps you should, *like* a child, be left in the care of someone a bit wiser and more mature. Grow up already. Learn to wait patiently. Be an adult. Practice what you preach, or *stop* with the preaching.

March 13

It seems that you live in the era of Nietzsche's "Last Man." The *Last Man* seeks comfort, safety, and steadiness above all else, and he is willing to trade away every vestige of actual manhood in exchange for his precious, cozy life of *ease*. The *Last Man* is a contemptible but all-too-common creature, and it seems that you bump into one of his number nearly every time you leave your home. Indeed, you have to consider the possibility that you need not leave home to encounter the *Last Man*. How much have *you* been willing to trade away for the sake of maintaining your home, automobiles for the family, health care, and ready access to quantities of food that your ancestors could scarcely have imagined? How easy, you really must ask yourself in *pointed* fashion, does your life need to be? The *Last Man* may be looking back at you from the mirror, might he not? That reflection is not exactly the image of the noble barbarian, nor is that an image of anything resembling Nietzsche's *Overman*. When Alexander the Great met Diogenes the Cynic, *you* were not there, and you would almost certainly have been spurned by both of those superior beings. Unless your mirror is hopelessly inaccurate, you must conclude that you see, in the looking glass, a figure that would cause Nietzsche to dissolve in hysterics. Diogenes went looking for men and found none—but he found *boys* in Sparta. You would not have qualified even as a boy by his standards. Chew on *that*, pal.

March 14

You have many chores to do today, and several ancillary tasks that are, in and of themselves, not particularly pleasant or rewarding. It is not a particularly unusual state of affairs, is it? This is *not* an excuse for complaint, nor is it an excuse for failing to do your duty. Every life is filled with time- and energy-consuming obligations, and no one benefits from whining about drudgery, or from listening to others carping about their lot. These complaints are not uncommon, nor are the consequences for the whiners or for those to whom they direct their wailing. Waste no energy in the childish and ignoble act of throwing a fit because you are not permitted to spend every moment at leisure, or to do only what you are naturally inclined to do at all times and in all circumstances. What is the great "injustice" about which you carp and complain to yourself? Do you have to work for money to sustain yourself and your family? Oh, how tragic! Be grateful for the job and the strength to do it. Be immeasurably *more* grateful for your spouse and your family. Do you have to prepare dinner for the people that you love? Be thankful for the food, and be *more* thankful that you have a family to feed. Do you have to die soon? Are you bent out of shape about mortality? Surely, you jest. Be grateful that you had a chance to live in the first place. Must you suffer? Does the world impose physical pain, psychological discomfort, and emotional unease upon you? Try to remember that you get to live a *human life*. Do so like a man. Stop quivering like a jellyfish.

March 15

No one ever derived anything of value from sloth, cowardice, and acquiescence to a vast majority that knows not what it does, or ever considers why it does anything at all. Never hesitate to venture out and forge a new path merely because the mob tells you that *it* cannot or should not be done. What is to be gained by mindless, shallow conformity to a standard that is upheld by the mediocrity of an amorphous mass of humanity that seems mostly incapable of producing anything of real or lasting value? History is neither made nor written by the average, the non-descript, or by the devotees of safety and stability. Indeed, there is something troubling about the contemporary fixation on ease, luxury, and safety. You live in a culture that is over-insured, overweight, and overworked. Why must so many people work so many hours in order to purchase so many goods and services that none of them actually need? The pursuit of ever more *stuff*, ever expanding insurance premiums to cover the stuff, and the life of wage slavery to afford it all, this hardly constitutes a life well lived. Take the time, and exert the effort necessary, to distinguish between a noble risk and an ignoble fantasy. Work aimed at nobility is time well spent. Work aimed at "keeping up with the Joneses" is *not*. Recognize the difference. Having done so, take the risk required for the ennobling endeavor at hand. Either that, or pick out a casket and get comfortable.

March 16

The cage fights tonight were competitive, compelling, and the combative skills on display were among the most impressive you have ever seen. The athleticism, grit, and endurance required are almost superhuman. The dedication to an artistry mixed with acute violence is simply astonishing, and you struggle to comprehend the kind of mind and the type of character that is not, even grudgingly, impressed by the elite participants in mixed martial arts and cage fighting. What kind of man does not, at least in *some* of the further recesses of his soul, long for the opportunity to test his mettle at least *once*, in the arena of physical combat? How is it possible, given the evolutionary history of your species, and given the cultural imperatives that have driven history, to find nothing compelling in a good fight? There are reasons that the Romans went to the Coliseum in throngs to watch the gladiators do battle. Boxing, wrestling, and the no-holds-barred *pancratium* were among the earliest Olympic contests for similar reasons. The contemporary vilification of violence, and the practice of raising children to "use their words" rather than learning how to deal with bullying "the old-fashioned way" are not in keeping with the martial spirit that inspired reverence for warriors and defenders of nations. Bring back the *agoge*! This age of sickening civility is *not* a period of admirable social evolution. You bear witness to the symptoms of sickness unto cultural death all around you.

March 17

There is news today that *another* member of the immediate family may have cancer. This is not, at this point, particularly surprising. Cancer of one form or another has accounted for more than half of the deaths of those "particular others" that you count among family and close friends. It is probably quite similar for most of the people of your nation, living in this day and age as your contemporaries, and as persons who indulge in behaviors that often result in one or another form of cancer developing. Of course, many forms appear to be congenital, and this provides good cause to be certain to choose your parents well. It seems that you have gone astray on this score, as your father died of lung cancer. Who would have guessed that smoking four packs of cigarettes a day for fifty years could possibly prove problematic in this regard? Ah, yes—*everyone*. We know the risks and so many of us choose the dangerous course nonetheless. You find yourself wondering if it has been thus throughout human history, but has only been recognized to be so due to progress in a diagnostic science, or if there is something peculiar to the modern diet, the modern environment, or the modern longevity rates that render your contemporaries more susceptible to developing this disease. Of course, you sometimes wonder if this is how *you* will meet your end. If you face this diagnosis one day, do so like a man. Self-pity is *not* permitted.

March 18

The news is, not surprisingly, still full of chatter about the recent terrorist attacks in the Southern Hemisphere. This is, at this point, another in a very long string of similar attacks with no apparent end in sight. On one hand, you regard it as unwise to give any more attention to this type of vile act than is absolutely necessary. What is to be gained, after all, by sharing the malefactor's demented worldview with the public at large? On the other hand, atrocities perpetrated against innocents cry out for something like analysis, explanation, or, at the very least, expressions of outrage. Perhaps there are persons who commit acts about which there is simply nothing to say beyond, "This is man's inhumanity to man yet again," and the expression can only be followed by some gesture of disdain or contempt. It becomes increasingly clear that terrorist violence is not going to end within your lifetime. The West and the Islamic world are going to dig away at each other, and the partisans in this conflict are going to wage sporadic warfare until one side or the other is destroyed. Any hope you may once have had to see its end can, at this point, be regarded as a childish bit of wishful thinking. Fanaticism is at war with modernity, and the worldviews involved are fundamentally incompatible. The problem with fighting against fanatics of this stripe is that many of them do not mind being killed. It is possible that the long haul may *favor* the fanatics. What does the West have to match against *jihad*? Foolishness is no weapon with which to combat mass murderers.

March 19

Walking is, in addition to being fairly good low-impact exercise, also an excellent stimulant to the creative process of generating ideas and contemplating possibilities. How many good notions and useful insights have occurred to you as you strolled around the neighborhood, or as you have taken a hike through the woods? Often, the dog comes with you on these walks and he seems both overjoyed and fascinated to encounter plants, persons, and various stray scents along the way. Indeed, your dog may derive even greater benefit from the walk than *you* do. His pure joy excited by the walk is certainly more apparent than is yours. The other great cognitive stimulant, in your experience, is a really satisfying bowel movement. This may seem crass, but there is no getting around the truth of it. You cannot even hope to track the number of occasions on which you have emerged from the restroom with a viable solution to a previously bedeviling problem, or with a new idea of what is or is not possible. A moment of clarity, of intellectual fluidity, is often a concomitant of resolved constipation. The flow of thoughts becomes undammed and unfettered by the absence of *intestinal* occlusion. The brain and the gut are not quite the entirely separate items that you might otherwise be inclined to assume. A cleansing in the one seems to lead to a clarification with respect to the functioning of the other. The dog cannot say *that*. Of course, the dog cannot really say much of *anything*.

March 20

The news of the day does not have the power to irritate you, confound you, or cause you to become miserable, without your complicity in the transformation. No event in the external world can exert direct causal control of your mental states or your general mood. This is fairly obvious, is it not? A person who has no interest in a particular state of affairs will not be troubled when that state of affairs unfolds. That person is immune to any psychologically discombobulating effects attaching to the events in question. It follows, does it not, that if you learn to develop the capacity to detach yourself, both psychologically and emotionally, from any events over which you have no direct control, then you will, thereby, become immune to discontent caused by the news of the day. All that lies within your control is your own mind, your own attitudes, the direction of your attention, and the management of your expectations. Stock markets, political affairs, talking heads on television and social media, environmental developments, and the behavior of all persons who are not numerically identical to *you*, are *not* yours to control, and you guarantee that you will suffer if you allow your concern to attach to anything that lies beyond your control. Such concerns constitute hubris. What kind of egomaniac allows his mind to obsess over the unfolding of events in an external world that takes no notice of him and does not obey his will? Stay within your proper sphere. As the kids say… *stay in your lane*, dude.

March 21

As an experiment, attempt to live this entire day without being noticed by *anyone*. See if you can manage to be so unobtrusive that absolutely *no one*, including the people who know you best, pays *any* attention to you at all. The prospect is both fascinating and forbidding, is it not? Presumably, you will have to refrain from speaking, and you will also have to decline all other mechanisms and media of interaction with your fellow talking apes. Send no text messages, no e-mails, and engage with no social media format. For just *one* day, do *not* talk to any of the other primates or communicate with them in any other fashion. You will also need to remain unseen, unheard, and inaccessible to all of the other senses. Can you make yourself *undetectable*? Perhaps you will be compelled to stay locked in your room all day. Then again, you will need to use the restroom at *some* point. Can you get there and back without detection? Maybe you should make your way to the woods and use the "facilities" you find there. Do you have the willpower necessary to forgo all comment upon the passing scene for *one* day? You will have to keep *all* of your opinions and observations to yourself for *one full day*. What does it say about you that doubts are already surfacing about your ability and willingness to pull this off? The prospect of being unseen, unheard, and otherwise not experienced by anyone is a source of a bit of anxiety. This powerful an urge to be noticed is something of a *disorder*, is it not?

March 22

It behooves you to consider the possibility that killing any living thing without just cause is *sinful* or, at the very least, wasteful. In the absence of just cause, *why* would you want to curtail *any* being's life? Certainly, the threshold of just cause is fairly low in many cases. If you contract a sinus infection, you have sufficient reason to take antibiotics and slaughter the invading bacteria *en masse*. That particular "genocide" should not trouble you in the slightest. If a fly or a bee makes its way into your home, swat the life out of the intruder without even a hint of hesitation or moral compunction. If, on the other hand, you find a snail making its way across a sidewalk somewhere, the urge to step on it should be treated with skepticism. What is to be gained by depriving the small creature of its life? Killing *anything* merely for the sake of killing is, at least arguably, an unhealthy and ignoble impulse. How much worse to kill "big game" and deprive the world of a noble beast merely for the "thrill" of the hunt? Stories of "big game" are, for the most part, stories of very small men. Why kill an elephant or a lion in anything other than self-defense? Only small, sinful men kill elephants. Perhaps all men are small and sinful, but most of us refrain from the needless slaughter of kings of the jungle. That does not justify any form of self-aggrandizement, of course. It is, however, at least one sin avoided.

March 23

More than anything else, today you find that you wish to be free of all invisible constraints and compulsions. For *one* day, you would enjoy the absence of obligations, and you would bask in the time and space to do whatever your heart, your soul, and blind happenstance moved you to do—completely apart from necessities surrounding your various roles within the construct that is sometimes called "community" or "society." How did these silly, amorphous abstractions ever weave a way so deeply and pervasively into the structure of every one of your days, your projects, your intentions, and your every exertion? It is difficult to recall the last time that you had no schedule, no expectations imposed upon you by yourself in deference to others, and no limitations artificially binding your time and your limited vital energies. Responsibilities always seem to hover around your every private moment, indicating that a mere *moment* of privacy is the most that you have coming. So much of the world is so *very* much *with* you, it seems. Do not complain about your obligations, though. Complaining does no good, and it reveals weakness that you had better keep concealed. Better yet, extirpate the weakness completely. A bit of longing for a bit more freedom is, however, not exactly the deepest, darkest sin ever committed. Who, among the chattering primates, does not yearn, now and again, to be a little freer, a little more at liberty to pursue interests and goals as the ape sees fit? This is perfectly natural, but not always attainable in noble fashion.

March 24

Do not posture, do not pretend and, for the love of God, do not demand posturing or pretense of others. If you find yourself pretending to believe something that you do not actually believe, or if you find yourself masquerading as something or someone that you are not, you must immediately stop talking and start thinking about *why* you are behaving that way. You can count on the fingers of one hand the number of people that you believe you know well enough, and with sufficient intellectual intimacy, that you feel confident in assessing the character of each one through and through. The other seven and a half billion people on this planet are all, more or less, equally no more than strangers to you. Some you recognize on sight, and most you do not, but this is a distinction with virtually no difference. You cannot see, or otherwise experience, the inner workings of the minds and souls of those with whom you are visually familiar. Thus, they are no less strange to you, in those respects that truly matter, than are adolescents on horseback crossing the bare stretches of plains in Mongolia. You can identify a *name* for some. *That* does not constitute *knowing* the person in question. What *is* a name? It is a sound or an inscription. What is *in* a name? What does a mere name actually tell you about its bearer? Whatever you may find there, it is not a rose, and it does not smell sweet. Do not wax Shakespearean without just cause.

March 25

You had better find something or someone that inspires in you the experience of sincere reverence and genuine awe. A life devoid of these types of experience is a life half lived at best. For many people, God serves this function, and He may very well be the ideal object of worship. Whatever there may be to say about awe, reverence, or faith, those characteristics are not proper objects of derision. Even if there is *no* God, no Creator, no Designer, you must still identify some type of phenomenon before which you cannot help but humble yourself and remember that you are small, fragile, relatively powerless, and ephemeral. You will not, in the grand scheme of things, last very long. On a cosmological scale, your life is not even equivalent to the blink of an eye. This cannot be said of the universe, the natural world, or the various manifestations of astronomical grandeur. These shall endure, if not forever, at least for billions upon billions of years. Already, they have persisted for eons. Surely, there is something in the natural world, in "creation itself" (if that term is permissible), to remind you that there is a great, great deal lying beyond your measly life and interests to revere and respect. A talking ape that regards nothing beyond its life, its experiences, and its interests as worthy of attention, thereby ties itself into a small, ignoble, and vaguely ugly package wound around with a ludicrous and needlessly gaudy bow. The world has no need of such a "gift."

March 26

The journey upon which you embark today is intended as an adventure, an exploration, and a bit of a vacation as well. You travel to a familiar place, but you seek something that you have not encountered before, either at today's destination or elsewhere. The object of your search is not a place or a physical entity in the external world. It is not to be found on any map, nor is it available in any catalogue. It cannot be purchased but it cannot be had for free either. This begins to seem like you are constructing something like a riddle, but you already know its answer. You know what you are after, but the question remains as to whether it will or will not prove attainable by your efforts. You are after an *experience* that has, thus far, eluded you across your entire life. Although you travel to a geographical location, the experience you seek is not an inherent feature of the topography, the geography, or the town to which you travel. Others have experienced what you seek, or so they claim. Some of the residents of the town to which you return today do *not* have the experience that you seek in the place where they reside. Perhaps some of them came to that place with the same intentions that you have, and in pursuit of the same object of your endeavors. You seek the experience of feeling *at home*—for, perhaps the first time in your life. You have never been quite at home in the world. The problem cannot be the world. Is the problem, perhaps, *in you*?

March 27

Another false and malicious allegation has been hurled at you today. This experience is neither new nor unique, and you are now accustomed to this kind of thing happening from time to time. Perhaps it occurs more frequently than that. In this instance, you have no doubt as to your innocence—though you cannot make the same claim in regard to *every* allegation you have faced. This time, a small man, both literally and figuratively, has cast the aspersion in question, and he has done so as, presumably, an intimidation tactic, or a threat of further harassment in the future. The accusation appears to be intended as something of a "warning shot" designed to encourage self-censorship on your part. The accuser appears to be "marking his territory," or staking something like a claim to "alpha male" status. In his case, particularly, it is all you can do to stifle a cackle at this ridiculous spectacle. You cannot help but wonder if, somewhere in the depths of this pathetic pipsqueak's subconscious, he wrestles with his glaring inadequacies as both a man and an antagonist in this imaginary struggle against you. Surely, he must understand, at some level, that he is a laughable caricature of what he projects himself to be. It is as if a mouse were to develop delusions of being a lion. His fantasies do not even rise to the level of an amusing charade. Try not to be overconfident in the coming altercation. It will not be *easy* to avoid overconfidence in this case, but you must do so nonetheless.

March 28

What is the difference between an attorney and a professional charlatan who will make literally *any* claim for sufficient remuneration? Sadly, this is not a premise for a lawyer joke. It is not a "setup" for a punch line to be delivered at the expense of one of the least reputable professions this side of the *oldest* profession. No, it is a genuine question that manifested after listening to an interview with a defense attorney representing a client who could not be more obviously guilty even if the crime had been captured on video. The experience was something like watching a man pointing at the blue sky while listening to him declaring that it is *obviously* a red and white checkerboard. Is there *nothing* that this professional prevaricator is *not* prepared to assert on the client's behalf? Is this level of dishonesty and shamelessness actually regarded as a *virtue* by practitioners of this profession, and by their clientele? You have heard as much asserted in defense of the lawyer's "art." If the term "virtue" can be perverted through such acts of semantic contortionism, perhaps words are even less trustworthy than are those who deploy them. To be fair, you have met *a few* honest lawyers, and you would not wish to paint all of them with the same brush. In your experience, however, the honest and forthright attorneys are much more the exception than the rule. Perhaps you are interacting with the wrong lawyers. As for the "right" ones, you do not know how to go about finding them.

March 29

It is possible that your life, or the lives of your loved ones, might depend upon you understanding, at the crucial moment, that there is no such thing as a "fair fight." To be sure, there are fair boxing, wrestling, and martial arts *matches*. There *can be* fair combat events in a parking lot, the back room of a bar, a basement, or out on a dimly-lit street corner. If the parties involved agree to a set of rules and abide by the rules to which they have agreed, and if some reliable character is entrusted to oversee the event and make certain that the rules are enforced, then a reasonable facsimile of fairness is established and enacted. That, however, is *not* a *fight*. A fight, by definition, has no rules, no holds or tactics are barred, there is no such thing as fighting "dirty," and the participants in the fight seek to *kill* the adversary. People do not *agree* to fight. Fights erupt spontaneously, or they result from an attempted attack with death as a potential consequence. All *true* fights are, at least in principle, *to the death*. Anything short of this is a sport, an assault, an altercation, or some type of misunderstanding. For this reason, it is advisable to avoid a *fight* whenever you are able to do so without sacrificing something that you value more than your own life. If you cannot or will not avoid a fight, you *must* fight to *win* by any means necessary, and to hell with the consequences. If your life is on the line, or if your family is placed at risk, you had better fight like *everything* that you have ever cared about is at stake.

March 30

When you enter into any competition, be sure that you maintain steady control of your psychological and emotional attachments pertaining to the resolution of the matter. Do not allow your peace of mind to become tethered to the *outcome*. Winning and losing are not within your control. If those matters were up to you entirely, you would *never* lose. Your adversary may be superior in the contest between you. Your opponent may prove to be smarter, stronger, faster, or more skilled than you. There is no shame in losing to an opponent who is simply better than you are within the arena in which the contest takes place. Should you wish to continue participating in similar competitions, learn everything that you can from each of your adversaries. Whether you win or lose, you are obligated to do your best to extract as much useful information from the contest as you are able. Perhaps you can, one day, surpass an opponent who had previously been your superior. Perhaps you will encounter someone against whom you will *never* triumph. There is no shame in this. You cannot be the greatest ever to have competed in *every* form of competition. If this is to be the way of things, learn humility and develop respect for the adversary you could not conquer. You may earn respect from this competitor, and you may not. This is also outside the sphere of your direct control. Your *effort* and your *attitude* are yours to govern. Embrace the result with fortitude. Do your best and acknowledge those who are better.

March 31

The last day of the month signifies absolutely nothing meaningful about the natural world, nor does it signify anything crucial about any important human construct. It corresponds to no ecological phenomenon, such as a solstice, an equinox, or even any particular phase of the moon (though the term "month" would seem to indicate otherwise). This is yet another arbitrary invention dreamed up as an expediency to address some trivial interest, real or imagined. Why must there be thirty-one days in March and only thirty days in April? Would the planet stop turning if the situation were reversed? Even *interests* can be imaginary, or can, at least, become epiphenomenal after the passage of many years, or after any and all of the lives in which the interest played any significant part have come to their various conclusions. So much of what is all too often referred to as a "culture" is, upon inspection, nothing more than years of accretions of pretense, surrounded by rumors of once-worthy goals, enwrapped in ancient, and now archaic, expectations. So much of this nonsense has *so* little to do with acquiring wisdom, attaining decency, and pursuing an honorable life. Why should anyone care if we all call this the end of March, the beginning of April or, for that matter, the twelfth day of Christmas? Today, you are informed, is the last day of March. Of course, it has not always been so. Hunter-gatherers cared not for "March" or for first or last days of "months," did they?

April 1

Is there some day of the year that is *not* dominated by fools and their foolishness? If so, you must have missed it. Why, then, does April 1st get to be called the "Fool's Day"? Yes, you have read competing accounts of the origin of the term and its association with this date. None of them have proved particularly interesting or edifying. That is not, however, the point. Can you not play a practical joke on (say) June 18th? Is there no "foolery" on (say) November 2nd? Anyone who needs to carve out a specific day, dedicated to a trivial purpose, and celebrate it by acting as a vague irritant, is simply failing to use time efficiently. There are twenty-four hours in every day, and the option of fooling people or playing practical jokes is nearly always available to any minimally industrious pain in the neck. Most people engage in trivial, irritating pursuits *many* times per day, if not per waking *hour*. Many people genuinely derive pleasure from being annoying, and from misleading gullible friends, coworkers, and relatives. Well, what is *that* to you? Trivial people do trivial things, irritating people irritate, and liars never tire of telling lies. You need not pay any of them any mind. Let them go about their trivial lives, and do not even bother to criticize them. What would be the benefit of doing so? They have found their level. They behave this way because they are incapable of conducting more useful lives. You seek *your own* level—and make certain it is a bit higher than theirs.

April 2

Rare is the day that you can live out fully in the absence of some sort of irritant, annoyance, or disruption of your serenity. This is, of course, your own fault, and it reveals the inadequacy and lassitude of your mental discipline. Your goal should be absolute emotional *imperturbability*. You should strive to be utterly unflappable. Turn yourself into the rock against which any potential irritants collide and shatter. This is a noble goal, but it is also very lofty and not *at all* easily attained. Indeed, it is not clear that anyone has *ever* managed such a level of self-discipline and psychological fortitude. Perhaps Socrates, the Buddha, or Epictetus attained such heights, and perhaps they did not, but there are precious few historical candidates for the title "Sage." No good, however, is so lofty that you may not attempt to approach it, consider it, and bend all efforts of heart, mind, and soul upon approximating it as nearly as you are able. Do not embark upon any endeavor in a condition of abject hopelessness. Hopelessness is not likely to spur you in the direction of improvement. Let your goal be *progress* rather than perfection. Even if the summit is too high to see, you can always aim for the next ridge or, at the very least, *one more step*. Just advancing that one more step is immeasurably preferable to remaining where you are and what you are. Stagnation is not exactly a noble goal, and the idea of remaining as you are, as *imperfect* as you are at the moment does not appeal to you. Even if your body gives out, let your *spirit* aspire still.

April 3

Some ne'er do well shall attempt to annoy you today, or otherwise impede your progress. That is simply the nature of the malefactor. Many people, it seems, do not feel as if they are really alive unless they can be really obnoxious, or unless they can hurl themselves as stumbling blocks athwart someone else's progress toward one noble goal or another. The motivation for this type of behavior is always either malevolence or boredom. These people are akin to the undead from zombie movies. They lack any drive or capacity of intellectual self-locomotion, and can only be moved by the sight, sound, or feel of an external agent in quest of something that the zombies dare not pursue themselves. They are dead inside, and they resent the living and the phenomenon of enthusiastic endeavor. Your life force is both enticing and revolting to them. They are drawn to it, but they resent the fact that you attempt to accomplish goals that they find far too intimidating to set as objectives for themselves. Knowing that they lack the wherewithal to enact honesty, nobility, and the quest for virtue, resentment impels them to do everything in their power to prevent *you* from experiencing improvements of character that they can never manage. They despise their own weakness—and are too weak to admit or acknowledge it. The weak prefer to direct resentment toward strength, as this is so much easier than learning how to become less weak and pathetic. The path of least resistance is the path most trodden by the sheep.

April 4

If you find that conflict is inevitable, you must wade *into* the conflict boldly and with absolutely firm resolve. Avoid needless conflict, and de-escalate the situation if it is possible to do so without debasing yourself, but if those options are not available, keep your antagonist constantly on defense by overloading your adversary with information. Give the antagonist too much data to process in the amount of time available. Advancing upon your opponent will diminish both the real time available, and it will also cause your opponent to underestimate the amount of time remaining to consider available alternatives. This will cause confusion and, most importantly, hesitation. In that moment of hesitation, you must seize the advantage and never let go of it until the conflict is concluded. Relentless pressure is too much for most adversaries to bear, and most will break and panic if presented with genuine risk to their interests. Do not allow your opponent to take on the role of aggressor for even one instant. *You* seize the initiative, *you* aggress, and *you* impose *your* will. Do so without hesitation, mercy, or compunction. Relentless aggression will cause most adversaries to retreat, turtle up, fluster, or surrender. If you fail to press forward, you will allow your adversary time to think, time to react, and the opportunity to dictate the pace or the terms of the conflict. If your adversary is able to seize the initiative, you will find yourself having to react to your opponent's aggression. *That* is a recipe for defeat and disaster. *Action* is always faster and more effective than reaction.

April 5

The next time you attend a funeral, be sure to notice how very similar the departed is to those walking, conscious corpses, not yet quite fully expired, who have come to pay their respects. Apart from the layers of makeup that cause the dear departed to resemble a cartoon caricature of the person who once inhabited the carcass in the casket, you will find precious little separating the dead from the not-yet dead, or the soon-to-be dead. This, of course, includes *you*. In the not-too-distant future, it will be you in the casket, and it will be you wearing the cartoonish face paint. That will be a fairly ridiculous look for you, but, on the bright side, you will be dead and, therefore, unaware of how silly you look. There is something else vaguely ridiculous about the average funeral. The purpose of the event is, to your way of thinking, never quite clear. Is the point of the funeral really a matter of "paying respects" to the recently departed, or is it largely a matter of making an appearance at a ritual in order to avoid disapprobation and pointless conflict with friends and relatives? The whole shindig is largely for show, is it not? It seems that a bit of pretense is necessary to pull off this strange end of life ritual. If you knew that no one else would show up at the funeral, if you knew that you would be the sole attendee, how many persons of your acquaintance would inspire you to attend the ceremony nonetheless? It is difficult to envision attending a funeral *alone*. You would not expect anyone to go to *your* funeral alone. Who would go to *your* funeral in *any* case? Why would you *care*? You *will* be *dead*, after all.

April 6

Some people are bound and determined to indulge in gamesmanship and dishonest dealing whether it is useful, necessary, sensible, or not. These are people who *enjoy* dissimulation, and these are people who regard honesty as something quaint and archaic. They get a rush out of con artistry even when they do not otherwise profit from their activities. How did "your" culture devolve to such a condition that it tolerates this kind of person, this kind of behavior, and this kind of childish interpersonal interaction? How do such persons not suffer uniform and intense condemnation and ostracism from every component of decent society? Any culture that tolerates lying, repugnant charlatans is beset by a sickness very close to the heart of that civilization. Surely, no society can long endure as these charlatans proliferate and metastasize. They should be treated like the cancer that they are. There *are* people who should *not* be tolerated under any circumstances. Those people should pay an immediate and very painful price for behaving in a manner that poisons the culture at large. When a society allows filth to move freely among its citizens, and when that society allows the miscreants to profit from their malevolence, or even to be tolerated without some type of sanction, you may safely conclude that the society in question has very little time left before it implodes. You can also be fairly confident that the society *deserves* what it is going to get.

April 7

Aristotle listed *magnanimity* as one of the cardinal virtues. What have you done to cultivate this state of character within yourself, or to encourage others to become more magnanimous? You seem to have something of a penchant for less than generous or forgiving behavior toward rivals and detractors— especially when you are proven right at their expense. This is not, arguably, the most admirable or virtuous of your qualities. You have a tendency to "rub the other's nose in it," do you not? Indeed, doing so might, with some justification, be listed among your choicest enjoyments. There is more than just a bit of the darkness within you, and you have not worked in a particularly assiduous manner to extirpate the blackness of which you are aware. You have a bit of a cruel streak in you, and it manifests most intensely, and most observably, when you find an opportunity to humiliate an adversary. Sometimes, you have positively reveled in opportunities of this nature. This is *not* one of your more admirable traits, yet you seem to have little interest in eradicating this tendency. Are you so petty that you derive genuine joy from this type of cruelty? Are you really so small, and are you really so far removed from magnanimity? If so, you ought to be ashamed of yourself. You do not ennoble your character by humiliating others. You know all of this, but you also know that you are not planning on improving this facet of your character. There it is.

April 8

Epicurus may have been onto something when he suggested that the best style of life is to go *unnoticed*. Anonymity has both its benefits and its charms. What, after all, are the alleged advantages of fame and notoriety, and is it really plausible that these benefits are sufficient to counterbalance the glaring detriments and needless challenges to one's sanity that appear to be part and parcel of being well-known? Fame is, perhaps, conducive to lucrative business arrangements in many cases, but those arrangements often involve dissimulation, undeserved flattery, and concealment of one's many flaws from the fawning public. The famous are subject to a degree of scrutiny that would drive the average person into fits of fury and frustration. Furthermore, why would you value money and fame more than decency and serenity? Mass attention to oneself and one's work is, at best, a double-edged sword. Your influence upon others is difficult to predict and impossible to control. Consider having the course of your adult life governed, in large part, by the wishes and whims of the masses and their fickle desires and interests. Some maniac might read your work and become inspired to, for some reason, become a murderer, a tyrant, or (God forbid) an *attorney*? Perhaps it is best not to run this risk. Lord knows that the world has no need of still more attorneys. What would happen if this profession claimed even more victims? Perhaps the world at large, and your nation in particular would *deserve* this fate. Who knows?

April 9

Beware the temptations of confirmation bias when you search, dissect, and analyze the available evidence. *Very* few people are able to look honestly at the possibility that long-held and deeply-cherished beliefs and values are, in fact, nonsense and nothing more than unexamined, dogmatic twaddle adopted through familial or cultural osmosis, as opposed to inerrant, self-evident truths written onto the tissues of the heart by the finger of God Himself. You *want* to be right. In this respect, you are just like everybody else. At least *admit* this tendency, if you wish to have *any* chance whatsoever of avoiding the pernicious psychological corollaries that seem, almost invariably, to attend it. Everyone likes to encounter evidence to confirm his or her preexisting biases and inclinations. Everyone likes being correct, being *seen* as being correct, and being able to gloat after having been *proven* correct. No one enjoys knockdown, drag-out evidence of limitations, inadequacies, and cognitive failures. No one, despite many protestations to the contrary, *loves* being proven wrong. No one parades his failures in public on purpose. No one declares, "Look at how wrong I was!" *You* are no different. You are not better. Do not pretend otherwise. You must guard against your *own ego* even more vigilantly than against external stumbling blocks. The most dangerous traps are scattered around your own mind.

April 10

You have no obligation to appease hypersensitive, irrational, emotional weaklings who live for the opportunity to express phony outrage or faux indignation. Nothing can be done to assuage their counterfeit concerns or quiet their *constant* cries of, "Injustice!" The class of professional victims has been growing for several decades and, unfortunately, the profession has proven fairly lucrative. It seems that pretending to be offended has become something of a cottage industry, with attorneys facilitating the transfers of cash, and the petulant cry-bully has become the ubiquitous terror now pervading "your" culture. Do *not* surrender to these pathetic reptiles, and do not indulge in self-censorship in an effort to avoid their disapprobation. If you have something to say, and you believe it to be both true and worthy of expression, you need not concern yourself with any form of condemnation or reprisal. Let the children wail to their hearts' content. What can anyone take from you that would be worthy of your concern? Can another person deprive you of your decency? Can anyone strip you of your honesty without your consent? You can be deprived of your job and of things that can be purchased with money. If *those* items are the primary objects of your concern, then you deserve to suffer the tortures of the damned when you are stripped of them. What do you care for trifles? As for those things that are acquired with a life lived with dignity—those cannot be *taken*.

April 11

Epictetus warned against keeping company with persons who do not encourage virtuous behavior, and with those who fail to serve the interest of your self-improvement. It is advisable to associate *only* with those persons who bring out the best and most admirable facets of your character. In other words, you should *avoid* people who are stupid, evil, dishonest, or slothful. All such persons are worse than useless to you—except insofar as they serve as cautionary examples of the kind of dissolute character that you must shun at all cost. You ought to avoid these types like the plague... that they are. Liars and charlatans abound in the contemporary world, unfortunately. Perhaps it has always been so, perhaps not. In any event, you associate with such lesser beings at your own peril and, almost certainly, to your own detriment. Beware the bad habit of giving "the benefit of the doubt" too promiscuously, or of allowing that benefit to linger too long after the signs of ignobility have presented themselves. It is simply not *that* difficult to spot an inveterate louse with nothing to offer but vice and idiocy. Once you identify a person of this stripe, get that *thing* excised from your life with all due speed and diligence. Any attempt to maintain good relations with a person who is *no good* will only serve to lead you into iniquity. Any association with liars will only lead you into the temptation to indulge in dishonesty. You cannot associate with filth and remain clean. Disinfect your associations. Cleanse your interpersonal relations.

April 12

Remember that freedom of speech entails freedom *from* speech as thoroughly as it provides the liberty to run your mouth. Not every thought is worthy of expression, and not every truth needs to be uttered. If a new mother shows you her ugly baby, it is not necessary to share with her your assessment of the infant's appearance. Neither the mother nor the baby can control what the kid looks like, and the mother does not deserve to hear the unpleasant truth in this particular instance. This is one of those truths that need not be told. Try to avoid facial expressions that reveal your internal states at such moments as well. You "speak" with your face and your posture nearly as "loudly" as you do with your voice. Discretion is not only the better part of valor, but it is also the better part of interpersonal communication and convivial relations. A remark about the beauty of motherhood and the creation of a new life should suffice to avoid any remark about the little gargoyle. Think before you speak, gain control of your mind before you make *that* face, and consider the likely consequences before you wave your hand dismissively. If you are even minimally creative, it is usually not terribly difficult to avoid utterances that are all but guaranteed to destroy an otherwise valuable friendship or collegial relationship. If something need not or *should not* be said, then maybe just shut the hell up and walk away. Remember your freedom *from* speech. Reason is generally preferable to *bile*.

April 13

The serpent convinced Eve to violate God's first command, and to eat of the fruit of the forbidden tree. Was it really so onerous to avoid the fruit of *one* tree while cavorting innocently through paradise? Was Eve really so gullible, or so greedy for the knowledge the serpent had promised her, that she was willing to defy her Creator, to whom she owes literally everything? Perhaps. This story is, of course, intended as an *allegory*. The serpent represents the voice of temptation. The forbidden fruit is the object of the indecent or the sinful desire. The violation of God's command is the act of self-abasement in the pursuit of selfish aggrandizement. Adam represents, among other things, the "collateral damage" that is the inevitable consequence of sinful selfishness. He is, of course, culpable in forbidden behavior as well as is Eve. The punishment that follows is the inescapable damage to your character every time you do something that you know you should avoid. Many "fruits" are "forbidden" for *very good* reasons. When you identify vice, accept *no* excuse for allowing yourself to succumb to its temptations. Do not rationalize your vicious behavior, do not concoct excuses for your failures of self-discipline, and do not too easily forgive yourself for *your* sins. The most elegant solution to the problem of temptation is to become utterly incorruptible and, therefore, never susceptible to temptation. Until you attain this condition of moral impregnability, you had better remain vigilant, and remember that *you* are your own worst enemy — *your own serpent*.

April 14

What did you catch yourself worrying about today? Take a few moments to consider the benefits and detriments of your stewing and the amount of time and vigor spent engaging in the fretting in question. Did your worrying, in and of itself, do you or anyone else any good? If so, demonstrate the benefits of your perseverating. Enumerate all of the goods with which the world has been endowed as a result of your anxious ruminations. Can you produce a list of the benefits that warrant the time and energy used up in the process? If not, then perhaps you would do well to spend less time and energy on impotent anxiety, and devote yourself to developing the kind of mental discipline that will obviate future bouts of pointless fretting. Mental discipline is what you need. Learn how to remain untroubled more often, and learn how to focus your vitality in more productive fashion. If the object of your concern lies within your control, then simply govern the matter in rational fashion, and there will be nothing to fear. If the cause of your worrying is some condition over which you have *no* control, then leave it up to whatever forces determine such matters, and focus your efforts on some condition that can actually be altered or improved through your focused efforts. Otherwise, you are inviting the misery that inevitably attends emotional or psychological attachment to phenomena that take no heed of your mental states. Irrationality is unhealthy. Stop *making yourself* miserable.

April 15

Has anyone ever *learned* anything at a meeting that could not have been conveyed in a two or three sentence e-mail? The needless proliferation of committees and the endless meetings to which members are subjected, or to which members subject *themselves,* is absolutely baffling, especially when you consider the uncontroversial claim that nearly *every* meeting of nearly *every* committee is nearly *entirely* valueless. The impulse to schedule and attend useless, pointless, and, all things considered, *counterproductive* meetings should be classified as a mental illness or, at the very least, a close cousin of sadomasochism. On occasion, you have wondered if the meeting exists for any purpose other than wasting your time and getting you to contemplate suicide. You have attended hundreds, if not thousands, of vapid congregations of humanity *en bloc*, and you have *never* exited the event thinking, "Now, *that* was time well spent!" What is to be gained by gathering people together in a room, droning on about the nonsense *du jour*, and posing as a purveyor of crucial information? *Everyone* in the room knows that they are wasting their time. Surely, this is nothing more than an exercise in delusions of grandeur mixed with a bit of truly perverse exhibitionism. If you find yourself authorized to schedule a meeting, simply decline to do so. Send out a two or three sentence e-mail to the parties concerned, and be done with the matter. The others will probably be grateful. *You* will have reduced the world's tedium just a bit.

April 16

If you cannot manage genuine gratitude for the many unearned advantages you have been granted, to say nothing of the unearned opportunity to be born and live a human life, then you are a sad sack indeed, and you ought to consider an alternative to continuing to inflict yourself upon other persons and upon the world at large. Here you are in an anthropic universe, on a planet that is just the right distance from the sun for liquid water, a viable atmosphere, sources of food, etc. You did *nothing* to earn your way to this astonishingly felicitous condition. Even among members of your own species, you have been endowed with opportunities that most could barely fathom. Consider the plight of the ancients, who had no access to anything that you would recognize as health care or any form of useful medical attention. Consider the plight of the millions of human beings destroyed in the womb and, therefore, never permitted to breathe, or reason, or love, or read your books (if *that* is a life "worth living"). Consider the plight of all of the non-human sentient animals that experience their final excruciating moments of life serving as a *meal* for some other creature. Consider a counterfactual reality in which *you* make no appearance at all, and recognize that but for the grace of God, or the blind laws and forces of nature, you need not have existed *at all*. Consider gratitude for this world and for your place in it. Either that or just curl yourself into the fetal position and wait for somebody to kick you down a staircase.

April 17

Just about everything tells a story, if you are willing to investigate a bit, and if you are sufficiently attentive. If you look carefully, listen closely, and introspect as you experience its other sensory properties, then you will learn something about the components of your current experience that would have escaped you without your best efforts to be mindful and aware. Pick up an old baseball from the backyard lawn, and you will find scuffmarks, battered parts, and gashes left by the dog's teeth. You will feel that some parts are smoother than others, and you will notice the smell of grass, and other detritus around your yard. You can probably guess roughly how old it is and how often it has been used. Perhaps you will find yourself imagining ballgames and laughing children. Similarly, if you encounter a new dog at the park, and you watch and listen carefully, you can probably tell a good deal about the dog's owners, the place it lives, and how much time it has spent among other dogs. Even a member of another species can tell you an interesting story, provided that you are heedful of all there is to see, hear, smell, and feel. Unfortunately, *people* will also tell you their stories, whether you are or are not interested and, unlike a ball or dog, many people appear to be *very* impressed with their achievements—and seem to be desperate to impress others as well. They love to tell the story, "This is *me!*" When a person describes his or her character, *watch* closely. You will usually find that the behavior you witness departs from the descriptions uttered. Believe your eyes, not your ears.

April 18

Your age is beginning to show, and there is nothing wrong with looking your age, although you struggle to remember that a bit more on some days than you do on others. Your scars, wrinkles, and gray hairs have been earned through visceral experience, and valuable lessons were secured along the way as well. If you could be eighteen years old again, would you take advantage of the opportunity? Consider reliving all of the years between then and now, and ask yourself if doing something differently would be worth the reliving. If it would, you have lived your life very poorly, indeed. Would you go through over thirty years of reruns just so that you could have intercepted that pass at homecoming? In retrospect, perhaps the homecoming game was somewhat less significant than all that has transpired afterward. Do not fall prey to vanity and attempt to conceal your age with lotions, creams, potions, or clothing designed to hide the parts that tell the tales. To be middle-aged and *still* vain is something like a sin compounded with perversion. The absence of vanity is not, however, a justification for allowing your muscles, your reflexes, or your physical functionality to atrophy before nature absolutely requires it. You have a family to protect and defend. You must also avoid allowing yourself to look like an easy victim. An aging wolf still has fangs. The sheep should still fear the old wolf. Sometimes, the wolf has to remind the sheep who is the predator and who is the prey. Which are *you* again? Still?

April 19

If you ever find yourself feeling *underappreciated*, take a moment to consider *why* anyone would be obligated to appreciate you *at all*, and take a second moment to ask why you would insist upon *being* appreciated. Is a human life and all the potential associated with the big primate brain insufficient to satisfy you? Pay attention to everything you have that you did *nothing* to deserve. You are either here because you are part of God's plan, or you are merely one product of a chance concatenation of scattershot, unguided events that could have produced innumerable alternatives that would not have involved *you* at all. If you exist because God made it so, then God is the only proper object of *anyone's* reverence, gratitude, or worship. Do not attempt to secure credit for the Maker's handiwork. You are merely a vessel, and you cannot even make the case that you are particularly confident about what, if anything, you are supposed to be doing. Play your assigned role, and expect neither applause nor thanks for doing so. If you are simply a lump of cosmological detritus that, due to neurochemical oddity, happens to have developed consciousness and something like a sense of self, then recognize that a lump of wet flesh really ought not regard itself as anything of note. A carbon-based robot with haphazard programming is nothing for which anyone owes gratitude. It is God or chance that runs this show. You are merely a player upon the stage. Break a leg.

April 20

Sometimes you simply have no alternative apart from waiting. At such times, you would be well served to learn to wait patiently and avoid complaining about the matter. If you really believe that whining and complaining will prove *useful*, then by all means get about it at once. Perhaps the world would benefit from reading your journal of complaints, gripes, and dissatisfaction. Then again, maybe it is best to set that thought aside for the time being. Remember that other people are going about their business, much as *you* are trying to accomplish your various tasks, resources and personnel are limited, and being compelled to do something like *standing in line* is neither an injustice nor a punishment. If you will a particular result, you must also be willing to endure the requisite conditions to bring that result into being. In some cases, the waiting is elongated and exacerbated by incompetence or inefficiency, and tolerating these phenomena has always been something of a psychological challenge for you. Waiting in line probably qualifies as one of your pet peeves. When you feel yourself growing impatient and agitated, remember that your mental states will not cause the line in front of you to evaporate, nor will your exasperation cause the incompetent to become any better at performing their jobs. Take a moment to turn inward, gain control of your emotions, reason your way back to a calm state of mind, and wait like an adult. Do not whine about it — not even in the confines of your own unruly and ungrateful mind.

April 21

Some challenges you overcome once and for all, other challenges remain with you as constant "companions" that periodically reassert themselves, but you learn to manage the degree to which they interfere with your progress. Finally, there are some challenges that cannot be overcome, and that will ultimately destroy your body and sap the life from it. Meh, what are you going to do about those? There is, as far as you can tell, no permanent cure for some of the less fortunate and less desirable components of your makeup. If there is a hereditary inclination, you cannot simply *reason* your way to altered genetics. You are stuck with your fundamental biological building blocks, and with the visible and functional consequences thereof. You can, however, learn to govern the psychological and behavioral manifestations of your inherited proclivities. If the challenge in question is a product of environmental impingements, past or present, you can work on the beliefs and expectations surrounding those events that have the potential to trigger dysfunctional or unwholesome mental states. Whatever the past may have been, your present attitudes *are*, with sufficient mental discipline, *yours* to control. You are *not* a *slave* to biology or happenstance. Well, you are not *entirely* enslaved in those ways. Develop the mental discipline to cope with anything that the world might throw at you, and also anything with which the world has saddled you. Discipline *is* freedom.

April 22

If you experience moments of self-pity, given all of the unearned benefits that you enjoy, it can only be the result of weakness, petulance, and irrationality. What justification could you possibly conjure for anything other than consistent feelings of good fortune, gratitude, and serenity? Your life is easier, less dangerous, and more filled with opportunity than at least ninety percent of the human beings that have ever existed on this planet. Indeed, even by comparison with your contemporary talking primates, you enjoy *far* more benefits than do most of the people on the planet right now. Having been born into a wealthy, Western nation in the middle of the 20th Century, and having never dealt with a lack of food, medical care, or opportunities to accumulate positive experiences, you *must* acknowledge the privileges that you have not worked to attain. While perfect, unwavering equanimity is probably unattainable or, perhaps, only instantiated in *extremely* rare sages who *very* infrequently appear on this planet, your duty is the attainment of the closest approximation of that condition that your limitations may allow. You are no Socrates, no Epictetus, no Diogenes, no Buddha, and no Marcus Aurelius, and this is clear to anyone paying the slightest attention, but you *must* learn from their examples. Do *not* pretend that no one has pointed the way. If you stray from the path, you have only *yourself* to blame.

April 23

Stop living as if you are not going to die. Remember that thou art mortal, and that thou hast lived more than half of the life that human beings are typically allotted. The end is *indeed* nigh, in some sense of "nigh." You do not, of course, know *how* nigh, but you are, at this point, almost certainly closer to the end than you are to the beginning. Surely, this fact must alter your priorities to some significant degree. You must waste no further time on grievances, real or imagined, concerning old interactions with family, friends, acquaintances, or colleagues. What is done cannot be undone, and you need not wish for any counterfactual past. Such a wish would be both pointless and self-defeating. Waste no time wishing for anything that never was and cannot be. There is no such thing as what "should" have happened, and you have no business complaining about the manner in which your life has unfolded to this point. Do you complain about birth as a human being, with a relatively healthy and properly functioning body and mind, in one of the wealthier nations on the face of the planet? Surely, you cannot allow yourself to be as peevish and absurd as *that*. You occupy the present, you plan for a future that may or may not conform to expectations, and you train yourself to weather any storm that may arise. You are to face the present and the future like a fearless explorer of the human condition and the various possibilities with which you have been provided. Let nothing deter you. Let not your heart be troubled.

April 24

At the end of the allegory of Adam and Eve in the Garden of Eden, God metes out punishments. Adam's punishment is *labor*. He will have to *work*, in order to feed himself, his wife, and his children. In the sweat of his face and brow, he will be compelled to earn his living, or some such translation as that, is the description of the sanction levied against Adam. Consider, however, the vapidity and emptiness of a life *devoid* of labor and struggle. Contemplate a life in which your "living" is not earned through your efforts and your struggle but, instead, everything you want and need is simply provided to you irrespective of your contribution. Would *that* not be *far* more tragic, all things considered, than a life filled with difficulty, challenge, suffering, and the gradual accumulation of such wisdom as you can manage? If you could choose between life as a consistently happy child who never understands anything that is not accessible to the mind of a toddler, or you could opt for your *actual* life, complete with pain, humiliation, frustration, and all the rest of your experiences, would you even *hesitate* to choose the latter? Socrates suffered far more than would a perfectly contented pig, but you would *never* choose the contented porcine life rather than the struggles and tribulations of Socrates. After the collapse of Eden, Adam is informed that he must spend his life in labor and he must suffer. Thank *God* that it is so. Human beings are not meant to live in constant, unrelenting bliss. Suffering is *essential* to a well-lived life.

April 25

The human race and the human condition are *not* improving. Technology is *obviously* making tremendous progress and providing opportunities that would have been unimaginable to prior generations. There can be doubt about that. The Internet and smart phones would have been indistinguishable from the miraculous to your not-very-distant ancestors. As for virtual reality goggles, even *you* find it difficult to understand *those* as mere products of technological advancement. It is, however, equally obvious that technological advancements come with societal and cultural trade-offs that are not particularly salutary or healthy for contemporary individuals or for the populace at large. The persons composing your society and generating the many facets of your evolving (or *devolving*) culture are, if you are to assess them honestly, not morally or intellectually superior to your ancestors and forbears. If anything, the most recent generations are, by comparison with those that came before them and made the contemporary world possible, a group of disproportionately weak, petulant, lazy, ungrateful, ill-informed, and pathetic creatures that mostly befoul the legacy that they have inherited. Yours has become a nation and a culture of weaklings and whiners. There *are* exceptions, but they are the *precious few*. Self-assessments are notoriously unreliable, but you cannot be much more impressed with your own character than you are with society at large. Your culture is dying.

April 26

Never trust *anyone* who seeks the power to govern you, regulate your life, or to arrogate to some external authority the wherewithal to compel you to say or do *anything* that you would not otherwise say or do. Perhaps you should be even more suspicious of those who seek to govern the populace at large. When you were a child, your parents had this type of authority over you, to a significant extent, and this was necessary to secure your survival through childhood and adolescence. That arrangement is, however, one of those "childish things" that must be "put away" as you become an adult. You did not spend all of that time, and expend all of that energy, and suffer all of the bumps and bruises along the way, just for the sake of allowing other adults to treat you as if you are *still* a child. Anyone who seeks power over you, *ipso facto*, seeks to infantilize you and to compel you to accept a relationship that was all well and good between you and your parents, but that is utterly inappropriate between you and the government, or between you and any specific government functionary, or between you and some other individual who is not, in fact, one of your parents. For practical purposes, you may *decide* to abide by laws that legislators pass, and to observe simple, practical cultural norms and mores, at least for the most part, but only insofar as it serves *your* interests. You have no inherent *moral* obligation to do anything that is contrary to your conscience.

April 27

Small, physically weak men, who rise to positions of political, economic, or societal power, are *not* to be trusted, as they almost always become tyrants or authoritarians of one stripe or another. Those who spent childhood and adolescence as powerless victims of the stronger kids and the cooler kids are psychologically incapable of resisting the urge and the opportunity to impose their weak wills upon others. You need not indulge in armchair psychological theorizing about this phenomenon in order to notice the regularity with which it occurs. Voting for a "man" who grew up getting bullied on a daily basis is, generally speaking, a bad idea and an invitation to corruption and despotism. A person who has felt powerless and susceptible throughout the formative and pubescent years, and who, as an adult, finds sudden access to mechanisms whereby he may impose his will on others, must almost always construct some rationalization to convince himself that the objects of his aggression *deserve* to suffer, or that he is now *entitled* to cause others to experience the misery that he has endured. They cannot, typically, exact revenge on those who bullied them, but they can certainly find proxies to fill the role. It is no accident that the loudest proponents of collectivism are, almost always, pencil-necked weaklings, whining tattletales, and fat slobs. Not all truths are "politically correctly" or comforting. Physical weaklings are *not* to be trusted with any significant degree of power or authority.

April 28

Very few people can be trusted with those things that are generally valued, prized or held up as sacred. If you allow your life's savings to fall under the control of an unscrupulous financial advisor or manager, you should not be surprised when you end up destitute. Money is, of course, not nearly as valuable as honor, decency, or wisdom, but it has its practical utilities, and it is much easier to abscond with your cash than to deprive you of your rectitude. If you allow your family to fall under the influence of depraved miscreants, then you are a failed parent, or spouse, or sibling, and you cannot be surprised, or you certainly *should not* be surprised, when your children are lured into discreditable behaviors, or your family is torn apart by needless internecine conflict. Do not blame the external threat if *you* left the gate wide open or, worse yet, if you actually *invited* the malefactor into the home environment. Finally, if you turn the governance of *your mind* or *your character* over to some charismatic character with malicious intent, then you will *deserve* the suffering and dissolution that *always* befall those who follow such Svengalis mindlessly. What could you *possibly* hope to gain from any external source that is worth putting the people that you love more than any others at risk? Never sacrifice the health, well-being, or sanctity of the family for *anything*. Eternal vigilance is your most reliable suit of armor.

April 29

Beware those who warn you against "being judgmental," and those who insist that all forms of deviance and filthy behavior must be "tolerated," or, worse yet, normalized and embraced by the culture at large. More and more, you cannot help but notice that behaviors that, up until half a generation ago, would have been all but universally regarded as anathema and shameful seem to be embraced more broadly, and decried less openly and not quite so vociferously. Abomination, it seems, loves company, and despicable people always seek to surround themselves with as much detestable human rubbish as possible. It is not, in *most* cases, appropriate for *you* to mete out justice to those who transgress, but there is *nothing* wrong with taking note of foul deeds, and there is nothing wrong with attaching the appropriate and proportional judgment. The *sin* in this arena is regarding yourself as an intrinsically *higher order* of being than those whom you behold indulging in degeneracy. You are no better *in essence* than the most repugnant persons ever to have walked the earth. You are members of the same species, you share the same ultimate origin, and you are as susceptible as is anyone else to the traps that culminate in hideous misdeeds and corruption of character. When you judge another, do not forget to assess *your* character as well. Be sure that your judgment is not an exercise in hypocrisy.

April 30

Do you believe that you ought to be excused for inappropriate or irrational behavior due to alleged trauma from childhood or other events from your developmental years? This attempt to construct a rationalization is a trap of your own making. All human beings face challenges, dangers, and opportunities to go wrong in indefinitely many ways. Certainly, you cannot claim, with a straight face, that your life has been more filled with trauma than have most of the other lives experienced in the "vale of tears." You have had it comparatively easy. Do *not* pretend otherwise. Perhaps you prefer to appeal to genetics or biochemistry as a pretentious justification for foolishness or ignoble lapses into bad habits and lassitude of integrity. That would be much more comfortable than an honest investigation into your character, your true beliefs and values, and the causative powers of the conscious states over which you have direct control. Though it may be comforting, it is simply not a viable explanation for anything like the totality of your inappropriate indulgences. It is much more difficult than that to slough off responsibility for *your own* habits of thought, and *your own* intellectual proclivities—and *failures*. Look at how excuse making seems to work out for those who indulge in it habitually. People who are good at making excuses are seldom good at much of anything else—and it is even *more* rare that they are *morally* good or admirable people. Take *responsibility* for *your* life.

May 1

The pervasive dishonesty of your culture is absolutely stunning, and there are no signs of mass sincerity breaking out any time soon. There are legions of celebrities, media pundits, and, tragically, academics, who have based their *entire* careers on claims that they clearly *know* to be untrue, and theories that have been discredited more times than ought to have been necessary. Yet, the nonsense persists unabated. There is also significant overlap between those who proffer *obvious* untruths, and those who regularly offer judgments, insinuations, and accusations for which they have precisely *no* evidence whatsoever. It seems that liars enjoy pointing the finger of blame even more than do the more honest among the talking apes. More distressing, perhaps, is the fact that large swathes of the public seem to believe these ludicrous claims and these unsupported accusations, or *pretend* to believe them, simply because they *want* to believe, or because they want to be on a particular "team" in some facet or other of the "culture war" or the societal battle of the day. Some uphold untruths because they actually derive enjoyment from contrarianism or dissimulation for its own sake. Are there no better hobbies to pursue? What has become of this culture that you once thought of as "yours," and that you now recognize as yours *only* in the sense that you reside within something like its geographical boundaries, because you were born there? There cannot be much time left for this pathological collective. Perhaps it *deserves* to expire. Let go of any residual attachments you may have to this dying "civilization." Its time is nigh.

May 2

Laugh a little when you can. There is nothing wrong with a bit of levity and a healthy chortle now and again. A life devoid of the occasional chuckle is, arguably, not even a life worth living, and it is, almost without the need for argument, a defective life by comparison. The feeling that you get from making other people laugh has always been one of your most enjoyable experiences. Though it may not last long, and though it may make less than a dent in the grand "scheme of things," a good joke, clever playfulness with words, or a good old-fashioned pratfall, will almost always prove to be worth the effort. We are, all of us, headed for the metaphorical gallows. Can we not enjoy the occasional belly laugh along the way? There is no good reason to exacerbate the feeling of absurdity or pointlessness to which nearly all persons are sporadically susceptible—unless, of course, the pointless absurdity of your condition can serve to momentarily alleviate somebody's doomed trek from cradle to grave. You have read that dwarves and midgets actually have *very little* in common. Surely, this is a nugget worth sharing. Any dwarf or midget who takes offense can be excused for so doing, but you have yet to meet one who did not get a *little* kick out of that gag. There are *far* worse ways to go than to die *laughing*. There are many wastes of time that cannot hold a candle to a bit of comedy shared among friends or strangers. Imagine a social engagement during which no one laughed or even cracked a smile. It is a funeral or a wake that you describe, is it not? Try giggling at Death when he comes for you. He might laugh along.

May 3

It is for good reason that the injunction against bearing false witness is included in the Ten Commandments issued to the Israelites at Sinai. There can be no justice, and there can be no trust in a relationship if one of the parties involved is comfortable with telling lies to the detriment of the other. A relationship built on falsehoods, playacting, and dissimulation is far worse than the absence of companionship. The punishment for false testimony *should be* proportionate to the sentence that would have been imposed upon the defendant in the event of a conviction. False testimony that, if believed, would have resulted in a life sentence for the defendant should culminate in the same life sentence for the witness, if the deceit can be proven beyond a reasonable doubt. Prohibited lies do not, of course, occur *only* under oath, or in courts of law. Malicious prevarication and gossip intended to impugn the reputation of another person, once the deception is uncovered, ought to result in ostracism at the *very* least. If you catch *anyone* engaging in this type of behavior, you are nothing but a damned fool if you continue to associate with the scoundrel. Lying is, with *very* few exceptions, a bad idea, and it is almost always deleterious to relationships and to society at large. Children will tell lies, and they must receive instruction about the misbehavior in question. Adults really ought to know better. An otherwise rational adult who lies casually is *lower* than a snake in the grass. Only a degraded being can tell a lie with indifference. Do *not* say anything that you do not believe. Do *not* associate with those who do.

May 4

In retrospect, there are *very* few experiences that retain the impact and the "feel" that you recall having undergone at the time of the impression in question. Indeed, David Hume argued that one of the fundamental distinctions between types of mental phenomena must be understood as the difference between the immediacy of current experience, and the phenomenological distance of the memory, the residual trace that remains in the wake of an impression as an *idea* of it. Many times, you remember having felt humiliation or embarrassment that now strikes you as utterly silly and prompted by something that now seems insignificant. In other cases, you recall thinking nothing of a particular remark or gesture at the time it occurred, but you have subsequently realized that it revealed a crucial underlying facet of an interpersonal interaction. Over time, you have come to understand much more than you grasped in the various moments you have experienced. You have come to appreciate that what you thought had transpired is, in fact, *nothing* like the event that you now perceive it to be. Consider all the experiences that you have *not* reevaluated in anything like a rigorous fashion. How many intentions have you misconstrued over the years? How many times have *your* words or actions been misinterpreted? Surely, such cases are legion. Can you be confident that misunderstanding is not, in fact, the *norm* in human interaction? Perhaps we are *mistaken* about each other more often than not. It is, after all, no mean feat to peer into the motives and expectations of persons who, as it turns out, are *not you*.

May 5

There are few endeavors that are more primal, more fundamental to the nature of your species, and more inherently fascinating, than combat sports and all of the surrounding theatrics. Neither books, nor music, nor travel, nor any other type of interaction or performance can compete with the spectacle of highly skilled, well-trained fighters trying to outperform each other in their chosen arena. It is more fascinating still if they are, in addition to competing against each other, genuinely attempting to smash each other into submission or unconsciousness, and sincerely interested in causing each other *genuine* damage. There is no shame in admitting this fascination. There has never been a purely non-violent culture in human history and, if one were to crop up, it would not long endure. Captivation with violence and combat are woven into the very fiber of your species, and your genetics are, in no small part, an inheritance from those most adept at imposing their will, and defending their lives, through the most efficient application of fierce methods. Is there a single human being alive today who has not even *one* murderer among his ancestors? The competitors in combat sports do not even need to be particularly skilled in order to make a fight compelling and worthy of your attention. *Blood* is always fascinating. No playground bout of fisticuffs has ever failed to draw a crowd. *Every* man wants to know if he is tougher than the next guy. Even if the answer is obvious, you cannot help but desire the *demonstration*. Why *lie* about this?

May 6

Any man who mistreats a woman, particularly any man who *strikes* a woman in anger or with the intention of doing violence to her, is nothing more than a pathetic coward and a craven, lowly weakling posing as a "tough guy" in his own mind and his own estimation. *Real* men do *not* hit women. You can, of course, imagine *very* rare exceptions to this rule, such as striking a woman as the only means of preventing her from killing you, or as the only way to stop her assault upon a child, but that kind of thing is mostly the stuff of fiction. Also, it is *your* fault if you allow yourself to associate with a woman of that stripe. What kind of "man," worthy of the title, would *ever* put his hands on a woman with the intention of causing her physical harm, or with the objective of humiliating her? A spineless dastard of that type deserves a beating *himself*. If *you* see an adult male abusing a woman, you can *only* judge him to be a repugnant, filthy creature, and you are *obligated* to expose the cretin as the vile snake that he is. If necessary you are obligated to turn his violence against him and make the proper purpose of applied brutality abundantly clear to the miserable miscreant. A *real* man will not harm a woman or engage in *any* form of physical violence against a woman. A real man *will*, however, bludgeon the barbarous abuser of women to within an inch of his life—*and* one inch further if necessary. Adult males who do not understand this are in need of instruction. They have lessons to learn and beatings to absorb.

May 7

With *what* do you concern yourself, and what justification can you offer for your concerns? So many people live their *entire* lives in pursuit of material gain, power, fame, influence, and notoriety of various forms. Do they imagine that the money, the houses, the cars, and the other trappings of wealth will follow them into the afterlife? Have they not been informed that power ceases at the grave, fame is as insubstantial as fog, and the people whom they hope to impress are all going to die in their own good time? No one, as far as you can tell, drives a Lamborghini to heaven or hell. The idea of "streets paved with gold" should be anathema to the true believer. What good is gold to the departed? All the money, all the fame, all the power, and all the adulation available in this "vale of tears," is worth less than *one* moment of genuine contentment born of virtue. If you seek some *other* reward beyond the state of decency and honor, then you have lost the plot entirely, and you are no better than those for whom you have only contempt. Your purpose, the "meaning of life" *for you*, is the pursuit of wisdom, virtue, and mastery of the methods for constructing the most admirable *self* that you can manage. All the trappings of fame, fortune, and power are as *nothing* compared to your *moral* purpose. Take care that you do not get caught up in the all-too-common pursuits of the multitudes. Let them live their lives as they wish, and do not try to impose your values upon the masses, but stay apart from them as well. Leave the *shiny things* to the children.

May 8

It seems that more and more people feel compelled to pretend to believe propositions that *no one* actually believes, and to pretend to *value* characteristics that *everyone* recognizes to be ignoble and brutish. A bizarre *inversion* of values appears to be gaining currency in your increasingly perverse culture. When did promiscuity become anything other than a cause for *shame*? When young women, indeed *girls*, boast about their numerous sexual encounters, successive generations *cannot* be entrusted to them safely. At what point did *ignorance* turn into a cause for celebration? You cannot count the number of people you have overheard *bragging* about never having read a book or written a paragraph. Why would *anyone* ever pretend to value *victimhood*, respect weakness, and regale listeners with tales about acts of abject cowardice? When men cease to be held to account as defenders and protectors of women and of civilization at large, you can be confident that civilization shall not endure much beyond the present. When women are no longer expected to serve the role of primary nurturers and caregivers, or to serve as the main counterbalance to the male inclination toward promiscuity, you can expect procreation to result in broad and pervasive mediocrity. This is, of course, precisely what you increasingly observe as the general trending of your culture. Men do not know *how to be men*, women cannot be bothered *to be women*, and children have no idea how to go about growing up to become *either men or women*. How is "inverted" modernity working out?

May 9

Spend *no* more time in the company of persons who do not ennoble your character, or those for whom you have little or no regard. This injunction will exclude the *vast* majority of the human race from your circle of voluntary interaction, but *that* is nothing about which you ought to be concerned. Did you really hope to develop companionable relations with the teeming masses? What in the world is to be gained through such wide-ranging associations? Most people are, at best, a waste of your time and energy, and they will sap your will to improve like parasites of the spirit. At their worst, most human beings are tantamount to a substantial dose of chlamydia. They drain away your energy and provide you with *nothing* that you need, and *nothing* that you ought to desire. They are encumbrances that chew up time, money, vitality, and offer only vapidity in return. Most people are, to be blunt, idiots, liars, and self-absorbed simians shrieking away about nothing. Some will regard this generalization as an undeserved and unjustifiable indictment of your own species. So be it. Let them complain as they wish. Your species is, frankly, no great shakes as far as living creatures are concerned, and the vast majority of your fellow talking apes is something akin to a massive walking biohazard. Encounters with the humans provide more opportunity for contamination than edification or self-improvement. Most people are a *waste* of your life. Ignore them, find the few that matter, and make your life among *those*.

May 10

Frustration sets in every so often as you make your way through the workday, and often enough when you are running errands, doing chores, or waiting for some expected event to unfold. This is not surprising as frustration besets everyone now and again, but it is crucial that you recognize frustration as a symptom of your own *indiscipline*. Had you restricted your desires and aversions to matters that lie within your control, vexation of this sort would not have befallen you. If you desire *only* conditions that you can bring into being through the force of your will alone, then none of your desires would ever go unsatisfied. You would simply produce the desired condition by act of resolve. If you allow yourself to be averse *only* to conditions that you can prevent or dispel simply by choosing that it is to be so, then you would never incur anything to which you are averse. You would simply avoid the undesirable condition by fiat of self-determination. When you find that you are frustrated it, therefore, follows that you *must* have allowed yourself to develop a psychological or emotional attachment to some state of affairs that you lack the capacity to control and to produce or prevent by will alone. It is unwise and unhealthy to allow your state of mind to attach to conditions that are left up to the dispensations of forces that lie beyond your direction. This is, as you well know, a recipe for dissatisfaction, frustration, and other unpleasant experiences that are avoidable with proper mental discipline. There is no such thing as *too many* reminders of this. Why *invite* irritation?

May 11

Keep your nose to the grindstone when distractions beckon, and when sloth or lethargy begins to creep into the periphery of your consciousness. The task at hand, the job before you, and the responsibilities with which you are confronted, these must be the objects of your efforts, and all ancillary considerations must wait until the task at hand is completed to the best of your abilities. Embrace your responsibilities, set yourself doggedly to the chore before you, and allow *nothing* to guide your attention elsewhere. Until your work is done, until the job is completed, and until you are satisfied that you have done the very best that you can manage, do not allow your attention to drift to easier or more comforting thoughts. Flagging attention frequently leads to disaster. Even if you manage to avert the *worst* consequences of inattention, you will still have failed to exert your *best* efforts, and the results will be less admirable than they could have been. A failure to attend to business may be expected among the mentally weak, and among those who lack discipline, but it is not permissible for a competent adult to suffer from childish distractions. If you *are* a child, a weakling, or an undisciplined scatterbrain, then stop *posing* as a responsible adult. What kind of spouse, parent, or professional allows cognitive lassitude to determine the course of the day or the culmination of his efforts? You are not here for the sake of taking up time and space while accomplishing nothing. Be an *adult*.

May 12

If you injure yourself doing something that *needs* to be done, then utter *no* complaint about the damage your body has suffered. Try to learn how to avoid a similar injury the next time a similar duty falls to you, but accept the current bodily damage as part of the price of discharging your obligations. No one promised you that the necessary work would always be safe, and you were issued no guarantee that your responsibilities would never lead you into danger. The safe and easy work is, in most cases, fairly far removed from the most satisfying and fulfilling tasks. If a danger presents itself, and if *you* are responsible for facing that danger, then you are to do so with every scintilla of resolve at your disposal, and you are to accept the consequences of doing your duty. You need not waste any further thought about the matter. You are, thereby, liberated to embark upon your next endeavor. Indeed, you ought to be *grateful* that you are entrusted with, for example, the obligation to protect and defend your family and other innocents in your charge. This can be a dangerous duty, but it is yours to undertake, and doing so is an honor within the family structure. You must place yourself firmly between any potential threat and those whom you seek to defend against that menace, and you must *not* allow your moral purpose to go unfulfilled because of fear for your personal safety. Your body is a *tool*. Sometimes the tool must be deployed and, in some instances, sacrificed to a noble cause. Do what must be done, and take whatever lumps you must endure. No complaints are permitted in such matters.

May 13

Never embrace the dominant narrative simply because it is dominant or simply *because* you hear and read it as it is repeated *ad nauseam* in the media or among your peers, colleagues, and acquaintances. The mere fact that "everyone" is telling, more or less, the same story constitutes scant evidence that the story in question is either true or worth repeating. History is replete with false claims and unverified theories that held sway for hundreds, if not thousands, of years. This planet was not, in fact, flat just because everyone believed it to be so, nor was this planet at the center of the universe just because people thought that they saw celestial bodies, such as the sun, revolving around it and crossing the heavens. Disease was not caused by malevolent spirits simply because that vaguely anthropomorphic explanation was the easiest theoretical reach prior to the discovery of viruses and bacteria. The fact that *"everybody"* believes a proposition to be true is inadequate evidence of its *actual* truth, and people are notoriously incompetent when it comes to figuring out underlying causes or thoroughgoing explanations. In the absence of evidence, remain cautious, intellectually humble, and circumspect about your beliefs. False beliefs tend to motivate actions that lead to needless confusion and readily avoidable trouble. It is probably impossible to avoid *all* falsehoods, but you can *try* to minimize the number of untruths to which you subscribe.

May 14

You are *never* permitted to fail to repay *any* debt under *any* circumstances. Such a failure would be dishonorable and a breach of faith. For this reason, it is worth noting, you have no business *acquiring* any debt that is not a matter of *practical necessity*. Do not borrow money for an education unless you *need* a college degree for your chosen profession, *and* you have a *clear* and thoroughly deliberated plan about your path through college, and into a career sufficiently lucrative and reliable to pay back your loans in a reasonable period of time. If you are not certain about what you wish to do professionally, or if you are drawn to a vocation that tends not to pay particularly well, then it is both irrational and irresponsible to take on a debt that you have no reason to believe you will be able to discharge in a timely fashion. Wanting the money, wanting the education, and wanting the benefits derived from a diploma are, in and of themselves, insufficient justifications for taking on a massive financial obligation on which you may default. Someone will have to repay the loans, and if it is not you, then the burden will be borne by persons who never agreed to pay your debts for you. Clearly, you have no business imposing such burdens upon strangers and fellow citizens. *Your* decisions should not create financial difficulties for anyone else. The guiding principle here applies to home loans, car loans, and other mechanism involving borrowed money. Do *not* borrow beyond *necessity*. *Lending* money is also notoriously problematic.

May 15

In *Deuteronomy*, Moses presents the choice of life or death to the Israelites as they prepare to enter the Promised Land—from which Moses, himself, has been barred. This is, arguably, one of the most heartbreaking events in Hebrew scripture. Moses is denied access to the land of milk and honey. His people, however, are provided with this long-awaited opportunity. They may choose the blessings and bounty that attend the virtuous life, lived in accordance with God's commands, or they can choose the curses and punishments that accompany the vicious life, lived in rebellion against God and the refusal to obey His commands. Moses then climbs to a place that enables him to gaze upon the land that God will not allow him to enter, and he dies before the Israelites cross the threshold into the region vouchsafed to their ancestors, to Abraham, Isaac, and Jacob. Moses can do nothing more for his people. His service is at an end. Are *you* not presented with the same choice laid before the Israelites of virtue or vice, obedience or rebellion against the dictates of decency? Do you not see that virtue is, in and of itself, a reward to your character, whereas vice degrades your spirit? This is *not* merely a quaint account about an ancient stiff-necked tribe. *You* can "enter the promised land," or you can die in the wilderness. You can live a life worth living, or you can opt for the easy path of dissolution and bestial gratification. *Choose.* Choose a life.

May 16

A good meal must *never* go unappreciated and it is always appropriate to give thanks, either before or after you consume. This is a ritual that seems to have become less common in recent decades, and that is at least a bit of a shame. You need not believe in God in order to say grace or give thanks, but you are certainly free to consider the possibility that the meal *is*, in fact, a product of God's generous bounty. You are, in any event, entirely at liberty to express gratitude to those who raised the protein, *produced* the grains, *grew* the vegetables, shipped the ingredients to your locale, and prepared the meal in a pleasing fashion. Reflect on how many people are involved in the entire process of generating the meal, and remember that you are fortunate to live in a place, and at a time, that allows food to be plentiful, nutritious, and comparatively inexpensive. Never lose sight of the fact that the food you eat is *literally* sustenance for you and for your family, and *without* that sustenance, you would be incapable of accomplishing anything else, and your family would literally perish. Preparing food for another's consumption is an expression of affection, concern, fellow feeling, and a manifestation of interest in the well-being of those who eat it. Even people who never meet each other can express mutual appreciation through the provision of, and consumption of, a healthy and physically nurturing meal. Preparing a meal that is gratefully received is enormously satisfying, and eating that meal with gratitude is the very least that you can do in return of the efforts involved. So, *Mangiare bene*!

May 17

The ignorant, the slothful, the weak, and, most importantly, the *dishonest*, are to be treated like human instantiations of the plague, and you are to avoid them as if the health and well-being of your *soul* depends upon it. Actually, it *does* depend upon avoiding human flotsam and jetsam. Every moment spent in communion with lowly miscreants is a moment spent in *shame*, and is also a moment devoted to self-destruction. Adults who cannot, or *will* not, conduct their lives after the fashion of adults in the pursuit of wisdom, self-improvement, and the attainment of virtue, are "adults" *in name only*. They are, in fact, children or adolescents, and they merely *masquerade* as genuine persons. Is participation in this insipid masquerade one of your goals? Do not partake in their ludicrous pretense, and do not *affect* a sham respect of this nauseating mass of rubble and detritus dressed in human clothing. Seek *honest* persons wherever you go. Only those who tell the truth are worthy of your respect, and only *they* possess actual rights and liberties that are worthy of your deference. Liars are *not* persons worthy of your respect, and you owe them *no* consideration, and you are not enjoined to enact concern for their welfare. Brutal honesty is necessary in this instance. Do not pretend that "everyone is equal," or any such nonsense as this. It is not true, it has never been true, and it never can be true. Nature does not concoct *equality*. People are no more "equals" than are dogs, horses, or, your close cousins, the apes. There are alphas, there are betas, and there are those who are unworthy of mention. *Everyone* knows this.

May 18

The Amish intentionally avoid associating with "the English," or "the Yankees," or just about everyone else on the planet beyond practical necessity. They are *not* wrong to do so, and they are seldom vilified for it. Indeed, you must admit that, in many ways, you admire and almost envy the Amish, their culture and, most importantly, their separate existence, apart from the collected pathologies that constitute the "culture" with which they find themselves surrounded. It takes a degree of fortitude to turn away from the dominant and pervasive norms and mores, and to reject practices that are anathema to, and incompatible with, decency, honor, and a life well lived as you and "your people" conceive of it. You cannot help but applaud those who reject mindless materialism and the unending pursuit of pleasures on a pointless hedonic treadmill. The Amish cling to traditions and values that hold their community together and, perhaps more importantly, hold them apart from outsiders. Maybe those values are quaint or archaic. Maybe they *fear* modernity. Then again, perhaps quaint and archaic values are the only antidote to the poison that is contemporary "culture." Perhaps the culture and mores that the Amish reject are well worthy of denunciation. A society not worth preserving is, in most cases, well worth avoiding. Is it time to go looking for a horse and buggy? Ah, they would never have you. In all honesty, you simply cannot blame them for rejecting the likes of *you*.

May 19

Disappointments have a way of insinuating themselves into your life, down your throat, and into your interpersonal relations. It is almost certainly so for everyone else also. Remember that your disappointments are, in *every* case, a result of some failure or other on *your* part. You have failed to restrict your desires and expectations to the sphere of your direct control, or you have done an insufficient job of strengthening your resolve to think and to behave in accordance with the dictates of reason, and correlate your will with the natural flow of events. When events transpire, it is not as if blaming the world is a sensible course of action. Was the world "supposed to be" different than it is? How would that work? By all means, get yourself a time machine as soon as it becomes practical, and pick up a device for altering the laws of nature at your local hardware store when one becomes available. Until then, you might be better off working on your beliefs, desires, expectations, and leaving the world to its own devices. Did it *request* your intervention? If any event occurs in a manner that is contrary to your desires, the defect lies in your desires and in your inadequate self-discipline. Events are *not* obligated to accord with your pre-reflective whims, or to satisfy your unguided impulses and drives. Govern your interests, your desires, your aversions, and your expectations so that the world, and the unfolding of events therein, *cannot* disappoint you, and *cannot* run afoul of your rationally governed moral purpose. It is *that* simple.

May 20

Know that *you* are *always* under oath. This is not a *legal* constraint or an injunction imposed by any court or any judiciary. No, the oath under which *you* are constrained at *all* times is the oath enjoined upon you at Sinai, thousands of years before you were born. You have been informed that you are *not* to bear *false witness*, and the highest "court" imaginable has issued this command. Your adherence to this command (or your *failure* to adhere to it) is set before the judgment of an infallible arbiter. There is no such thing as "getting away with" any form of sin. You are *not* permitted to lie, and every lie that you have told (and you are guilty of telling *more* than your share) will be noted, and you will be held to account. This, in any event, is what you *believe* to be the case. You may well be incorrect. It is notoriously difficult to attain certainty about the existence of God, and the nature of divine intentions or commands. This is a limitation of the human condition that you must acknowledge if you are to be brutally honest with yourself. Indeed, claiming to *know* that there is a God would, in *your* case, constitute a *lie*. Do not tell *this* lie either. Do not claim to *know*, but feel free to *hope*. Feel free also to *act as if* God is watching and judging you at all times. Surely, so doing can only improve your behavior and your tendencies regarding your assessments of other persons. Many of your thoughts are less than charitable toward the human race. Watch how you think about God's children.

May 21

Every time that humanity, or any segment of the human race, has arrogated to itself the authority to determine what is good and what is evil, or to decide who counts as a fully-fledged "person" and who does not, the result has been utterly disastrous, and the culmination of human arrogance has been genocide, slavery, oppression, and depravity. *You*, and your fellow psychotic, talking apes, have proven to be entirely incapable of governing your affairs without some form of assistance, and as for interacting within the moral sphere, or avoiding degradation, you have proven time and time again that you need divine guidance, real or imagined. The blathering primates are entirely unfit to identify objective moral facts, and to impose moral law, in the absence of an allegedly transcendent wellspring of moral good and evil. Human beings simply *cannot* be trusted to govern themselves, or to govern others, if they do not believe that someone or something more powerful than mere humans is watching them and cracking the whip as a threat against malfeasance and self-centered obsessions. If God is dead, humanity is left adrift on a sea of vile bestiality. Perhaps this is, in fact, your lot, and perhaps the entire human race is similarly doomed to meaningless ignobility. You are, of course, permitted to *hope* that it is not so. Do *not* trust *people*. Misanthropy is *not* entirely unwarranted.

May 22

Nietzsche's *Overmen*, the geniuses who are willing and able to impose their will upon the world, have provided humanity with works that the rest of the species, the pathetic herd, could never have produced. So says Nietzsche, and not without reason. No one other than Beethoven could have composed the *Ode to Joy*. No one other than Shakespeare could have written *Hamlet*. No one other than Isaac Newton could have decoded the riddle of gravity and the laws of thermodynamics, or at the very least, no one else could have done so under the same circumstances and in the same period of time. No one other than Alexander could have risen from Macedonia to conquer virtually all the world insofar as he knew it, or again at the very least, not in the same manner and the same length of time. No one other than Nietzsche could have revealed, explained, and alerted the rest of us to the necessity of recognizing and admiring the contributions that are unique to the *Ubermenschen*. Well, in any event, no one else *did* alert us in quite the way that Nietzsche did. This contribution to intellectual history should not be overlooked or undervalued. Either all of that is correct, or *you* are prone to illusions concerning the proper valuation of human accomplishment. Are you distrustful of reliance upon God for everything that makes life worth living? Nietzsche was. *Someone* is confused about the ultimate nature of the human condition. Perhaps *everyone* is confused in this way.

May 23

The average intelligence and the average degree of integrity across any collective are, invariably and inevitably, lower than the intelligence and integrity of the most cognitively excellent member of that group. It is, therefore, unwise for any person endowed with intellectual prowess and admirable character to associate with or participate as a member of any collective predominantly peopled by inferiors. Why would anyone with genuine integrity wish to associate with morally lesser beings? What is the advantage, for the intellectually superior person, in associations involving cognitively lesser beings? *You*, of course, need not worry a great deal about such questions. Finding persons superior to you by both of those standards of measure is no great struggle. If you realize that *you* are the smartest person in the room, or the noblest person in the room, you need to *leave* that room as soon as you are able, and you probably ought to pity those who cannot get away. Avoid lesser persons like the plague... that they *are*. Consider the probability that *you* are an element of that plague as well. The noble are *always* a *very* small minority. It is *impossible* to form a *large* collective of people consisting only of the upright. Thus, all collectivists pursue inherently ignoble projects and are, without question, doomed to abject failure. As much as possible, avoid participation in collectives, altogether. That is probably the simplest solution.

May 24

If the alternative to being a "good member" of your largely sick and depraved society, and ingesting the pathological, perverse "culture" that it spews out of every medium, is exile from "your" culture, then you lose absolutely *nothing* by embracing this exile. It would be worse than a shame to be a "member in good standing" of a culture that embraces the repugnant phenomena that you encounter on a daily basis. Indeed, self-imposed exile may be a moral obligation given that you are confronted with a "culture" that embraces the legalized slaughter of unborn human beings, the glorification of criminality, and the normalization of depravities that can lead to *nothing* wholesome under *any* circumstances whatsoever. Consider, for example, the continuing sexualizing of younger and younger children. Can there be any doubt that the normalization of pedophilia is already well underway? The day that you shrug and tolerate grown men *raping children* as "just one of those things" that happens from time to time is the day that you need to wander off into the woods and never return. Any attempt to "heal" this moribund culture or to drag it to the path of righteousness and decency is, at best, a quixotic fool's errand and, at worst, a perverse leaping about as a poor impersonation of a *court jester* in a contemporary Babylon or Gomorrah. Do not allow your life to serve as a *show* for those who befoul everything that they touch. Yours is, unapologetically, the way of *exile*. So be it.

May 25

No human being, no collection of human beings, no human construct, and no human intellectual creation, is worthy of worship or unconditional allegiance. Indeed, there may be *nothing* that is worthy of unconditional allegiance, but *if* anything fills that bill, it is *not* of mere human origin. If people are, in fact, the "highest," wisest, and most advanced beings that you are *ever* to encounter, then you are forsaken indeed. Some persons have their charms and their intellectual virtues, but the species is a woefully flawed assemblage of matter and energy. If the solely naturalistic account of your world is correct, then feel free to abandon hope of any attainment greater than wise self-governance, and recognize that *you* are *not* wise and, thus far, you have governed yourself fairly *poorly*. Indeed, you have *never* met a genuinely wise person, nor have you encountered anything approaching ideal self-governance. Forlornness in this regard does not strip your life of purpose, but it does rule out any possibility of a *transcendent* or *ultimate* meaning of life. Perhaps this *is* the true condition of your species. Perhaps the natural world is the *only* real world, and all rumors of the transcendent realm are empty superstitions concocted by your benighted ancestors. You may forgive yourself for hoping that there is something *more*. Indeed, there appears to be fairly compelling evidence that this universe was engineered to be habitable by complex, intelligent creatures. Either that, or your assessment of such probabilities is way off. How can you *know*?

May 26

How reliable are history's narrators? As frequently as contemporary media sources lie, distort, fabricate, and misinterpret events of the day, you cannot help but consider the *volumes* of potential misinformation stored away in the many reports that constitute what you think of, perhaps erroneously, as *history*. We are told that, for example, Brutus and Cassius conspired to assassinate Julius Caesar, and carried out the deed on the Ides of March. Perhaps this is precisely what happened. Perhaps the proffered motivations for the assassination are, more or less, as they have been described and explained to the ages. Of course, it is not as if the event was captured on audio and video camera. For all you know, Brutus and Cassius managed to take credit for someone else's "wet work," and sought to capitalize on stolen "glory." You have read many accounts of events that strike you as, to say the least, hard to believe. Is the alleged meeting between Alexander the Great and Diogenes merely apocryphal, or did the two actually engage in a brief and illuminating conversation? The event seems unlikely, but it is not chronologically *impossible*. Perhaps the old Cynic philosopher really did ask the great conqueror to move out of his sunlight. How confident can you be about what *has* and has *not* actually occurred? Lee Harvey Oswald assassinated John F. Kennedy. Okay. Why, however, did Jack Ruby *really* kill Oswald? If he was "taking out the button man," then there is a lot more to the story, and there is some reason that powerful people want to conceal it. How much of history is like *that*?

May 27

If someone asks you for your advice, and *only* if someone *asks* you, then you are obligated to offer the best, most *honest*, and most helpful advice of which you are capable. You are obligated to do so *provided* that a minimally decent and honorable person makes the request. There is no such thing as an obligation to advise indecent, repugnant filth in a helpful and felicitous manner. Those reprobates can go straight to hell without your assistance. Sometimes, of course, you will realize that you are in no position to offer *any* helpful advice whatsoever. On such occasions, simply *admit* that you can be of no service in the matter, and do not waste anyone's time with phony deliberation that will come to nothing. *Never* pretend to be in a position to offer helpful counsel, if you cannot, in fact, do so. Ill-informed advice is usually *worse* than no advice at all. When you sincerely believe that you *can* provide valuable counsel, do so in the most direct, clear, and unvarnished fashion that you can manage. Parables, allegories, and metaphors are all well and good for scripture, novels, or communication with posterity. No one, however, asks directions to the hospital in the hopes of receiving an exegesis of the *Book of Job* in response. Try to avoid being the kind of person that runs off at the mouth because you so desperately love to hear yourself speak. There is, perhaps, a time for oratory and complex analysis, but it is relatively rare that either of these is requested of *you*. Say what needs to be said and be done with it. Keep it simple.

May 28

You woke up this morning with that vaguely familiar feeling of something scratching at the back of your throat, and clogged sinuses, a bit of fatigue, and a bit of fog surrounding your consciousness, accompanied this feeling. As you went through your morning routine, you noticed an extra layer of difficulty performing basic tasks and an increased cognitively discombobulating stupor. Though you tried to thrust it out of your mind and rouse your full energy and attention, by lunchtime you could no longer attempt to deny that you were sick. The evidence had mounted past the point of plausible deniability. It may be a cold, a sinus infection, or perhaps the early stages of the flu that has colonized your upper respiratory system. You had hoped that it might prove to be nothing more than allergies asserting their indications in stronger than usual fashion. Alas, some form of virus or bacterium has clearly invaded and caught your immune system at a loss for the onslaught. The little bastards slipped by the guards under cloak of darkness, and launched an assault upon you as you slumbered. Cowards! Infiltrators! It is too late to stave off the illness, but there is ample time to bear your condition without childish complaint. Do your job, discharge your responsibilities, blow your nose, and keep your *whining* to yourself. No one needs to hear about your problems, and no one needs to witness your suffering. Do not make a show of your symptoms in an effort to garner sympathy. Just go about your business and let nature take its course.

May 29

Is there a unifying narrative, a single unbroken thread, running throughout the entirety of your life? If you hold up a baby picture and say, "This was me an hour after I was born," is that statement *literally* true, or is that just a loose and oversimplified way of speaking about the complexities of personal identity over time and through physiological and psychological changes? If you are the same person as the baby in the photograph, what is it that makes all of your first-person experiences attributable to the same "self" persisting diachronically across all of the changes that have taken place with regard to your body, your mind, and your external relations to the world? What makes *you* the *same entity* over time? Your DNA has not changed, but that is a matter of biochemistry that can be represented by any single cell from your body. A clone could have the same DNA, but it would not be *you*. If there is *nothing* that serves the necessary unifying function, then *what* is the relationship between the earlier temporal phases of what you have *thought* of as "yourself," and the current locus of experience, memory, and perception that you think of as *you*? The self is either a genuine phenomenon, or the *idea* of "self" is a misconception or an illusion that is, for some reason, almost completely ubiquitous. Everyone you have ever met behaves as if a persisting identity underpins the thoughts, actions, and plans for the future that they call "theirs." Can it be that *everyone* has fallen prey to the *same* error?

May 30

A politician's stump speech is always at least fifty percent bullshit. Everyone knows this, but the politicians suffer no negative consequences for their lying, dissembling, and misrepresentations of fact, because they *all* debase themselves through relentless dishonesty, and the voting public perceives *no* viable alternative. Every election devolves to a choice between one bullshit artist and the other. Thus, the voter casts a ballot for the lies that are most appealing, or the bullshit that is packaged in the most appealingly verbalized bundle of nonsense and agitprop. The candidate that is the more skillful liar, the more "charming" candidate, and the more likeable prevaricator usually comes out on top. Do you prefer the liar from column "D," the liar from column "R," or the liar who cannot win because the vast majority of the voters take only liars from columns "D" and "R" seriously as voting options? Thus, the nation chooses its leadership, and the cultural degeneracy continues unabated. Why continue to participate in this idiotic and ignoble charade? You cannot do much about the public, the politicians, or the system that continues to reward liars, charlatans, and those who are most efficient at exploiting the mechanisms of corruption. You *can*, however, disentangle your interests from the whole sad charade. Stop voting for people you would not allow into your home. Democracy contains the seeds of its own destruction. The voters *deserve* what they get.

May 31

Many best-selling books, top-grossing films, and songs that top the charts for weeks on end are worthless garbage that appeal to the idiot multitudes, and the masses of adolescents (of all ages) that seem to dictate the market for these forms of public "storytelling" (to use that term *very* loosely) and other forms of popular culture. How many superhero movies have made hundreds of millions of dollars in revenue, without departing *one* iota from a formula that had been used too many times well over half a century ago? They are *all*, more or less, the *same* movie with slight changes to the title. Look at all the authors who get rich by writing the same narrative, presenting the same basic characters, and massaging the same plot, over and over again, while simply changing titles and the names of the interchangeable characters. What, exactly, is the difference between *one* love song and the next, or one pop ballad and another? The public, however, just keeps *devouring* the same dreck, the same pabulum, and the same bullshit. Perhaps they derive comfort from repeatedly hearing, seeing, and otherwise experiencing the same things that they associate with the innocence and freedom of youth. Maybe they are incapable of imagining anything new or interesting, and maybe the producers, writers, directors, etc. just keep giving "the people what they want" because the "creators" have long since run out of ideas. Fine. Let them all keep rehashing the same dish again and again. Let them *choke* on it. What difference does any of that make to you? It is zombies feeding zombies.

June 1

Cato killed himself and, if the legend is to be believed, thwarted attempts to save his life, because his only alternative, as *he* understood his circumstances, was to accept and submit to the illegitimate and despotic rule of the virulent Julius Caesar, or so the historians and philosophers tell us. As for Caesar's *actual* character, you are content to maintain a degree of healthy skepticism. Perhaps he *was* as terrible as Cato believed, and perhaps he had compensatory virtues as well. *That* is beside the point. How certain, however, can *you* be about Cato's motives? You have long regarded this ancient Roman statesman as a hero and a moral exemplar worthy of your admiration and your best attempts to emulate him. If those histories most genial to Cato and his motives are accurate, then he was heroic and admirable, indeed. *Are* those histories, *in fact*, accurate? This is, to say the least, difficult for you to determine. Other, less noble motivations for Cato's suicide are readily imaginable, and a few have been suggested by competing analyses of the events and individuals in question. Indeed, how confident should you be that he even died by his own hand? Perhaps Caesar had Cato assassinated, and the suicide narrative was fabricated by Cato's acolytes in an attempt to lionize a man who was, in reality, just another victim of ancient despotism. Did Cato *really* pull out his own entrails after an attempt had been made to save his life, or is that just a more compelling narrative than reality offered? How can you *know*? Does it *matter*?

June 2

Sloth has become so common and so pervasive that you are now pleasantly surprised any time you encounter anyone who is not, to your way of thinking, *shamefully* and *stunningly* lazy. This applies across the various fields of physical *and* intellectual endeavor. Intellectual sloth is no less repellant than is physical indolence. You frequently encounter "workers" in various fields and disciplines who seem to become vaguely aggravated when they are simply required to *do the job* for which they are being *paid*. The attitude that one is *entitled* to a paycheck irrespective of the quality of one's work and, indeed, irrespective of whether one has or has not actually *done* one's job is simply inexplicable. How do these jellyfish masquerading as humans get as far into their lives as to even attempt an *occupation*? Most of your colleagues do everything within their power to put as little effort as possible into the execution of the professions that *they* have *chosen*, and if the truth is to be told, *your* chosen profession is one of the *least* intrinsically burdensome vocations known to humankind. There is very little "heavy lifting" involved. The diligent, responsible college *student* is also, by now, the *rare* exception to the *wretched* rule. A task *half* completed appears to satisfy most of those undertaking various assignments, and a drowsy, mediocre effort is almost always sufficient to pass through the system, retain a job, and slouch all the way to retirement. Do not allow yourself to "blend in" to this cultural *miasma*.

June 3

Unless it is thoroughly well earned, your participation in a standing ovation is a perverse display of the herd instinct married to disingenuous pseudo-appreciation of the mundane and unimpressive performance in question. You have *no* obligation to stand and applaud mediocrity just because an auditorium full of reflexively imitative primates chooses to rise upon their hind legs and slap their paws together, more or less, in unison. If you are moved *sincerely* to this show of appreciation, then leap to your feet, by all means, and applaud with all of the gusto that you can summon. If, however, the event you attend is supposed to "honor" some aging factotum at the culmination of an utterly unremarkable career, feel free to offer a "celebration" in proportion to the *actual* impressiveness of the phenomenon with which you are presented. There is no need to get carried away by the odd behavior of those among whom you find that you are surrounded. Perhaps sitting and tapping a thumb and index finger together might suffice. In other cases, leaving the room altogether may be the appropriate expression of your honest attitude regarding the entire matter. An ovation *can* be an exercise in bullshit just as can any other disingenuous public act. *Why* would you want to contribute to the world's current quantity of malarkey?

June 4

How is it that there are people who make it all the way through medical school, spend all of the requisite time and money, and endure all of the sleepless nights before exams, and then decide to specialize in *proctology*? This is, of course, a necessary medical function, and you are grateful that there *are* proctologists in the world. You feel compelled to stress that there is nothing wrong with, nothing defective about, and nothing shameful about this specialization. Indeed, you will probably find yourself a patient in such a physician's care someday (probably in the, regrettably, not-too-distant future). The *need* for proctologists is no mystery. The *demand* is not difficult to explain. Beyond this demand, however, what explains the seemingly adequate *supply* of those physicians that perform the relevant services? Why, to put the question a bit more bluntly than is entirely necessary, so many *ass doctors*? Is it just a fairly well assured stream of patients, and a reasonably lucrative position that attracts doctors to this field, or is there some *intrinsic* fascination that simply (and thankfully) escapes your powers of imagination? You regard dentistry such a sufficiently repulsive occupation that you struggle, at least a bit, to imagine ever having seriously considered it as a career, but a vocation devoted to the opposite terminus of the alimentary canal is altogether *too* alien for you to contemplate. God bless the proctologists—but where *do* they come from?

June 5

Is there *any* reason that you should *not* be forgotten very soon after you "shuffle off this mortal coil," and someone places your remains in a box underground or in an urn upon a mantelpiece somewhere? Should your name outlast you by more time than it takes to produce an obituary? Does your life even *warrant* an obituary? If so, produce the *evidence* that you merit a "legacy" or an enduring place in anyone's heart or memory. What is *posterity* supposed to do with you and the sum total of your life's work and your paltry efforts? Perhaps your life might serve as a cautionary example for those inclined to delusions of grandeur, or maybe it constitutes a bit of comic relief, but beyond serving as a footnote in the story of some more significant phenomenon, you should not anticipate posthumous fame or admiration of *any* kind. You should expect the entirety of your existence to disappear into oblivion, and to do so "not with a bang, but with a whimper," as foretold in "The Hollow Men." Indeed, that fate is pretty well assured not only for you, but also for all of the other "hollow men" at the end of the world. If not in the immediate aftermath of your demise (likely as that seems), then certainly over the *long* term, you are destined for *erasure*. This is neither good nor bad. It may not even rise to the level of *indifference*. You can "rage against the dying of the light" all you want. In the end, you die, that light goes out, and the world is shut of you. Is this *not* as it should be? Is this not the way of all living things? *You* are *not* special.

June 6

If you had to write a *eulogy* at the end of your career, as if that portion of your life had died, what would you be inclined to say on behalf of the occupation at which you had spent the better part of your adult life? Having spent over thirty years at a particular occupation ought to afford ample occasion to contemplate the value and purpose of the work you have done. Perhaps you would tell the assembled audience that you are a better person for having known this career and spent so much time in its company, and learned so many edifying lessons about your tiny slice of the human condition. You might have to admit that, in some respects, you did not get to know this occupation as well as you might have known it, had you just put in a little more effort, or had you been just a little more attentive and receptive to all this career offered to teach you about yourself, about others, and about the world at large. Maybe you would say that although there is *something* sad in parting ways with your job, there is also a hope that this transformation will usher in fresh possibilities that you cannot quite grasp before "crossing over." Then again, maybe the whole idea of eulogizing your career is just pretentious bullshit. You worked a job for a long while, you decided that you had performed this job long enough for your tastes, and you realized that you could stop doing it without going quite completely bankrupt. You decided to retire because you had *enough* of your profession. What more is there to say?

June 7

Is there still some mystery about the use of potent narcotics and the likely consequences for those who use hard drugs? If someone has sincerely declared, "I am *so* glad that I got addicted to methamphetamine," then you must have missed that utterance. Who has ever said, with a straight face, "My life was going nowhere until I discovered heroin," and then held a Nobel Prize aloft? If people want to degrade themselves, ruin their lives, wreck their families, destroy their careers, and put themselves into early graves, then you have no particular objection to offer. Live and let live, or live and let self-destruct. You are *not*, however, required to indulge in sympathy for those who make moronic, self-eviscerating, indefensible choices over and over again. It may well be true that they cannot help themselves. From this fact, *if* it *is* a fact, precisely *nothing* follows about your "obligatory" compassion for these disastrous human beings. You have nothing to gain through empathy with creatures that are inherently self-hating, or congenitally catastrophic. A rattlesnake can do nothing to alter its nature, and its deadly venom is part of its biological makeup. Do *not*, for this reason, pick it up, clasp it to your bosom, and sing it a lullaby. It *is* a *snake*, stupid! It *will* kill you if you give it the chance. What kind of imbecile embraces a serpent? Do *not* latch onto the human equivalent of a rattlesnake and expect better results. Self-destructiveness *loves* company. These people love to drag others down with them. Do not allow yourself to be dragged to hell.

June 8

What would happen if you told everyone that you encountered *exactly* what you were thinking over the course of one full day? What, in particular, would happen if you told your interlocutors what you were thinking about each of *them*? Imagine allowing your *every* thought to spill out of your face without any self-censorship, without any editing, and without ever biting your tongue. Consider what percentage of your utterances that day would constitute insults, imprecations, and general expressions of disgust. How many times would you say, "Shut up," and "I do not care," over the course of that day? A betting man would probably do well to place a great deal of money on the "over" for nearly any suggested finite number. The number of "Shut up!" utterances might only be exceeded by the number of expletives that would explode out of you, many in rapid succession and absolutely *dripping* with venom. You are neither a "gentle soul" nor a greater lover of humanity. Indeed, your misanthropy has rarely been matched in other persons of your acquaintance. It is quite reasonable to regard this cast of mind as unhealthy. Nonetheless, you have little or no interest in divesting yourself of it. You have no desire to learn to love your fellow human beings. Any suggestion to the contrary is just bullshit. You do *not* like *people*. In retrospect, you realize that you have *never* liked people. If this misanthropy of yours is a defect, so be it. Embrace your distrust of humanity. How many counterexamples have you encountered?

June 9

So much of the dreck that passes as "entertainment" these days is, in fact, just a set of symptoms of a decaying, dying culture, and consuming the "entertainment" in question is tantamount to watching lemmings rush giddily toward a precipice. The various "entertainment" industries are tinged with filth, stupidity, and several varieties of degeneracy. You watch throngs gathered for a football game or a concert, and you experience a powerful, palpable disgust as you see thousands of your fellow citizens indulging in some mindless chant, or performing a "wave" across the stadium, or applauding some display of juvenile self-indulgence on the part of a player who has done nothing more than his *job*—for which he is, for some reason, ludicrously overpaid. Is dancing in the end zone after a touchdown worthy of cheering, hooting, and expressions of approval? People who get paid millions of dollars to catch passes, and leap about like lunatics because they have managed to do nothing more than the job for which they are being paid, should be recognized as clowns, jesters, or imbeciles. No cheering is warranted. Is scoring touchdowns *not* what receivers and running backs get *paid* to do? Crowd surfing a concert audience is an expression of the vapidity of the artist's songs. If the music is worth hearing, a stage dive is unnecessary. Did Beethoven surf atop the crowds? The crowd, today, *pretends* that they are part of the show because pretending is the best they can do. Public "amusement" is mostly bullshit. Unfortunately, it also pays well.

June 10

Even a dog can indulge in a bit of bullshit if the mutt believes it can get what it wants through surreptitious machinations. You have witnessed *your* dog engaging in the back turned, over the shoulder, "I am not *really* begging, but I am here for you, if you cannot finish that entire steak," maneuver. This indicates the depths to which bullshit penetrates the very marrow of your bones, and the evolutionary adaptability of deceit, pretense, and bald misdirection. If a dog deploys such tactics, with its rudimentary (at best) ability to assess a situation and adopt an advantageous posture, then your ancestors *must* have developed dissimulation to something like a form of art. Surely, you are descended from effective liars, cons, and charlatans. If lying "works" today, and sometimes it does, then it has probably been useful for most of human history. You cannot know who the *first* bullshit artist of your species may have been, but you can be fairly confident that this skill enabled its masters to increase their likelihood of surviving long enough to procreate. The survival of the fittest may, in some cases, amount to survival of the best bullshit artists. Cain possessed "the gift," did he not? The response, "Am I my brother's keeper?" uttered by the man who was first to *murder* his brother is, arguably, the earliest recorded resort to bullshit as an alibi for homicide. It did not *work* in Cain's case, but he *did* survive long enough to procreate. His children inherited the bullshit gene. Since then, who has been spared this inheritance? Certainly, *you* seem to have been endowed with "the gene," have you not?

June 11

Were you to be "weighed in the balances," like the king from the *Book of Daniel*, would you not also be "found wanting" in the same manner that this judgment was rendered against Belshazzar? Indeed, you are neither a king nor a moral or intellectual exemplar and, if you are brutally honest with yourself, you are *far* removed from the type of character that *anyone* ought to emulate. Were you to list your faults on one side of a ledger and enumerate all of your virtues on the other side of the page, there can be no doubt that the one side of the page, the "unfortunate" side, would show a *far* longer list than the other. Perhaps this is true of everyone, but not *everyone* has been left in the governance of *your* will. Others must struggle with their own failings, and their success or failure to do so effectively is simply *none* of your business. You do *yourself* a disservice, to say nothing of the disservice to *others*, when you focus on the vices and transgressions of other persons rather than bending your will on improving *your* character and rooting out the source of your *own* inadequacies. How easily you are drawn into criticism of others, and how reluctantly you turn your critical gaze inward. Obviously, this is because you fear what you will find upon honest introspection, and sincere analysis of the intellectual and moral malformations that you can expect to find there. Who died and made *you* the Messiah, pal? Remember that no one asked *you* to wash away *his or her* sins. Do you not have enough of your own to occupy your time?

June 12

Never stop reading books, articles, and commentaries, or watching documentaries, and seeking other sources of useful information with which to improve your understanding of the world, current events, history, science, and your place in the cosmos—as a miniscule, insignificant speck of an ephemeral species on a tiny planet in a vast ocean of space and time. The amount of information available to you surpasses the totality of all the accumulated knowledge of the human race from the dawn of history up until about ten years ago. Any source that reminds you to remain humble and accept your allotted role as *no one in particular* is well worth your time and effort. Who are you compared to Socrates, Diogenes, Epictetus, Alexander, Michelangelo, Mozart, the Buddha, Jesus, or Shakespeare? If you were offered the job of holding the hem of Socrates' tunic out of the dust, and keeping your mouth shut while doing so, you would be woefully under-qualified for the position. What have you accomplished compared to those aforementioned giants of intellect and spirituality, and to innumerable other figures that have shaped the course of history, the evolution of cultures, and our understanding of the human condition? Even the "immortals" of your species must pass away, and *all* of them are to be swallowed up by time, space, and the eternal expansion of the universe. Even your heroes go "the way of all flesh" in the end. *Your* life comes to *nothing*. Now, *live* it!

June 13

The lights are going out all across the Western World, the superstructure of this civilization is crumbling, and it is the *leaders* of Western nations that bear the primary responsibility for the incipient death of the West. Pay no attention to those who deny that the West is dying. These people are either very poorly informed, or they are compulsively disingenuous. There were probably Romans who denied the collapse of the empire up to, and beyond, the undeniable death of all that they had known. In the name of globalism and a hopelessly misguided version of cosmopolitanism that insists all people and all cultures are both equal and mutually compatible, the West offers a ceaseless absorption of millions upon millions of "migrants" who *despise* the West, its values, and its traditions. Those inhabitants of the West who resist being assimilated by the migrants obviously seeking to *supplant* Western culture with a "new order" that will, quite clearly, prove unpalatable and, quite possibly, fatal to those who value the culture that sprouted from Athens, Jerusalem, and Rome will be decried as "xenophobic," or "racist," or whatever might be the ludicrous shibboleth of the day. You struggle to remain emotionally detached as you watch this suicidal stupidity unfold. Though you know that you can do nothing to forestall the incipient collapse of the culture you had hitherto called "yours," the temptation to despair is powerful indeed. Nonetheless, you *must* resist *this* temptation. *You* must *not* collapse along with the West.

June 14

Some days, you feel a bit lost and *more* than *just a bit* out of place, out of sorts, and far less than comfortable interacting with your contemporaries. Sometimes you experience any form of company as vaguely oppressive or, at least, needlessly unsettling. Perhaps *all* men feel as if they are "born out of time," or as if they have emerged from a cave and do not recognize this "new world" all around them—maybe, at some point or other, all men feel like *exiles* from their own culture or their own historical epoch. You cannot be certain about the rest of the human race, but the feeling of exile visits you on a nearly *daily* basis, does it not? Indeed, you cannot be certain that you have spent more time in a condition of serenity, or in a state of general discomfort. The problem is *not* the world in which you find your experience unfolding. The world was here *first*, the human race was "in business" *long* before you were conceived, and people were engaging in interpersonal interactions for hundreds of thousands of years before anyone had the "pleasure" of *your* company. Live in exile if you must, but you are to blame *no one* for this, and you are to utter no complaint about your circumstances—not even in the confines of your own consciousness. The world is as God has designed it, or the world is as it is due to the laws of nature and the unguided behavior of matter and energy. Do you find fault with God or with nature? Do not be ridiculous. Your exile is self-inflicted. By the way, is it *really* so terrible?

June 15

Television pundits are, with very rare exceptions, charlatans, liars, spin-doctors, and bullshit artists. *Everyone* knows this but, for purely partisan and ideological reasons, many are willing to *pretend* that they believe the liars who work at the behest of the party or the corporation to which they pledge their allegiance. A culture that accepts a ludicrous kabuki dance as a method of gathering and analyzing news of the world, and allows the normalization of partisan *lying* as the *standard* mode of political discourse and communication, is a culture that staggers upon its last legs and begs enemies, both foreign and domestic, to take advantage of its pervasive societal stupidity and degeneracy. It seems as though much of the public *insists* upon being either uninformed or badly misinformed—but in a manner from which they derive psychological and emotional comfort. Moreover, the culture that tolerates this state of affairs *deserves* the consequences that are all but guaranteed to ensue. Of course, you find it difficult to know what really transpires in the back rooms and barrooms of Washington DC. The purveyors of "spin" (a euphemism for lying and dissembling) control the "messaging" (a euphemism for telling the idiot public what it wants to hear), and the politicians dance to the tunes called by the highest bidders. Collective karma is simply the law of cause and effect writ large and manifested in lost blood and treasure. Create a duplicitous culture, and *live* among *liars*. It is practically a law of nature.

June 16

What is the good, what is the benefit, what is the great virtue to be derived from *fame*? Is it not laughable and pathetic that so many people pursue fame as if it is an intrinsic good, and as if it is the most worthwhile pursuit under the sun? Indeed, many of those that pursue fame most doggedly appear to be willing to sacrifice decency, honor, and every virtue imaginable, for anything that they believe to be necessary for the attainment of this strange condition of wide-ranging notoriety. Fame is rarely achieved, it seldom lasts for very long, it often does *far* more damage to the famous person than could ever have been caused by anonymity, and it nearly always creates needless complications for those who attain the stardom they seek. What *is* the appeal of being recognized by strangers or idolized by people with whom one shares no kinship or attachment that even approaches viable affinity? In other words, why would you want to be revered by persons whom you do not know, or recognized by persons with whom you would not voluntarily associate? It is foolish enough to concern yourself about what *anyone* thinks of you, but concern with what *everyone* thinks of you is, at least arguably, a full-blown mental illness. This desire to be recognized everywhere you go is an unhealthy fetish. If you wish to experience the "world's embrace," you might try burial without a casket. The very *earth*, the soil, will *embrace* you indeed.

June 17

Never deploy a straw man, an ad hominem, or a red herring, in the context of *any* debate. If you find yourself tempted to resort to any of these fallacies, know that you are not confident that you are on the *correct* side of the debate, and the impulse to deploy a *non sequitur* is an act of cowardice or intellectual sloth. Engage with your opponent's *actual* position, without offering up any mischaracterization of it, without aiming your criticism at your opponent's character, circumstances, or alleged hypocrisy, and without attempting to change the subject, in subtle, deceptive fashion, from the subject of the debate at hand. If you are defending a true proposition, and if you have the capacity to marshal evidence in persuasive fashion, without resort to semantic or rhetorical trickery, then you have no *need* for fallacious arguments or tactical machinations hidden behind a shroud you have woven with words. If you are correct and you can prove it, just do so without the needless and cowardly trickery. Furthermore, you should not *want* to win a debate by dishonest means whether you are defending the correct side of the dispute or not. You *sully* the position you are advocating when you resort to some devious stratagem in your attempt to convince your opponent or some audience. Do not make it seem as if your position cannot stand genuine scrutiny. Finally, you degrade *your character* by dissembling about the matter at issue. Tell the *truth*. Deploy *reason*. That *must* be enough.

June 18

How much time does your species, how much time does *humanity*, have left before its inevitable extinction? The short and simple answer is, of course, no one knows. Certainly, *you* do not know. Has humanity *earned* a long-lasting tenure as the dominant species on the planet, or has your species managed to persist this long *in spite* of itself? Consider the possible states of affairs for your species five thousand years into the future. Can you tell whether it is more likely that people will have caused their own extinction through warfare, whether environmental collapse will have made the planet uninhabitable for humans, or whether your species will find that they are flourishing because of its elevated intellect and mastery of technology? Perhaps humankind and all of its technological wizardry will prove paltry by comparison to another power, of a different order and origin, and perhaps all of the humans will be laid low by this power that finds humanity to be unimpressive, disappointing, or unworthy of continuing its journey into the future. In other words, maybe aliens will wipe us off the planet. Surely, *some* kind of apocalypse *must* occur at some point. Nothing, after all, lasts *forever*. The human race will *not* prove to be an exception to this rule. What you have encountered, in your life on this planet, is clearly not made for *eternity*. Indeed, you are not particularly confident that eternity will be better off with people in it than without them. Perhaps eternity needs a bunch of puppies.

June 19

There are, in fact, people buried in holes in the desert, the woods, and under the foundations of buildings because someone said the wrong thing, or did the wrong thing, or showed up in the wrong place at the wrong time. A variety of relatively innocent mistakes actually *can* culminate in you getting yourself murdered. This is not just a myth sustained by Hollywood gangster films and television police dramas. The world is peopled with a variety of personality types, and *not all* of them are interested in working and playing well with others. Some people will kill you with less hesitation or compunction than you might wish to imagine. The next time you step on a snail, take a moment to consider the fact that there are people who would eliminate you with no more emotional engagement than you experienced when you snuffed out that snail. You are both a fool and a sheep if you assume that you will never encounter the type that does not respond to reason, or to plaintive cries for mercy. Learn to identify the signs that you have happened upon such a character, or resign yourself to the probability that you are likely to be victimized. If you are *not* prepared to become the thing that even the "bad men" fear, and if you are *not* prepared to make that transformation within the blink of an evil eye, you invite all sorts of abuse, up to and including your murder. Anyone who offers an invitation should refrain from shock or outrage when the invitation is accepted. If you *ask* for it, you just might *get* it. The world *is* a rough place, after all.

June 20

Beware the danger of having *too many* ideas percolating at the same time, and of pursuing too many contemporaneous interests. Learning about a variety of subjects is all well and good, but be careful that you do not *dilute* your progress in one area of inquiry with the ill-conceived pursuit of expertise across an overly broad range of topics. Nobody gets to be an expert in *everything*. Even Aristotle remained ignorant of *a few* disciplines. *You* are no Aristotle, and you clearly lack the intellectual wherewithal to master *all* of the disciplines that you find intriguing. It is better to enhance your understanding of *a few* related fields of study in significant fashion, than it is to make nominal gains that provide negligible advantage in multifarious areas of endeavor. Would you prefer to develop genuine, adamantine mental discipline that renders you imperturbable, or to develop that aspect of your character only moderately, while also making modest progress toward understanding long-term investment strategies and developing competence at playing the ukulele? What good will the extra money for retirement do you, if you are too easily susceptible to anxiety, depression, and fits of rage? How much joy will you and your audiences derive from your strumming away at a miniature guitar, if you are incapable of maintaining the mental discipline to remember how to play the instrument and sing at the same time? Prioritize self-rectification and the improvement of your character. If you can manage *that* and also learn to play expert backgammon, then that is all well and good.

June 21

You need not concern yourself over gaining a few pounds or an inch or two around your waistline. At your age, this condition is difficult, though not *impossible*, to avoid. It is not a mere happenstance that there are very few professional athletes in combat and collision sports over the age of fifty. *Morbid obesity* would be worthy of some attention and correction, and you have not yet slid into *that* degree of lassitude, but the mere loss of the washboard abdominal muscles from your youth is hardly a tragedy. Do not *obsess* over fine physiological details such as the mere aesthetics of your torso or the development of skin that reveals an aging body. That is nothing but a manifestation of an ignoble and petulant vanity. Having a "six-pack" never made anyone wiser or more virtuous. The ability to perform backflips on command is not exactly a prerequisite for living a decent and honorable life. Are you training to be an underwear model, or are you training for healthy functionality and competence if it is needed in the defense of yourself and your loved ones in the event of some emergency? If you want to look like a statue of a Greek God, you should probably reconsider that desire and try to extirpate the narcissism that motivates it. It is one thing to "keep in shape," and something else altogether to want to impress people with your physique. What do you care for how your body is *perceived*? Never concern yourself with how you *look* to others. What can your body *do*? That is the only interesting question in this area.

June 22

It is important to recognize that your children, your students, the children of your friends, neighbors, and associates, and other young people you encounter, *watch* you and observe other adults as they develop their conceptions of what it is *to be* an adult, and how to go about developing their character and governing their behavior. Boys watch men to try and figure out what it *means* to be a man, and girls watch women to develop their conception of what womanhood *amounts to*. Feel free to *talk* to young people until you are blue in the face, but the youth learn by *modeling* far more efficiently and effectively than they learn through verbal instruction or discourse. They imitate in "monkey see, monkey do" fashion. You *are*, whether you like it or not, a role model for at least some of the youths that you encounter. This responsibility is not to be shirked, and you fail to serve as a virtuous role model at your own peril *and* to the detriment of your civilization. Given the pervasiveness of depravity and stupidity among your culture's adults, you had better do what you can to serve as a model of decency, honor, and diligence. You cannot *control* how anyone responds to your conduct, or whether any particular youth is paying attention to your attempts to be honorable, but you *never know* when you are being watched, and you are, therefore, obligated to do your best to model decency at *all* times. Do *not* add to the cultural dissolution that afflicts your society. Do not contribute to the West's loss of faith in itself.

June 23

Are you misperceiving something, or is your culture increasingly sexualizing younger and younger *children*? A society that indulges in this form of perversion is simply not worth saving. If elements of your culture are actively trying to normalize pedophilia, and this certainly seems to be the case, then a sickness, a *very* deep depravity is eating away at the very *concept* of *minimal decency*. What will *not* be permitted, if the utterly obscene, vile, and depraved phenomenon of *raping children* is to be tolerated by *any* segment of the populace? When *child rapists* are not treated like the repugnant *monsters* that they so *clearly* are, there can be no form of behavior that remains *illicit*, and there can be no hope of a morally viable future for those that tolerate this insidious, filthy cultural deformity. Why defend your nation, if your nation is willing to countenance the most scarlet of all sins? The *unthinkable* is unfolding right before your eyes. Whatever the Supreme Court may say about the matter, raping children clearly warrants execution if that punishment is *ever* warranted by *any* deed. In prisons across the nation, even mass murderers refuse to tolerate the presence of child molesters among them. They are *not* wrong to enforce this policy. There can be no reform or rehabilitation for the filth that rape children, and *nothing* is gained by allowing these vermin to continue to draw breath. They are the most prolific violent criminals, and they *never* stop perpetrating their chosen crime, and *every* minimally decent human *despises* them. Again, this attitude is *not* defective. Let them *all* dangle.

June 24

You can almost *taste* the corruption today. It is a most curious, and unpleasant, instance of synesthesia, but the experience borders on the undeniable. Like drinking grapefruit juice from a metallic thermos, the news this evening provides a mixture of the unpalatable and the irresistible. You want to look away, but the spectacle of sheer, naked, obvious duplicity compels your attention. It is a bit like finding the rotten food that has been causing that putrid odor in the refrigerator. One whiff is never sufficient. You stick your nose in at least twice, and then you find the nearest person, thrust it toward her and say, "Smell this!" You want to do the same thing now. You want to find someone and say, "Listen to *this* bullshit!" Ah, where is that metal thermos full of grapefruit juice? At least you can spit *that* out and be done with it. Would that you could do that with corrupt people in positions of power. Imagine a world without politicians and merchants of mendacity. Of course, this world will never come to pass, but the fantasy is pleasant, is it not? Plato was correct about democracy. It is nothing more than appetitive grasping manifest as a political system, and the long-term prospects of any such system are far, far less than promising. The voting public is an unruly beast, and it cares for nothing more than stuffing its fat face and avoiding payment for the meal. Would a philosopher king be a wiser and more benevolent ruler? Let us give it a try. How much worse could this arrangement possibly be?

June 25

It is not uncommon that other persons mistreat you without provocation on your part and without any other rational justification that you can identify. Like everyone else, you have suffered various forms of abuse or inappropriate treatment. Clearly, your experiences of this nature hardly constitute something new under the sun, or anything about which you ought to expend a great deal of intellectual energy. If you live in the world, you are bound to get a few bumps and bruises, and some of the damage may afflict your ego or your psyche. So what? Try not to take such incidents personally, as the behavior in question is generally the result of some irritant, or other event or condition that has beset the mischievous party. When people suffer, some of them are only capable of responding to that experience by trying to make others suffer as they have. In most cases, *you* just happened to be in the vicinity when the frustration or anger erupted. Though the wrath is *directed* at you, or at something you have done or said, it is not actually *about* you. Moments of emotional indiscipline strike just about everyone. This includes *you*, by the way. You cannot reasonably demand *perfect* mental discipline from everyone at all times. Indeed, it is unwise to expect *perfect* mental discipline from *anyone* at *any* time. Consider all of the occasions on which you have "blown up" at persons who had done nothing to warrant such treatment. It is hypocritical to hold others to a higher standard than can be met by your own comportment. Cut people a little slack. Hold *yourself* to a higher standard.

June 26

You have already lived enough years to accomplish most, if not all, of your central or primary life goals. The fact that so much of what you have sought to bring into being remains unaccomplished is a testament to your sloth, and to the staggering amount of time you have *wasted*. Take a few moments to contemplate the amount of time you have used about as poorly and unproductively as it could have been used. How many of your waking hours have you frittered away on watching idiotic television shows? You have literally spent *years* of your limited life in front of that idiot box, and most of that time, you did not even particularly *enjoy* what you were watching—much less learn anything from the experience. How pathetic is *that*? You have thrown away valuable time cognitively marinating in televised sewage that has, if anything, dulled your wits and produced ludicrous expectations that bear little resemblance to rational assessments of any real world likelihood. The world of television is *not* the world in which you actually *live*. How many *reruns* have you seen? There is simply *no* excuse for watching the same episode of some sophomoric sitcom for the *twentieth* time. There is no excuse for the *fifth* viewing of the episode. How many game shows have you watched? If you derive enjoyment from watching perpetual adolescents leap about a stage after winning some trivial prize, then you *really* need to reassess your values and your interests. If *that* is the best expenditure of your limited time, then yours is largely a wasted life.

June 27

Do not be impressed by phony claims about the trivial "diversity" so frequently championed by those who are, or those who pretend to be, fascinated by skin color, ethnic association, sexual proclivities, or regions of ancestral origin. Why chromosomes and melanin should be determinative of your beliefs, values, and behaviors is not at all clear to you, but the merchants of multiculturalism never tire of trying to compel you to think in these terms. The only *diversity* that is *not* insignificant bullshit involves differences in worldview, values, ideology, and patterns of thought. Nothing about genitals, skin color, or ethnicity conclusively determines any individual's worldview, ideology, or overarching interests. A room full of people who all agree with each other about politics, morality, religion, and socioeconomic issues is *not* a *diverse* collection of humanity, no matter how many different races, ethnicities, or sexual orientations are represented in that room. An ideological monoculture is nothing to celebrate, it is not an admirable attainment, and no rational adult should desire or pursue its manifestation. You must point out the hypocrisy of faux "diversity," especially when it is held up as a noble or essential societal goal. It is, of course, nothing of the sort. It is not particularly wonderful to convince people to express only *one* point of view, or to encourage fear of challenging prevailing orthodoxies. Facts, and admirable virtues, do *not* stand in need of verification by plebiscite.

June 28

You might think there would have to be some type of upper (or perhaps *lower*) limit to human depravity, but as you observe your nation, its culture, and the world at large, you can find no boundary that is not transgressed and, increasingly, transgressed casually, publicly, and with a stunningly perverse display of *pride*. You have, for example, seen and heard abortionists *bragging* about the *thousands* of unborn human beings that they have snuffed out in the womb. They, and their fellow travellers, recount these deeds in *televised interviews*, and they smirk and laugh at those who regard them as mass murderers committing infanticide as a *profession*. What kind of "physician" chooses to specialize in *that* procedure? You have, as another macabre example, seen interviews with people openly supporting and defending terrorists who slaughter the innocent on trains, at restaurants, or in nightclubs, and concoct the most ludicrous rationalizations for regarding this behavior as something *other* than abject villainy. You cannot help but boggle at the legions of apologists for the mass murder of the innocent. Compounding their repugnance, they concoct "arguments" to justify these behaviors so *patently* specious that *no one* can find them to be genuinely compelling. These people are willing to resort to casuistry and dissembling in the defense of murdering innocent human beings. They simply have *no shame*. Human beings of this stripe are, arguably, not *persons* at all. Is that not reminiscent of the claims that some make about the "fetus" as opposed to the infant? It travels three feet, and becomes morally significant. Does *anyone* believe that?

June 29

You often find yourself wondering if you will live long enough to see your various tasks and projects through to their completion. Although there is nothing special about you or your work and avocations, you still find that you sometimes worry about not being able to finish everything that you have started. This is, of course, a needless and unhelpful bit of speculation. You have no idea if decades of life remain for you, or if you will drop dead before your next birthday — or the next *sunrise*. There is not much chance that you will ever know how much time remains for you to breathe in and out. This is probably the wrong way to think about your concerns surrounding mortality and the limitations imposed by your demise. You should *hope* that your death *would* curtail *some* project or some worthy pursuit, should you not? If your death does *not* interrupt some noble endeavor, then that will mean that you were doing *nothing* of value when death came for you. *That* would be a *real* shame, would it not? Do not, therefore, concern yourself that you will not have sufficient time to complete your various tasks, but rather set yourself the goal of *always* engaging in some worthy project or other, so that death will *have to* prevent you from completing *something* worth doing. Let yours be a life of engagement, effort, and diligent endeavor unto its very end. In this way, you can meet your end knowing that it took *death* to stop you. Do your best while you can. Embrace the rest. Live until you die. *Amor fati.*

June 30

Never embrace or accept servitude or submission to *any* worldly agency, or to any individual, or any concept that lacks at least a suggestion of the transcendent or the divine. No person, no collective, no nation-state, and no natural phenomena are worthy of reverence, or of any other attitude approaching worship. All of these are just the physical "furniture" of reality, they are things into which you might bump or fall, but they should not command anything like the attitude of devotion. Do not commit yourself to *unconditional* allegiance, or to doing *anyone's* bidding irrespective of the motives or consequences as they are explained to you, and as they are provided a rational defense. Even your loved ones can go mad or request some type of indecent conduct due to a fit of rage or momentary lapse of reason. Even your nation can go off the rails and become tyrannical or ignoble. Indeed, this seems less and less unlikely with each passing election. Even your long-held beliefs and values can, in principle, be proven false, flawed, or inadequate to future contingencies. Only God, if there *is* a God, may lay claim to unconditional submission and commitment on the part of those He has *created*. Though God can insist upon unconditional obedience, it is not clear that the God of scripture does so. Indeed, scripture includes *several* accounts of God's servants engaging him in something like a bargaining relationship. Are we not told that Moses convinced God to exact a lesser penalty against the Israelites who worshipped the golden calf? If even *God* allows dissent, let no mere human entity tell you it is impermissible.

July 1

Cooking a huge meal to feed the extended family on a holiday, or just for the sake of encouraging a family gathering, is a truly rewarding experience and, although that may seem like sappy, corny bullshit to some, it happens to be *true*. It is enormously gratifying to know that *your* efforts have produced pleasure and sustenance to those people about whom you care most deeply. It is a legitimate source of pride and joy. You used to believe that housewives told themselves things like that in order to rationalize the onerous responsibility of feeding an entire house full of people, and that most of them secretly resented the responsibility of preparing food for the family on a regular basis. This may be an accurate diagnosis in *some* cases, but you now believe these to be the exception rather than the rule. Since you have learned to cook (a bit), you have experienced the fulfillment associated with feeding the people you love, and witnessing the genuine satiation and gratitude expressed for your labors. When your spouse looks at you with a surprised and happy "yummy face," and you are confident that she is not faking it, you cannot help but feel as if you have done something good for your wife and your marriage. You now find it difficult to understand cooks who do *not* derive satisfaction from a job well done, a meal well made, and a family well fed. With the exception of professional chefs on the job, cooking is a selfless expression of love, intimacy, and mutual appreciation. What is wrong with that? Eat, drink, be merry, and give thanks.

July 2

It is unwise to offer an invitation to premature frailty and failure of body, mind, or character. If you live long enough, your body will deteriorate in terms of physical strength, stamina, flexibility, and general functionality. Given a sufficiently long life, this kind of decline is, more or less, unavoidable. Do not eat, drink, and conduct yourself in a manner that needlessly hastens this slide into frailty and dependency upon others. A long enough life will, very often, culminate in cognitive decline, and your capacity to reason, to remember, and to marshal complex thoughts, may be impaired by natural processes that cause deterioration of various neurological functions. Try to avoid turning your brain into a frequently malfunctioning organ before nature does the job on your behalf. Once your brain "goes," you will be of little use to yourself or anyone else. As long as your mind is functioning within normal parameters, you have *no* excuse for allowing your *character* to degenerate. Similarly, you need to keep your body in properly functional condition for as long as you are able to do so. Already, you are experiencing the effects of your various injuries, the surgeries you needed to repair those injuries, and there are early symptoms of arthritis, declining eyesight, and significantly diminished stamina. Exercise to maintain the functionality, coordination, and integrity of your body, but work even more diligently to maintain the integrity of your *character*. Contributing to your own debasement may be the greatest sin of all.

July 3

Those who are loath to contemplate loss, and what most people regard as catastrophe, are thereby inviting *far* more intense suffering and much greater susceptibility to despair when loss is inevitably incurred. There *will* be events that test your resolve, and challenge your fortitude. People who avoid danger at all costs are also much more likely to identify certain types of loss as "catastrophic" than can be rationally justified upon sober analysis. There is nothing intrinsically *catastrophic* about, for example, the loss of your job or permanent damage to your reputation. Many, many means of supporting yourself and your family remain open to you even if your career is ruined. Can you *not* secure a job washing dishes or doing janitorial work? Do you believe such occupations to be "beneath" you? If so, starve—and lose your family. Contemplate *that* loss. Consider the genuine loss that you can impose upon *yourself* as a result of irrational pride or unbridled hubris. As for damage to your *reputation*—what did you ever *believe* yourself to be that the opinions of others could possibly constitute *harm* to you? Are you a figment of someone else's imagination? Peer not into the minds of others. *That* is impolite. Finally, you know that death is how the story of your life on this planet ends. You can only regard your impending death as a catastrophe if you believed yourself to be immortal, or you maintained hopes of immortality in physical, human form. Surely, you are not as foolish as *that*. What is your death to *you*? It is not as if you will have to *live through it*, after all.

July 4

The experience of tasting blood should not be underestimated or underappreciated as an opportunity to learn about your psychological situation and about the general human condition. The taste of *your own* blood reminds you that you are susceptible to damage and death. It is a *memento mori* opportunity, and you should not waste the chance to remind yourself that your time here is limited and that death awaits you. Humanity is a fragile species. Its fragility applies not only to individual members of the species, but also to the species *itself* as a biological phenomenon. All indications are that the species and its members shall not long endure. This includes *you*, of course. Blood reminds you that you are susceptible to both injury and mortality. In combat, you have tasted your opponent's blood on more than one occasion, just as your opponents have tasted yours on more than one occasion. Let these memories serve as reminders that we are all fundamentally made of the same elements. The ancients believed that we were made of clay, air, and blood. Everyone bleeds, and everyone's blood is red. Thus, we all face the same fate in the end. You have eaten beef heart and noted the unmistakable metallic taste of this organ that your species shares with so many others. This should prompt acknowledgement that something *inside* of us ties all life on this planet together. The expression "life's blood" is pregnant with implications, is it not?

July 5

You are inclined to side with the country mouse in his dispute with the town mouse about which environment provides the preferable living conditions. Simplicity, in and of itself, is superior to anything that noisy, needless complexity could ever hope to provide in terms of "cultural opportunities" or "diversity of distractions." Even the availability of more diverse cuisines is insufficient to get you to choose the city life over the comforts of the places where there is no need to lock your door upon leaving home. The country mouse must subsist on simpler food, and less of it, than the delicious smorgasbord available to the town mouse, but his crust of bread is readily obtainable with no excessive expenditure of energies that are better used in other endeavors, and he has far fewer ravenous cats against which to contend. Aesop, like Epicurus, the Stoics, the Cynics, and Socrates, understood the inherent value of a simple life, simple desires, simple tastes, and a clear set of values and interests. There is some part of the human soul that longs for a return to humbler times and the clarity of roles, needs, and interests that seem to attend the simpler life. There is a *lot* of pointless bullshit "in town," and you should not be seduced into valuing the trappings of "the big city," more than you value the serenity and the ability to *hear yourself think* that evades city dwellers all too often. No, it is certainly "the simple life for you," and if that makes you a *simpleton,* then embrace that role with an open heart.

July 6

It seems that irreligion or, at the very least, disenchantment with religious institutions is on the rise in the contemporary world. Indeed, religious belief is increasingly treated with derision, and "persons of faith" are increasingly perceived as benighted bumpkins in the grip of archaic superstition. Whether there is a God or not, this trend is bound to have lasting consequences, and you have no reason to anticipate a better or more noble culture manifesting as part of the "death of God" and the cultural consequences that seem bound to ensue. If civil law and public disapprobation are insufficient to prevent incipient scoundrels from bringing their malevolence to fruition, how does removing a general acceptance of God's laws, and God's potential to punish *even* those scoundrels that *escape* man's justice, contribute to a *decline* in malicious behavior? A malefactor who does not take seriously the possible existence of an ultimate and inescapable Judge will, almost certainly, commit heinous deeds more promiscuously. Once God is *believed* to be dead, once the masses no longer *fear* God, what prevents them from demonstrating the lengths of depravity to which the talking primates are susceptible? Dostoyevsky indicated that *all things* would come to be regarded as possible or permissible. Is this not the attitude you perceive to be on the rise? Indeed, there already appears to be an unspoken competition to *surpass* the most evil deeds yet accomplished. This form of "freedom" may prove to be our final undoing.

July 7

You have never, to the best of your knowledge and understanding, experienced a revelation. Indeed, you do not even have a clear enough conception of the phenomenology of revelation to understand what it would be like to experience one. It does not, of course, follow that *no one* has experienced a divine exposure, or some form of communication from God or some agency working at God's behest. It is equally obvious that you do not *know* that anyone, anywhere, has *ever* encountered the divine or, indeed, that the divine or the transcendent exists outside of the human imagination. The natural world might be the world entire, and it might be that there is some transcendent realm that you can hardly imagine, if you can imagine it *at all*. You simply *do not know*. Though you must confess your ignorance in this area, you are not, therefore, completely stymied where the question of God's existence is concerned. Unless and until you encounter conclusive or compelling evidence that *no deity* exists, you are free to embrace, as a default position, the pre-reflective inclination to regard your presence in the world, and of a world *habitable* by intelligent creatures, as conditions *crying out* for explanation by reference to a designer, a mind, a creator... a God. Has this not been the default position of the humans in your ancestry for, at the very least, the entirety of recorded history, and has this default position not been challenged only in the *very* recent past? Check for a baby before you throw out the bathwater.

July 8

As you get older, you find yourself more and more frequently on the periphery of the culture that you no longer think of as "yours" in any sense beyond geography and happenstance. Being further from the center and further from the mainstream of this largely depraved culture is not a condition that you are inclined to lament as some type of misfortune. Let society contort itself into any kind of morally misbegotten bastardization of traditional values mated to narcissistic, relativistic nihilism that might rear its ugly head—you need not tether your hopes or your values to *any* of it. The effort to normalize pedophilia and other forms of depravity proceed apace, and most of your society chooses to look the other way, or to regard these phenomena as harmless bits of fun. This is, on the one hand, tragic and, on the other hand, precisely what you have come to expect from this decaying collection of pathologies masquerading as a "culture." If your civilization is bent on self-destruction, you probably cannot do much about it, and you cannot have an *obligation* to do anything that you lack the *capacity* to do, but you can certainly relinquish psychological and emotional attachments to the societal goings-on that tend to turn your stomach. Depraved people do depraved things, and they have no interest in learning the errors of their ways. Incorrigibility is one of the central features of depravity. Find likeminded *decent* people if you can, but do not allow *your* mind to become like the psyche of the *masses*.

July 9

The temptation to be frustrated by ignorance, sloth, stupidity, and dishonesty is particularly powerful, and it is even more so today than on most other days. When you are compelled to evaluate the work with which you are presented, the incompetence simply *leaps* at you, and the utter contempt for diligence or honest *effort* is simply impossible to ignore. How often are your orders botched, incomplete, or filled with shoddy product? Increasingly, you seem to encounter people who just *refuse* to *try*. A *mediocre* effort is, at this stage, superior to the *vast* majority of the service with which you are bestowed. Any work that is not completely *worthless* constitutes a happy and unexpected deviation from the norm. Does *anyone care* about the quality of his or her work anymore? Is *no one* ashamed of slapdash, pathetic workmanship? Someone, somewhere, *must* still take responsibility, diligence, and quality workmanship seriously. Someone *must* still take pride in a job well done, and someone *must* still suffer humiliation if work proves to be half-baked, halfhearted, or *entirely* unworthy of approval. There are, after all, *some* quality products and services, and there are still *some* important tasks being accomplished, and getting done on time and within the prescribed budget. These kinds of things still *occasionally* occur. *Where* do you find the people who still have integrity, and where are the people who still take pride in producing quality goods and services? You need to start looking harder.

July 10

You *cannot* expect liars and imbeciles to conduct themselves as if they are honest, rational adults without inflicting needless frustration, anger, and other forms of emotional suffering on yourself and, at least potentially, on others as well. Imbeciles are absolutely legion, and they seem to reproduce in astonishing numbers. What kind of behavior do you expect from these idiots? Surely, you cannot justify *any* expectation that they will *improve* your nation or its culture. How, after all, are dimwits supposed to improve *anything*? They will inevitably bungle any meaningful task or endeavor they might undertake, and if they are left in the condition of having the proverbial "idle hands," they will prove to be "the Devil's playthings" indeed. Thus, it is foolish to entrust them with any position or power with which they can do real damage, and it is also foolish to leave them unoccupied. What is the reasonable way to handle these people? Perhaps there is no viable answer to this question. Similarly, liars will *always* destroy decency and undermine any societal expectations of honesty or insistence that dishonesty should meet with disapprobation and, in *some* cases, *punishment*. Liars will do everything in their power to make sure that lying incurs no punishment and no disapproval. What else can they do if they insist on continuing to lie about everything that matters? Given all of these observations, how do you explain the current makeup of Congress? Who *votes* for these lying imbeciles? Ah yes, the voting public does this! Your democracy is, after all, a *representative* system.

July 11

This is, in the culture you occupy, something of a radical consideration, and it will certainly not receive a fair hearing, but just how "crazy" is the notion of *theocracy*? Look around and consider the many failures of democracy, monarchy, dictatorship, and all other forms of governance that have ever been enacted. Where are the noble and ennobling societies produced by these methods of societal organization? Where is the just and decent culture produced through the imposition of human constructs? Surely, there is room for improvement. Is theocracy unworthy of even *consideration* as a potential option? If there is no God, then any theocracy is bound to be devoid of foundation and will likely guide the nation to one form of disaster or another. This is difficult to deny. Of course, the *current* mechanisms of governance are not exactly on the cusp of generating some utopia either. If, however, there *is* a Creator, a Designer of the cosmos, an ultimate *Lawgiver*, and if God, in fact, issues commands to those who populate His creation, might it not be worth a bit of time and trouble to try to *understand* those commands, their proper applications to your life and your culture, and to at least *try* to codify some of the divine rules and regulations into law — or to, at the very least, advocate norms and mores that concur with God's will? There are, to be sure, dangers in this approach, but are there *not* dangers in *all* approaches to governing millions of people? There are dangers in all human interactions with each other, are there not? Maybe... God knows.

July 12

Moses did *not* want the job. Can you blame him? Carrying the burden of God's will, God's commands, and God's plans for a people in bondage cannot be a burden borne with a light heart or an untroubled mind. Add to all of that the difficulty of bearing these burdens with a speech impediment or the condition of being "slow of speech," and it is easy to understand his reluctance. Moses knew that *anything* might be required of him, and Moses knew that, in the end, he could only do his best to obey and to enact God's will. It is *crucial* to remember that Moses, though chosen, was just a man. He was not liberated from the various constraints imposed upon the human condition. He could not *know* the ultimate fruition of God's plan. He could not *know* that his efforts would culminate in the liberation of his people. He could not *know* that the Lord would *speak* to millions gathered at the foot of Sinai. He could not *know* that his name would be proclaimed throughout all of the ages from his time until today. Moreover, he could not know that God would prohibit him, despite all of his efforts, from entering the Promised Land after all his years of tireless service. Nonetheless, he placed one foot in front of the other, and did his imperfect best to do God's bidding. He did not even rebel against God when his punishment was revealed to him. Imagine his heartbreak at finding out that he would not lead his people across the Jordan. *That* is a real man. What are *you* compared to Moses? What is your excuse for being merely what you are?

July 13

What frightens you today, you irrational coward? Do you fear bodily injury or dissolution? Who told you that you were impervious to such damage? No one. Do you fear malevolent conduct on the part of other persons? Who told you that you had the capacity to govern the behavior of other persons? No one. Do you fear the collapse of the culture you have known all these years? Who told you that you could rule over the multitudes? No one. Do you fear illness, old age, and death? Who told you that you were immortal and impervious to viruses and bacteria? No one. Do you fear the mocking and disapprobation of the persons you encounter? Who told you that you could control opinions other than your own? No one. Your only *real* fear, your only legitimate fear, is the fear of *your own* weakness and inadequacy? Who told you that you were not malformed, not weak, not flawed, or not inadequate? No one. You are *precisely* as God, or as nature, or as chance has made you to be. What then is your complaint, ingrate? Look around the world at people who are born with congenital defects, look at people who contract dread diseases, look at people who exist under the hobnail boot of oppression and tyranny, and look at people laboring under the burden of the kind of grinding poverty that you cannot even imagine. Observe all of *that*, and try to construct a rational justification for your fears and your complaints. Can you not just work on becoming a better person? The rest is *not* your business.

July 14

You must learn to laugh even at *fear itself*. What can *anyone* or any *thing* do to you that you ought to tremble before the possibility presented? You *cannot* be ignorant of your impending death, and you cannot be sufficiently delusional to ignore its hovering presence in the background of every moment of your life. What is it to you that you know not when, where, or how death comes to you? You know that it *will* come when, where, and how Fate, or chance, or God decides. You have little or no say in the matter, and you have no business wishing it to be otherwise. As for the life you shall experience between this moment and your death, you have been offered *no* promises and *no* guarantees. Indeed, no one has any guarantees concerning the amount of life on offer in their case. Events transpire as they will, and the world in which those events transpire is *not* tethered to *your* will or *your* expectations. *None* of the universe depends upon you. How dare you *insist* upon *anything* at all? The world is not *your* creation and need not take *any notice* of you or your interests whatsoever. Only laughter is appropriate to the unfolding of events over which you have no power at all. Pay attention, learn what you can, and be grateful that you were here at all. Laugh because you are granted a life you never *earned*. Laugh because the banquet has been prepared for you though no one was required to prepare it. You are, in some cosmic sense, an *accident*. Do not make yourself a needless difficulty. Laugh with *gratitude*.

July 15

That nagging internal "whisper," that has been with you for as long as you can remember, seems a bit more assertive today than is usual, and it seems significantly more *urgent* than on most other occasions. It is not literally a *voice*, and you do not *hear* it, but it presents itself to your consciousness nonetheless. Some cognitive phenomena are ineffable insofar as communicating them to other persons is concerned. Our species has not developed words for *everything* that we can experience. There are *some* things that we must pass over in silence. This has, at least on some occasions, the effect of dampening or darkening your mood somehow, and you do not know why. The feeling that all is *not* well with you takes on a bit more exigency at times. It demands to make itself known to *you*, at least, and insists upon being shared with others. Is this a matter of insufficient sleep or a bit of low blood sugar, perhaps? Might it be a slight alteration of brain chemistry due to some subconscious environmental impact on your neural self? You are not *aware* of rational justification or warrant for this slight increase of anxiety, or this vague iota of dread, or whatever you might call it. Nothing special has happened, as far as you know. Perhaps even just this brief rumination on the phenomenon serves only to exacerbate it. Countermeasures are hard to come by for this illusive visitor. Something is not quite right, and you know not what is to be done about it. A grilled cheese sandwich, perhaps?

July 16

Compassion and empathy have their places and uses, but both are, arguably, quite overrated. Do you *really* want to empathize with everyone that you encounter or, worse yet, everyone that you read about, or everyone that you see depicted on video? The value and utility of "putting yourself in the place of the other" is, on occasion, fairly evident. It is, for example, useful in competition to have some idea of what your opponent is thinking, and what he is likely to do next. It is also very helpful to understand conditions that cause people pain and emotional suffering. This is a condition with which it is worth your while to become acquainted. Apart from such cases, what *is* the benefit of trying to adopt the perspective of another person— particularly, the perspective of a complete *stranger*? Why should you care what it is like to be a North Korean working for the "Dear Leader," or a department store cashier at a pretzel stand? It is both impossible and inadvisable to try to understand *every* perspective that has ever been occupied by every human being under the sun. There are *far* too many versions of the human experience to contemplate more than an insignificant *fraction* of the lives on offer. You have enough difficulty just trying to understand family and a few friends. Why add to your cognitive burden by trying to get "inside the heads" of those who are *utterly alien* to you. How does that provide any benefit to either you or to the other person? Let them have their privacy.

July 17

If you identify some act or some project as unwise, immoral, or pointless, simply refrain from indulging in it. You are *not* obligated to persevere in idiocy or to continue participating in endeavors that do no good for anyone. If someone asks for your opinion about the matter, explain your reasons, marshal your evidence, or shrug and walk away, but there is no need to badger people around you with ceaseless hectoring. No one benefits from relentless scolding, or persistent bickering over phenomena that do not lend themselves to conclusive resolution. What do you care if someone else is making a poor decision? How does it get to be *your* business to assuage the concerns of all those around you, or to govern the lives of people who never requested your intervention? No one gave you the authority to run any life apart from *your own*. Adults will do as they choose, and they will either suffer for it, or not, irrespective of *your* beliefs or desires about the issue. Furthermore, how many times have *you* been *wrong*—within (say) the past *week*? If you really believe that you are in a position to dole out advice like some as yet unheralded oracle, you may be *worse* than delusional. It is possible that you belong in an institution wrapped in one of those fancy jackets with sleeves that tie in the back. Try keeping your mouth shut, paying attention, and minding your own business. Give *that* a shot. Govern *your* own behavior. That is enough. It had better be.

July 18

If you give in to temptation *one* time, you cannot claim to be on the road to improvement in the area in question. The moment you slip, you are as far from the ideal state as you have ever been. You already *know* that what you are doing is wrong or unwise, and you do it *anyway*. This means that you are *weak*, or that you are *not* serious about self-improvement. What other explanation can you conjure for this obviously irrational behavior? If you know what not to do, and you do it anyway, do not call yourself an adult. Lay no claim to rationality or even decency, if you *intentionally* do what you know to be irrational or indecent. There is no such thing as a moral holiday. You do *not* get to "take a break" from the pursuit of truth via the mechanism of reason. You must be committed to this pursuit with all that you are, or you actually pursue nothing in particular. When you behave like a child or a low beast in pursuit of base pleasures, you thereby make a lesser being of yourself or, perhaps, you reveal that you have been, all along, a lesser being than you ever claimed to be in public. Do not become a bestial calamity. Whether you owe *yourself* better or not, you certainly owe your family, your friends, and those with whom you come into contact, a better effort than the merely casually brutish. Aristotle claims that you are a member of the species that is the "rational animal." He argued that reason is the essence of our species and that it separated us from the rest of the natural world. Try not to make him out to be a liar.

July 19

How does the mass of *meat* encased in your skull generate or sustain the phenomenon of *consciousness*? Is this an evolutionary adaptation that emerges upon the attainment of a certain level of neural complexity? If so, what is the mechanism of the transition from "mere meat" to *conscious* meat? If, on the other hand, consciousness is a non-physical phenomenon, you need an explanation of the apparent causal interaction between the physical and non-physical realms. How does immaterial *thought* "touch" the brain to cause events in your skull? Can there be *causal* interaction without *physical encounter*? If causation is *not* the mechanism explaining the correlation of mental states with brain states and other bodily conditions, *why* do they coincide? A broken bone will be attended by *pain*. Is the pain *in* the skull, or is it non-physical? This is something *more* than a riddle. This is a riddle that emerges from the deepest places within the phenomenon that you have, perhaps erroneously, regarded as *yourself*. This can of worms seems to open only from the *inside*. Are you better off leaving this question alone? Perhaps you are, but you simply appear *not* to have been made for leaving such cans of worms left unopened. This may be your fatal flaw. So be it. You will marinate in cognitive conundrums such as this whether it is fatal to you or not. You have to be who you are made to be. Otherwise, you end up alienated from your own nature. No one needs *that*. Here you go exploring again.

July 20

You have always been something of a misanthrope, and you have *never* encountered any evidence to disabuse you of this inclination. Obviously, *you* are a member of the species for which you mostly experience contempt. This is a fact worth remembering. Indeed, your misanthropy may be as much a commentary on *your own* character as it is a matter of the rest of the human population. Do you not spend more time in your own company than you spend with anyone else? Nonetheless, this attitude has always seemed well warranted as it regards most of the rest of the population. Keeping company with other jabbering primates is a *taxing* affair, and you prefer to avoid doing so more often than is absolutely necessary. Time spent in the company of others always seems to incur the necessity of subsequent time spent alone. A hermit's life would probably suit you quite well. Perhaps you will take up a staff and wander into the woods someday. Perhaps you will not. You will *never*, however, be enamored of your fellow human beings. Can you learn to find some form of peaceful coexistence with them? *Should* you do so? At the moment, you must confess that you can find no good reason for attempting the project. Tomorrow, you may find yourself in a different frame of mind. You may despise people even *more* than you do today.

July 21

What, if anything, makes you the same individual, the same *entity*, over time and throughout the full gamut of physiological and psychological change? Is it literally true that *you* were once a zygote, a single-celled organism, or is that just a loose way of speaking, or just a useful linguistic convention for organizing a viable account of a human life? The only physical feature of you that remains unchanged is your *genome*. That, however, is just an enchainment of chemicals. It could be extracted from any of your cells and placed in a petri dish. Surely, that substance in the dish would not be *identical* to you. Is the soul a unifying agent over time? Does the soul actually exist? If so, can it be *you* in a disembodied state, with no brain or sensory apparatus? What *is* this entity that allegedly goes to heaven or hell after you die? Is there any *evidence* of its existence, or is it nothing more than a bit of wishful thinking? Perhaps the Buddha was onto something. Maybe the persisting "self" is just an illusion. This is an interesting consideration. If you hold up a photograph from your third birthday party, and you say, "This is a picture of me celebrating my third birthday," are you speaking in convenient falsehoods? It seems that you have ruminated over this question before. Was *that* person *you*? You do not, at the time of the utterance, believe yourself to be speaking falsely, but perhaps your unreflective cognitive inclinations regarding this matter are less than perfectly calibrated. Perhaps *you*... do not exist. Well, that is probably *not* a particularly helpful way of putting the point. Language appears not to be designed for inquiries such as this.

July 22

A life *without* broken bones, lacerations, torn ligaments, or other forms of significant bodily damage, would be something of a shame, would it not? After all, most of your injuries have been sustained in the pursuit of experiences that proved to be worth the pain resulting from the endeavor. Combat and collision sports are bound to produce some bumps and bruises, but consider how much you have learned about yourself through participation in dangerous exercises. Furthermore, consider how much you have learned about yourself, and about other persons, by virtue of your suffering and your *response* to suffering. Would you really want to live an entire lifetime completely devoid of pain, anguish, and grief? That kind of life strikes you, upon reflection, as something of an anemic existence, does it not? You must learn to "make friends" with the dark and frightening aspects of the human condition, if you are to appreciate fully the pleasurable and fulfilling elements of your life. No one ever promised anyone a rose garden. Well, some gardener may have made such a promise to a homeowner, but try to stick with the *metaphor* and leave the literal to one side. Gratitude ought to extend beyond the *easy* parts of your time on this planet. Anyone can manage gratitude for the good times. Being grateful for the birth of a healthy child is not great achievement. It is gratitude *even* for difficulties, challenges, and suffering that indicate genuine progress toward wisdom. Are you making progress toward wisdom? Are you getting better at this "life thing" as time goes by? No... really.

July 23

How much of your experience of the external world is colored, impacted, altered, or otherwise shaped by the nature of your perceptual apparatus and, more importantly, your *conceptual* apparatus? The "visible spectrum" is, after all, that segment of the electromagnetic spectrum that is visible *to human beings*. There are animals that can see wavelengths of light lying outside of the limited phenomena available to members of your species. Dogs can hear dog whistles, whereas human beings cannot. Bats shriek and use the echoes to concoct something like an auditory "map" of their environment. You have *no* conception of this process or the phenomenology that attends it. It is probably an impossibility for you to have *any idea* what it is like to be a bat. The human brain appears to lack the equipment to perform any similar function. If you and a bat are locked inside of the same room, you clearly share the same objective environment. You *can*, after all, shoot the bat dead or swat it with a tennis racket. The manner in which you will organize the room conceptually will, however, depart in significant ways from the bat's conceptualization of the same room. Is the bat's account of its environment *wrong*? It seems to navigate the space at least as successfully as you do. Evidently, there is more than one way to experience and understand the same environment. How much of the rest of your understanding of reality is species specific? How much of the natural world lies beyond the reach of your species' perceptual and conceptual apparatus? You may never know.

July 24

There is nothing wrong with, nothing defective about, and nothing inherently problematic with "life in the slow lane." Indeed, the contemporary obsession with speed and immediate gratification is, almost certainly, unhealthy and contrary to most of the evolutionary development of your species. Any form of land travel faster than walking is a relatively recent development, and even the advent of riding horseback did relatively little to alter the fundamental parameters of getting around the planet. Today, however, you can board an aircraft on one continent, cross an ocean, and step out into a place that would have been unimaginable to your not-so-distant ancestors, and you can do so in the space of less than a day. The act of driving in an automobile at seventy miles per hour would have been regarded as attempted suicide or daredevilry just a few generations ago. The instantaneous access to the nearly unimaginable quantities of information, *and* disinformation, available at your fingertips would have required a Faustian bargain in *any* previous age. Would your great-grandmother have regarded the iPhone or a *flying carpet* as the greater flight of fancy? Surely, your species' brain and nervous system cannot have adapted fully to these alterations to your environment and circumstances given the speed with which the changes have taken place. Take care that you do not end up as *roadkill* on this new superhighway of blindingly rapid experiential change. Your mind is not made for *this* much input at *this* rate of intake. Careful.

July 25

Consider the benefits of a central set of organizing principles around which *all* of the most significant elements of your life and your worldview are structured. Inviolable principles tend to simplify decisions by excluding large swathes of potential options and eliminating most possibilities without the need for specific, individual consideration. Having decided, for example, that theft is *not* an option, you can immediately dismiss any and all actions or options that would constitute theft as a means of dealing with *any* material difficulty or shortage of funds. Once you accept the principle that adultery is forbidden under *any* circumstances whatsoever, all potential temptation in this arena evaporates. *No one* other than your spouse is *ever* worthy of a moment's consideration when it comes to sexual or amorous desire — to say nothing of other forms of intimacy that are reserved *only* for the person to whom you are married. There is *no decision* to be made when presented with *any* offer that encroaches upon your marital vows. Once you identify behaviors that you *forbid* yourself even to *consider*, the field of viable options narrows dramatically, and does so in a fashion that enhances the quality of your character as well as the quality of your interpersonal relations. The moment you recognize anything as *forbidden* by your root values and commitments, no further consideration is required regarding that option. It is immediately off the table. Identify rules that you will *never* break. Doing so makes life both simpler and more wholesome.

July 26

Why concern yourself with the beliefs, opinions, and values of persons for whom you experience indifference, at the very least, and outright *contempt* at the far end of the continuum of conviviality (or the absence thereof)? There are people, and their numbers are not insignificant, whom you would not allow your *dog* to approach at a community picnic. There are people to whom you would not offer the half of your submarine sandwich that you knew you could never finish before it spoiled, even if the persons in question had not eaten in days. There are people whose *deaths* you have openly applauded, in public, without the slightest hint of shame or reticence. When it comes to this band of filthy miscreants and their ilk, there simply is *no* reason to venture even a vague, stray inquiry into their assessment of *anything* whatsoever, and certainly no reason to investigate their "values" or their opinions about anything that you *ever* do or say. A villain like John Wayne Gacy is not worthy of the slightest concern. His well-being should never be part of any hedonic calculus whatsoever. People are *not*, in fact, all equally important. There are persons who are manifestly *less* morally significant than your dog, your cat, or a potentially viable *fungus*. The next time you hear someone declare the sacrosanctity of "humanity," try not to burst out laughing at the poor sap. You cannot help but wonder if the "lovers of the human race" have actually spent a good deal of time interacting with *actual* human beings. Are they just meeting *different* people than you are? *Hitler*… was a human being. Big deal.

July 27

No society in history has been more saturated with law and lawyers, and no society in history has purchased more insurance for life, health, property, and various contingencies that afflict the human enterprise—and no society in history has been prescribed more antidepressant and anxiolytic pharmaceuticals than *yours*. This *might* be a coincidence. Somehow, you suspect that the correlation is more than a matter of happenstance and the greater availability of lawyers, insurance, and mood-altering drugs. Not so many generations ago, your ancestors had access to nothing that you would recognize as "medical care," they had not conceived of a "legal system" in anything like the contemporary sense of the term, and the concept of "insurance" would have been unthinkable in the midst of predators, illness, accident, and a bewildering array of unavoidably lethal possibilities. What might have constituted "insurance" against another band of hominids with superior numbers and weaponry fixated upon scarce natural resources that they declined to share? Gathering rocks with which to kill as many of them as possible might have been the first order of business. Seeking a *liability policy* would not have been an option. All of our contemporary technology has, evidently, not managed to set our souls at ease. We are the most psychologically and emotionally troubled species on the planet. You cannot help but wonder if it was always thus, or if the "advancements" attributable to the big human brain have not also robbed it of its capacity for serenity.

July 28

The perpetually "offended" professional victims are at it again today. What else is new? They are, of course, entitled to pretend to be aggrieved by plain English, simple statistics, or any other phony phenomenon of their whimsical choosing, but you need not, indeed you *cannot*, take their grievances seriously. Has someone been "mis-gendered" again? Horrors! Did someone refer to the "developing world," in an attempt to explain some portion of an economic or political theory? Well, let us, by all means, string that wrongdoer up and invite the world to watch. Imagine using the term "developing" to describe a portion of the world that is *less fully developed* than the West! Someone is, no doubt, shouting, "Racism!" somewhere. Do not bother trying to figure out what is allegedly objectionable about the expression "developing world," just embrace the fact that pathetic charlatans have decided to pretend that it is so. The stupidity of "political correctness" appears to be boundless in every direction. Shouting shibboleths is, after all, *so* much easier than constructing an argument. So be it. You are free to laugh at the lying imbeciles and their bizarre conceptual contortionism. You are also free to avert your eyes, mutter a brief lamentation for your moribund culture, and get back to the business of trying to improve your own character so that these idiots and their childish ravings no longer cause you to grind your teeth. They are *not* going to disappear. They are *not* going to become honest or rational. Do not concern yourself with all the things that *they* are not going to do. Concentrate on *doing* what *you* must.

July 29

The Peter Principle is on display in politics and in "higher" education even more pervasively than it is in any other hierarchy. In the political realm, this is easier to understand, given that democracy (or what *passes as* democracy) is a representative system, and *every* eligible voter gets an equal opportunity to *one* share in choosing representatives—no matter how much of an imbecile that voter happens to be. Of course, the masses are going to choose incompetents who just look good on television, or who merely possess the gift of gab, or who manage to come across as *charming* (whatever that means). When it comes to the rank stupidity, incompetence, and utter dishonesty of the *vast* majority of the professors and other academics at colleges and universities, the explanation of this peculiar phenomenon is somewhat more difficult to explain to those with only a passing interest in what is, it seems ironically, referred to as "higher" education. Had *you* had no experience in "the academy," you would probably find this matter somewhat baffling. Are educators at the level of college professors *not* supposed to be endowed with elevated intellectual capacities? Perhaps they are "supposed to be," or "generally assumed to be," but you are well aware that some of the dumbest and most dishonest human beings you have ever encountered hold doctorates from prestigious universities. A doctoral degree is evidence that its possessor has spent more time attending graduate school than the average citizen—and it is evidence of precious little other than that. Most "intellectuals" are, frankly, not very bright.

July 30

How much of the foundational values and worldview that constitutes Western culture can be found in *Genesis*? Of course, the rest of the *Torah*, the rest of Hebrew scripture, the *New Testament*, the Greek and Roman philosophers, Shakespeare, and so many other sources are indispensable as well, but nowhere is the West presented in more efficiently condensed form than in the first book of the *Old Testament*. The first rebellion against authority, the first murder, the first near extinction at God's hands, the first attempt to build an empire, and the first devastating collapse of an empire, and *so* many more forms of human interaction, organization, and analyses of the human condition that are either unique to the West or constitutive of what you think of Western culture as it stands today, all of these are to be found in *Genesis*. God offers humankind the option of obedience attended by a promise of flourishing, or disobedience and the inevitability of suffering and civilizational collapse. Actually, God makes this offer *several* times in this origin story of humanity. The humans try, or *seem* to try, for a relatively short while. Somehow, the flourishing human society does not last very long before the temptations of greed and self-aggrandizement ruin everything. You *almost* get the impression that human moral frailty is an *indispensable* part of the story. It is almost as if someone is issuing a *warning* of sorts. You cannot help but wonder if your culture is currently falling into the same unfortunate pattern. The truth, of course, is that you do not *wonder* about this at all. The day grows late, does it not?

July 31

You would have made a terrible prophet, and you should be grateful that you have *not* been chosen for the job. On one hand, you lack the requisite love of your fellow human beings that ought to be part of the prophet's charge. Then again, many of the biblical prophets appear to have been somewhat less than enamored of humanity or, at the very least, less than enamored of the leaders they encountered in the place and time to which their missions attached. Prophets were seldom embraced by the masses at large. Perhaps this has something to do with the fact that part of the prophet's charge is calling the masses on the carpet for their sinfulness and their violations of the covenant. Sinners often bristle at those who shove their faces into the muck of their sinful lives. *You* might be inclined to react similarly to someone pointing out *your* many sins, might you not? That, of course, indicates the other minor problem with your imaginary and counterfactual prophetic career. You are *such* a disastrous human being that *no one* who ever met you, or read anything that you have written, could possibly take you seriously as a purveyor of the Lord's righteous messages and commands. Leave the prophecy gig to others who are *far* more qualified for the job. See if you can manage to *find* a legitimate prophet, and see if you can manage to live in accordance with the messages conveyed through some genuine medium to the divine. Of course, the divine *may* be fictitious. Thus, you understand your third difficulty in this arena. Your faith is not exactly unassailable, is it?

August 1

Pay no mind to accusations, insinuations, or allegations in any form, especially if you know that the charges are without merit, and those issuing the charges are motivated by malice or envy. Even if your accusers *actually believe* that you are, in fact, guilty of some misdeed, or of some dishonest dealing, you need not concern yourself about *their* beliefs. They are free to believe what they will, to say what they want, and to smirk as they please. Your only legitimate concern attaches to the actual *truth* or *falsity* of claims about your character or behavior. Whether someone *calls* you corrupt is not of any special significance. See to it that you are *not*, in fact, corrupt of character, and that you engage in *no* crooked or unethical behavior. Those matters *are* within your control. Having done your best to secure decency in your character and your behavior, you are free to remain blissfully indifferent to anything that other people say or believe. Why would you care what goes on between *their* ears? Make sure that you tell no lies. Beyond that, you can allow people to *call* you a liar as much and as loudly as they like. Do nothing of which you are ashamed, and you need trouble yourself no further about those who cry, "Shame!" and point fingers at you. What do you care for the direction in which persons point their various appendages? Guide the behavior of *your* body, *your* mind, and *your* soul, as best you are able. As for other persons and their conduct, comportment, and values, you should simply pay them no mind.

August 2

Travel is a potentially valuable form of experience, and you *can* learn a great deal about cultures other than the one from which you originate, or with which you regard yourself as most closely associated. Unfortunately, the travails, discomfort, and feeling of dislocation that often accompany the experience of travel to far-flung lands is often, in *your* experience, more trouble than the potential benefits are worth. This is odd given that contemporary travel is *so* much easier, and *so* much less dangerous than it was just a few generations ago. Though you know that this is so, you find that the calculus of psychological and emotional consequences of a few weeks overseas usually renders a decision to forgo that eleven-hour flight, and to take a two- or three-hour drive into the foothills or up to the mountains instead. Perhaps you will miss out on some valuable experiences by cordoning off your travels to a few hours' radius from your home, but there are also benefits to gaining a more thorough, and deeper, and a more full-blooded understanding and experience of the nearby environs. You need not hop a flight to meet interesting people. You need not board a cruise to see beautiful sights. You need not consult a map of another continent to experience delightful cuisine, or fascinating experiences of the natural world. Do not pine needlessly for the strange, the different, or the exotic. Nearly every place on this planet has its charms. That includes places in driving or walking distance.

August 3

A life devoid of purpose is a fairly horrific state of affairs, and it is worth avoiding at all costs. In the absence of some central, organizing meaning or some overarching project, life is little more than a series of tedious, painful, and disorienting experiences culminating in a *death* of quiet desperation. If you have no clear, identifiable values, and if you do not put those values into practice as diligently as you are able, your life will contain *far* too much drifting, *far* too much aimlessness, and *far* too much despair. Nietzsche referred to the experience of "staring into the abyss," and though his conception of abysmal experience is not easily captured, it is clear that a life without purpose is guaranteed to be *abysmal* indeed. You do not want to find yourself "staring into the abyss" only to realize that you are simply observing your own life, and your participation in it. Even if you feel compelled to *invent* a meaning to guide you, it is still better to indulge in that invention than to refuse to exert the effort, and to allow your vital energies to spill out in a directionless splatter of ill-conceived, petty, short-term goals, and formless blotches of dribbled capacities wasted on nothing in particular. A Rorschach blotch is not much of a guide to constructing your life's purpose or planning out the expenditures of your energies. Life is hard enough and sufficiently punishing when you know (or *think* you know) what you are doing and *why* you are doing it. Without *that*, life is a slowly unfolding nightmare that does not *terminate* in the experience of hell. That kind of life *is* hell.

August 4

Never allow culture, your peers, or the voice of the masses to dictate the "proper" or "acceptable" use of terms or concepts. No matter how many people insist upon indulging in Orwellian semantic contortionism, you are *not* required to accede to their pretensions. Any aficionado of slaughtering the unborn in the womb who denies that a fetus is a *human being* should be presented with the definitions of "human" and "being," and challenged to explain how a fetus fails to satisfy the relevant criteria. It *is* a being (an *entity*). It has *human* parentage and DNA. What this interlocutor *means* to claim is that the fetus is not a *person*. Presumably, the category "person" involves characteristics relating to self-consciousness, sentience, reason, or some other cognitively complex phenomena. Once this confusion is clarified, then you can hope, perhaps, to engage in a rational debate about the morality of abortion. If, on the other hand, your debate opponent *insists* upon denying that the fetus is human, or insists upon denying that it constitutes a *life* separable from the mother, then any subsequent argumentation is a waste of your time altogether. Never bother trying to reason with a charlatan, a liar, or an imbecile. Your opponent was once a fetus, and your opponent is now living a human life separate from your opponent's mother. Whence the magical transition from lifeless, non-human entity, to disingenuous, independent, human charlatan? Perhaps emergence from the birth canal magically imbues the fetus with personhood. That *is* a neat trick, is it not?

August 5

Be mindful of the manner in which you conduct yourself at all times, whether you are engaged in a significant enterprise or a fairly trivial chore. Even *the way that you walk* will communicate a great deal about yourself to anyone who is paying attention. If you walk and act like easy prey, someone will, sooner or later, put you to the test and select you as a victim. If you *are*, in fact, easy prey, you will not emerge unscathed, nor will your pride remain intact. If you are, in reality, a *hard target*, you will be compelled to demonstrate just how formidable you are, and the consequences of so doing are likely to land you in criminal court, or civil court with potential liability, or in a condition of having to look over your shoulder for friends or associates of your would-be assailant. The best way to avoid the worst is to appear to be a *very* poor selection for any potential perpetrator of violent assault. Your bearing and demeanor should communicate, very clearly, to any ne'er do well, "You are *not* looking at a victim. Look elsewhere or *you* are the one that will *not* walk away unscathed from this encounter." If the threat does *not* look elsewhere, and insists upon attempting his assault on you, be certain that you either put him down *hard*, or that you can escape without being followed. In the event that the former option is the only viable choice left to you, weapons will prove enormously useful. Know how to use them, and train yourself to do so with crippling efficiency. Running is not *always* an option. Walk like you *do not need* to run.

August 6

Work on maintaining presence of mind and keep your attention focused upon the job at hand, or the immediate experience with which you are confronted. Do not ruminate about some past unpleasantness when you have the opportunity to *enjoy* the present moment. Similarly, do not miss out on opportunities staring you right in the face because you are concerned about future calamities, or enthralled by some triumph not yet accomplished. The proper object of your attention is the *here and now*. No one ever experienced a yesterday or a tomorrow. The *only* experience that will ever be available to you is *this moment*. The present becomes the past as quickly as the future becomes the present. The ceaseless flow of time, as you know, waits for *no* man, *no* woman, and *no* collective. Time will have its way with all of us, and there is *nothing* to be done about it. Planning and preparation in the present may well assist you in facing the future, as it *becomes the present*, but the future *itself* (if that expression is permitted) is not to be had by you or by anyone else. The future is always beyond the scope of your *present* experience. As far as the past is concerned, what, precisely, do you hope to do about *that*? You cannot un-experience anything, it is difficult to un-know what you have learned, and you cannot alter conditions long since expired. Nostalgia is a double-edged sword, is it not? The pleasant *current* experience of time gone by tends to occlude your experience of the only time to which you have immediate access. The time is, always has been, and always will be... *now*. Pay attention *now*.

August 7

The public is a loud, ill-mannered, fickle, irritable, obnoxious, and nearly ubiquitous beast. It will not be tamed. Perhaps the most important thing for you to remember about this beast is that it does *not* care about you or your interests and pleasures one bit, unless it designs a means of *using* you for its own purposes. There is a sense in which you are now, always have been, and always will be *alone*. You have family, you have friends, you have colleagues, you have associates, and you have fellow citizens of the world, but not *one* of them can ever live a single moment "in your shoes," or occupy your unique first-person perspective for even the blink of an eye. Similarly, you can never take a breath as any person other than yourself, nor can you die anyone else's death, or so much as sneeze another person's sneeze. Not for one moment can you know what it is like be anyone else, *really* know, from the "inside," the inner life of *any* other creature on this planet, nor can any of them ever really know the life inside of *you*. It is in this sense that you are destined to be alone, as is every sentient creature that has ever existed or ever will exist. This is neither punishment nor anything worthy of lamentation. All of the "huddled masses" can do their best to squeeze as close to one another as they are able, and *none* of them can, thereby, stave off this fundamental element of the human condition. What, therefore, is the purpose of all the "huddling," and why would you wish to participate in such a sad spectacle? Stand somewhat away from the beast. It has *nothing* useful for you.

August 8

Happiness is wildly overrated and, in and of itself, hardly worthy or admirable as an overarching life goal. Consider the life of a happy, sociopathic underworld kingpin who *delights* in causing innocents to suffer and profiting from purveying drugs, prostitution, murder for hire, and protection rackets. Imagine that his bliss is entirely sincere, and do *not* kid yourself about the existence of persons who derive genuine joy from vice and violent criminality. Surely, the life led by a person such as this is neither praiseworthy nor flourishing merely because he is happy with his success in deriving enjoyment from human misery, and exhilaration from his ability to stay one step ahead of the authorities. Again, do *not* kid yourself about the existence of criminals who never meet up with justice at the hands of their fellow citizens. Consider the kings and military despots who were never dethroned or assassinated. Consider the organized crime figures that lived to ripe old age and never even appeared in a courtroom. It *is* possible to "get away with" villainy at least insofar as terrestrial consequences are concerned. It is *not*, however, possible to perpetrate villainy without degrading your character, and that is what *karma* really means. You are, inescapably, what you make of yourself. For this condition, no courts or juries are needed, nor can lawyers or plea deals save you from this fate if you allow yourself to indulge in vice. Your character is, inevitably, what *you* make it. You need not get "caught" to suffer the harm you do yourself. First, do your own *soul* no harm.

August 9

If you are not willing to subject yourself to rigorous training, and if you are not willing to put yourself through painful and difficult circumstances, then you should not expect to succeed, and you should *certainly* not allow yourself to become convinced that you are *entitled* to any special degree of self-esteem or any feeling of accomplishment. Where does anyone get the bizarre idea that self-esteem is supposed to *precede* attainment or success? Obviously, any self-esteem that is unearned can *only* be regarded as some type of delusion or, at the very least, an oxymoronic state of affairs. How does anyone manage to have high regard for a person who has accomplished *nothing*? That is a question that *you* need to ask *yourself* any time you *esteem* yourself while having done nothing to earn that experience. No one is *born* entitled to any special degree of respect or admiration. Birth is *not* an accomplishment. You did not *earn* your place on this planet. The very concept of *earning* anything requires you to exert effort, overcome obstacles, and push against limitations. You do not *earn* the air in your lungs. You do not *earn* your faculties of sight, hearing, etc. Those manifested without any effort on your part whatsoever. Consider everything else about yourself that you did not earn through any effort at all. The list is, upon consideration, somewhat longer than you might have thought before reflecting about the matter a bit. A great deal of your physical and intellectual makeup is attributable to blind luck, is it not? What, exactly, *have* you *earned*?

August 10

At one level of description, the sun is just a sphere of hydrogen, helium, and a relative handful of other elements in trace amounts. It is just the biggest, hottest thing in our neighborhood of the cosmos. On the other hand, the sun is an absolutely indispensable precursor to any possibility of life developing on this planet. You would *not* exist were it not for the sun. This ball of gas that is roughly 93 million miles away from you is, in some sense, a kind of a *parent* to you and to every other human being that has ever existed or ever will exist, not to mention the rest of the life on this planet. Without the sun, and the requisite distance, and the availability of the various elements within this planet's atmosphere, and so many other specific conditions that are far too varied to enumerate, this planet would be an awful lot like Mars, or Venus, or any other spheroid whirling around any other star that you might care to consider. The concatenation of conditions that had to fall within almost unimaginably narrow ranges in order for life to occur on this planet is nothing short of astonishing. Yet, here you are. There, above your horizon, sits the sun. All around you, there are wildly improbable creatures living within an almost unthinkably improbable ecosphere. *One* species of animal, under that sun, has managed mastery of complex technology. One *member* of that species writes these words. So, is *this* the best that you can manage with all of your "good fortune," or are you saving your "good stuff" for an encore?

August 11

Surely, a *conservative* must, by definition, hope to *conserve* something, and it is worth asking yourself *what* it is that you hope to conserve. There are noble traditions and admirable aspects of your culture, your society, and the massively complex phenomenon that is often referred to as "The West." Anyone who *reflexively* responds by pointing out the flaws and misdeeds of your culture is not to be taken terribly seriously. *All* cultures, all societies, and *all* peoples are, of course, hideously flawed and indulge in shocking misdeeds, because all cultures are composed of collections of *persons*. People are largely disastrous animals with just enough intellectual prowess, and sufficiently functional opposable thumbs for deploying the kinds of schemes that they manage to conceive, for the sake of causing genuinely terrible ideas to come to fruition. All persons are talking apes given to spates of barbarism and psychosis. What does anyone *expect* collections of primates to do that will *not* be filled with all sorts of darkness and stupidity? Nonetheless, some of the jabbering primates have, in fact, produced works and lives that are worthy of special note, and some of them have been *your* cultural ancestors. It is *not* irrational that you wish to attempt to preserve some of the advancements in science, literature, art, and elements of the socio-political sphere that have made life more interesting and, at least arguably, better for so much of the world. See if you can help conserve *some* of the virtue, wisdom, and nobility that have issued from Athens and Jerusalem. Can you *embody* those virtues? *That* will have to do.

August 12

Vanity is irrational, unhealthy, and it ought to be embarrassing to anyone with even a vaguely realistic conception of the human condition. Whence the excessive pride in *your* achievements, for example? Surely, you cannot believe that your physical appearance is anything that warrants special attention. There *are* mirrors in your home, are there not? Those mirrors do *not* need recalibrating. What you see is, in fact, an accurate reflection (literally) of your body. Do you see the problem with vanity attaching to *that*? Is there anything about your accomplishments that justifies allowing yourself so much as *one* moment of narcissism? Is self-conceit supported by *any* facet of your career, your interpersonal relations, or products and services you have provided to your fellow human beings or their posterity? Hold it up before a stranger, all the accomplishments of your life as one unified endeavor, and explain why the stranger should regard you as a superior being. Once the laughter dies down, and do *not* hold your breath waiting, you will have a clearer idea of the way that your paltry life and attainments appear to others. Though you need not concern yourself with the thoughts and beliefs bouncing around another person's consciousness, a bit of contact with someone who instantly regards any excessive self-regard on your part as *laughable* may serve to keep your ego in check. The mirror really ought to be sufficient, but you tend to look away a bit too soon. A conceited ape is a pathetic creature. Remember that.

August 13

There are far, *far* too many people enrolled at colleges and universities these days. Somehow, the public has become convinced that nearly every citizen possesses the intellectual wherewithal to benefit from a college education, and the masses seem also to believe that an adult without a college degree is consigned to the bread line or a hand-to-mouth existence. Both claims are, of course, entirely false and demonstrably divorced from reality. The vast, *vast* majority of the population is incapable of assimilating intellectually challenging information about the sciences, mathematics, philosophy, or comparative literature, and the vast majority of the population has little or no *interest* in attempting to ingest information from the more demanding levels of these academic disciplines. Very few people are sufficiently fascinated with quantum phenomena to pursue the works of Heisenberg, Planck, or Einstein. Indeed, most academics or "intellectuals" are incapable of such pursuits—though many seem to delight in pretending otherwise. Furthermore, there is nothing deficient or defective about working in manufacturing, the service sector, or any of the seemingly limitless opportunities for entrepreneurialism. *Most* high school graduates would be *far* better off entering the job market as soon after graduation as possible. The "next academic step" is pointless for most of them. College was never intended for persons of average or sub-normal intelligence. When and why did "your" culture decide to pretend otherwise?

August 14

The next time you find that you are summoned to an interminable and patently pointless meeting about "empowerment," "diversity," or some other topic designated by this or that meaningless buzzword, try using the time and setting to a productive purpose. It is, for example, relatively simple to adapt isometric or isostatic exercises to nearly *any* place and a *wide* variety of postures. Sitting at a desk or a table, while those conducting the meeting posture and virtue signal for all that they are worth, you can get a fairly full upper body workout. The biceps, triceps, deltoids, latissimus dorsi, pectoral, and abdominal muscles are readily susceptible to flexion, strain, and hypertrophy with nothing more than the body itself, the chair on which you sit, the desk or table before you, and a bit of ingenuity. Supposing that you do not have the time or opportunity for a workout simply betrays a paucity of imagination. The relevant exercises are difficult neither to learn nor to execute. A one-hour meeting can serve as an *opportunity* to improve your physical functioning even if it holds out little or any hope of cognitive or intellectual advancements. Do not allow bureaucrats to dictate that *you* must waste your time and energy in the manner that *they* choose to waste theirs. If the *content* of the meeting is actually valuable or interesting, then, by all means, engage with those around you. Of course, you *now* embark upon consideration of counterfactuals that rarely appear manifest in reality. What meeting has ever been worth the time and trouble taken to plan and attend the accursed thing?

August 15

A new criticism was directed at you today and, as an interesting departure from the norm, you can be very confident that this criticism is *entirely* without merit. You have been accused of participating in an event that took place over one hundred miles from the location in which you spent the entire day. Indeed, you have literally *never* been to the town in which the event took place. So, this particular accusation of participating in a nefarious deed is, quite clearly, *false*. Your initial impulse was to declare your innocence, express righteous indignation at the baseless allegation, and shame your accuser in public. You even toyed with the idea that you might insist upon extracting a public apology for the false accusation. You *resisted* these impulses. You considered the alternative of simply pointing out the relevant facts in this matter, presenting the irrefutable exculpatory evidence, and sitting back to await a voluntary apology or witness the backlash against your accuser. You decided to forgo this alternative as well. In the final analysis, you chose to do *nothing*. You offered *no* response of any kind. Had people *believed* the accusation would *their beliefs* have made the claim *true*? Certainly, they would *not*. Perhaps the accusation will be withdrawn. Perhaps it will not. What is any of that to you? Put the entire matter behind you as nothing more than a series of sounds emanating from the mouth of someone who is either poorly informed or lying. So? Who promised you that there would be no ignorance or dishonesty placed in your path as you tried your best to make your way from here to there?

August 16

A very small *minority* of those people who attempt to produce useful, creative work will almost always produce the vast *majority* of all genuinely useful, creative work. Most people are not very good at creating anything of value. This observation is likely to be rejected because the majority will regard it as unpleasant, but they will *not* be able to demonstrate that it is *false*. It follows fairly naturally that the lion's share of rewards will flow to those persons who are most prolifically and usefully creative. To oversimplify somewhat, those who are most productive and efficient are very likely to reap the majority of the available benefits, and they are probably going to hold a disproportionate share of the most coveted goods at any moment in time. This state of affairs is not properly regarded as lamentable. This is not a "problem" standing in need of rectification. This is simply the way that effort, ingenuity, and reward tend to be parceled out across the members of any society in the absence of artificial interference. It is not terribly surprising that the vast majority of the masses, almost all of whom produce very little of any unique significance or value, will develop a deep and abiding resentment at the disproportionate success of the creative and efficient minority. The resentment of the masses is not *evidence* of genuine impropriety or any morally pernicious imbalance. The resentment of the majority is simply a manifestation of envy and discontent among the weak and the stupid. This envy cannot surprise anyone who has been paying attention. The dim resent the bright. What else *can* they do?

August 17

You can *see* and *feel* the world of matter and energy. From this, it does *not* follow that the world of matter and energy is the only world that matters, or the only arena that is worthy of the exertion of your vital energies. Perhaps the naturalists are correct, and there is nothing beyond, apart from, or transcendent of this allegedly closed, homogeneous, and self-regulating universe in which you find yourself embedded. Of course, there is, even in principle, no hope of *demonstrating* conclusively that the world as you experience it, or as your species experiences it, and conceives of it, is the world *entire*, and all the world that is worthy of your notice or your consideration. The world of *matter* is not necessarily the only world that matters. There are various long-standing wisdom traditions that hold out conceptions of the divine, the transcendent, or the otherworldly as possibilities and hopes for meaning, for purpose, and for a foundation of moral value. Do you *know*, *can* you know, that the super-naturalists are incorrect, or that the naturalists can make the more compelling case for their worldview rather than one that includes the transcendent? Perhaps the totality of the available evidence leaves this debate in the condition of stalemate. How, after all, are a few billion primates, most of whom are only slightly smarter than the other, language-lacking primates, expected to discern the origins or underpinnings of the cosmos? Do not deny your inherent leanings or the traditional default position of your species. You know where your *hopes* lie. Perhaps *that* is enough.

August 18

Much of what you say, much of what you write, and much of what you have done and will do, is troubling to many other persons. Thank *God* for that! Imagine living a life that offends, troubles, and perturbs *no one*. Can any such life be worthy of living? Socrates, the Buddha, Jesus, Confucius, Gandhi, and Abraham Lincoln troubled and irritated *many* of their contemporaries. Do *you* regard yourself as *superior* to any of those socio-cultural and intellectual forebears? Surely, you would declare yourself to be both a fool and a delusional character by saying so. You know that you are not fit to handle the hem of Socrates' tunic or to carry the Buddha's sandals. If you were to meet Jesus, you would hurl yourself down at his feet and beg forgiveness for your many sins against his teaching, and against his Father's commands. It follows, therefore, that those people for whom you have the highest regard have *not* led lives that left the masses, the powerful, or the status quo undisturbed. Confucius may have been, for much of his life, a government factotum and a figure fairly far removed from anything like a rebellion or a revolt. As you observe the arc of history, however, you can see that his work changed, fairly dramatically, the culture into which he was born. Sometimes, the bull that *walks calmly* down the hill gets to reproduce most prolifically. It *is* your role to be the *bull*. The bull need not, however, rage through the proverbial china shop. Perhaps you *are* the raging bull. Perhaps you will stroll gently down the hill and speak calmly to the cows. This metaphor becomes strained, does it not?

August 19

Why *is* there something rather than nothing? One possible answer is that God made all of the "something" that you know as the universe or the cosmos. That answer, of course, does not explain why there is a God rather than no God. Perhaps God exists of logical necessity as Anselm's ontological argument contends. Why then does logical necessity exist, *if* it is correct to assert that it "exists" in the relevant sense here? Perhaps there is something amiss in your conception of *nothing*. Might it be that nothingness is a defective concept, and might it be logically (or otherwise) necessary that there has never been, and never *could* have been, a condition of nothingness? You have read, have you not, that nature abhors a vacuum. Perhaps this claim is even more pregnant than you had hitherto considered. It is, of course, possible that the original question is simply imponderable, either in and of itself, or due to the limitations imposed upon your mind or your circumstances. You *are*, after all, part of the something that exists, and you are not aware of having had any experience of nothingness. There may have been some time, prior to your conception perhaps, when you were *not* something, but you cannot coherently claim to have *experienced* the condition of *being nothing*, nor can you make sense of having had experiences prior to becoming something. Perhaps Lewis Carroll could have made more progress with this question than you ever will. What good does *that* do you? Lewis Carroll is *dead*.

August 20

Optimism has never suited you, and you struggle to understand how there can be so many optimists or, at least, so many people who *claim* to be optimists. What is it about reality that they perceive, or conjure within their minds, that makes these people so sanguine about the future? Apart from the rapid advancement of technology and the attendant ability to access more information, what has the recent arc of history provided to convince these optimists that the future of humanity, or culture, and of international relations will be preferable to the manifestations of these phenomena in the not-too-distant past? Are politicians becoming *more* honest and *less* corrupt? If so, evidence of this development eludes you *entirely*. Are political and corporate entities doing *less* damage and exhibiting *fewer* authoritarian intentions than they have previously? As the population expands, even if it will level off at around nine billion, as several theorists have argued, natural resources seem likely to become more scarce, more polluted, and the competition for these resources seems quite likely to become more intense, almost certainly to the point of touching off warfare. If you think that the finite supply of oil has caused more than its fair share of suffering and conflict, just wait until the masses begin to realize that there is also a finite supply of *potable water*. Nine billion thirsty people are, it seems, quite likely to become a bit anxious and irritable. Maybe none of these problems will come fully to fruition, but what evidence is there to support that hypothesis?

August 21

Do not underestimate the potential advantages of being underestimated. If an opponent or adversary regards you as a soft target, an easy mark, or a pushover of no consequence, then you thereby gain a significant benefit in any incipient conflict with that rival. Indeed, it may be advantageous to conceal your strengths and accentuate your weaknesses, or perhaps even to make yourself *appear* to suffer from weaknesses that are actually *not* part of your makeup. Consider a physical contest such as a wrestling match. Clearly, you are in an enviable position if your opponent believes that you have, for example, deficient takedown defense when, in fact, your defense in this area is quite competent, or even excellent. He will almost certainly use up a good deal of energy in misguided and, probably, failed attempts to take you down, when he would be far better off deploying some other strategy. Similarly, if your opponent in a debate erroneously believes that you are unprepared for a particular line of attack, then she will probably be thrown off balance when you present her, and the audience, with an utterly crushing refutation of the argument she has hurled at you. Appearing to be strong provides benefits across *many* contexts, but there *are* instances in which you might be better off concealing your strengths, and convincing your adversary to notice ersatz weaknesses. The trick is recognizing when your circumstances call for the one approach as opposed to the other.

August 22

Do not assume, and do not conclude too readily, that other persons you encounter are motivated, either primarily or, indeed, *at all*, by the pursuit of truth. People have a stunning ability to cling to beliefs that comfort them, irrespective of evidence to the contrary. If you encounter a person, or group of persons, whose livelihood depends upon *not* understanding, or not *admitting* any understanding of the available facts, then you will find that marshaling all available evidence, even if that evidence is absolutely overwhelming, is not particularly likely to compel public assent to the truths you utter. Inconvenient facts are easily overlooked or denied by charlatans. If an academic has staked his entire career on the defense and promulgation of a particular theory, then you should not expect him to admit that he has been wrong all along, merely because you present him with *conclusive evidence* that he has, in *demonstrable* fact, been wrong all along. The evidence you provide at your command will, in many cases, perhaps even in most cases, prove to be *entirely* beside that point from that interlocutor's perspective. Many people are busily *distorting* the available evidence, and doing so quite intentionally, precisely for the purpose of standing *athwart* the pursuit of truth. Unfortunately, your culture's commitment to the pursuit of truth, especially as manifested in its media and its institutions of higher education, seems to be eroding rather rapidly. Lying is, at this point in history, arguably more advantageous than is telling the truth. This is *not* a good sign for future cultural developments.

August 23

Attempting to maximize your experience of pleasures and enjoyments, or to repeat specific pleasures in ever increasing intensity, is a very poor strategy for attaining happiness, fulfillment, virtue, or flourishing. Eat all the chocolate you can shove into your face, and keep expanding your search for finer quality, and more ingenious confectionary concoctions, and you will, in all probability, wreck your body, and cause those portions of your brain that are *not* related to the pursuit and enjoyment of chocolate to atrophy and hibernate. Sometimes, organisms slip into hibernation and never wake up. If you choose to pursue sexual experiences with as many people as possible, or in as many permutations as you can manage, or as relentlessly as your body will allow, then you can expect a variety of genuinely uncomfortable consequences to follow in the wake of that course of behavior. There is a finite amount of blood in your body at any moment in time, and if you are almost constantly behaving in such a fashion as to cause an excess of blood flow to areas that are not particularly close to your brain, you should not be surprised when you become less and less capable of entertaining complex thoughts about subject matters other than the explicitly carnal. This is dangerous and unwise. Other dangers of promiscuity are amply compiled elsewhere. Sometimes, you need to cross a busy street. Do not allow yourself to end up as roadkill due to your obsessive pursuit of hedonic gratification. Look both ways and try to avoid stepping in front of a bus.

August 24

It seems that another of your heroes has been exposed as a very significantly flawed, arguably even depraved, person. There are credible reports, supported by fairly compelling evidence, that this person was a serial physical abuser of women, a serial adulterer, and, most troublingly, a rapist. This is, of course, not the first time that you have encountered feet of shattered clay that can no longer support one of your golden cultural idols. The lesson here is not that human beings are all flawed. You have known that since you were five years old. The lesson is also not that your beliefs, ideals, and values leave you susceptible to disappointment, or that they often fail to conform to a reality that will never be what you once thought it could be. That particular brand of disillusionment settled over you at least as early as your high school years. Humanity, you have understood for a long time, is a wretched *mess* of a species. If you expect the world and those who populate the world to satisfy your hunger for decency or honor, then you are absolutely begging for the world to break your heart and smash your face in. No, the lesson here is one that you should have learned and internalized a long time ago. It is a lesson at least as old as *Exodus*. No being other than God (if there *is* a God, and if there is not, then *no* being) is worthy of worship or veneration. All finite, created beings are properly excluded from the field of this special degree of reverence that must be reserved *only* for the *ultimate source* of all that is good or valuable. You shall *not* indulge in *idolatry*.

August 25

The expression, "Chivalry is not dead!" seems to be, increasingly, divorced from most of the reality that you find yourself inhabiting. The last time that you got up from your seat on the train and offered that seat to a woman standing nearby, you were treated to a lecture about your "sexist presumption that women are weak," and only *one* person, a woman other than the one whom you had offered your seat, spoke up in your defense. You remember thinking, in the immediate aftermath of this train ride, as you walked to your destination, that the hectoring nitwit on the train should be *grateful* for good, old-fashioned "sexist" chivalry, because it was the only thing that prevented you from punching her in the face. You are not the kind of pathetic, cowardly "man" (using that term loosely) that strikes women. Some incidents, of course, test that principle a bit more acutely than do others. Indeed, you did not utter a single word in *your own* defense, because the bile that would have (though it *should not* have) erupted from you on the occasion in question would have been entirely inappropriate language to direct at a "lady" (another loose use of terminology), or to utter in the presence of women and children. You might have chosen to use the word "lady" in the previous sentence, but should you not be disinclined to use terminology *that* loosely? It is a tough call. If chivalry *is* dead, the murder investigation should focus on militant, screeching feminists as the murder weapon. Is that *irony*, or is it just your culture dying?

August 26

If you incur any debt, of any kind, for any reason, irrespective of circumstance, you are to repay that debt, and only death, coma, or paralysis from the eyeballs down is to prevent you from repaying your debts, *yourself*. In the event of any of the aforementioned eventualities, make certain that you have someone you can trust to pay back your debts, posthumously if necessary. This is not merely a matter of "making whole" the party to whom you owe the debt, but it is also, and more importantly, a matter of maintaining *your* character in an honest and healthy condition, and doing your duty whether anyone notices or cares, or not. Acquiring a debt and declining or failing to repay it is *theft*. You could engage in all of the semantic contortionism that you might like to attempt, but *that* is the bottom line, and you are *not* permitted to pretend that you believe otherwise. It should be fairly obvious that the most effective and reliable way to avoid failing to repay a debt is simply avoiding the acquisition of any debt in the first place. This is not *always* possible. You owe a debt of a unique type to your parents, as you would not have existed without them, and that debt is difficult to discharge fully while either of them is still alive. Apart from that case of unavoidable, and not particularly onerous, debt, you will be well served to *avoid* debt as much as is practically possible. *Any* debt you do not avoid incurring, is a debt you *must* discharge without fail. You are *not* to steal. You seem to remember reading that somewhere.

August 27

It is a *very* hot and humid day, and nearly *any* outdoor activity is bound to entail sweating, discomfort, and an extra degree of physical exertion. If you should find yourself complaining about the weather, even if you do so just within the confines of your own consciousness, then you really are guilty of looking the proverbial "gift horse in the mouth," and you *really* ought to resist that ungrateful, petulant, and ignoble tendency. What you think of as "the weather" is one component of the vast, complex phenomenon that is the ecosphere of your home planet on a given day in the region that you happen to inhabit. Take a small step back from your conscious experience of this particular moment in your tiny, insignificant life, and *everything* that had to transpire in order for you to *exist* at all, and you should realize that carping about the heat is a bit like complaining about having to pay extra taxes because you have *won the lottery*! Are you *really* going to allow yourself to be discontent because the temperature is less than ideal for your current interests and projects? If you are incapable of making your interests and projects compatible with the weather, do *not* blame the weather! The planet and its ecosphere were here long before you showed up, and this planet neither invited you to join in the festivities, nor does it prevent you from taking your *leave* from the festivities. If you decline to stay inside, or to kill yourself, do *not* whimper about the heat. It *is* August. What were you expecting?

August 28

Anyone who claims that the poor are poor because the wealthy have intentionally consigned the poor to the fate of impoverishment can *only* be a demagogue or a dimwit. *How* do billionaires benefit from the fact that the homeless do not have houses or apartments in which to live? Was there some period in history when the ancestors of those who are currently living in poverty controlled all of the money and the natural resources, and did the ancestors of those who are currently wealthy wrest control of the goods from the noble progenitors of today's poor? That was a neat trick, was it not? Suppose that wildly implausible scenario actually took place at some point in the past. How, exactly, would *that* entitle the poor of the contemporary world to *any* of the acquired wealth of those living in mansions? It is fairly odd that so many people seem to imagine that the wealthy somehow acquired their wealth, position, and advantage by robbing the poor and powerless who, as it turns out, do not control a great deal of money or power, and whose ancestors mostly had very little money either. That is a genuinely extraordinary turn of events, is it not? Perhaps the wealthy and powerful have been fortunate, and the poor and powerless have not. How does *that* amount to an *injustice*? Never begrudge the wealthy and the powerful their good fortune. It is *not* as if *you* would be *better* off if *they* were *worse* off. Even if that *were* true, would that justify ill will toward them? How so? *Envy* is *not* a virtue.

August 29

Why is it that no one *ever* insists that Guatemala desperately needs an influx of immigrants from Mongolia? Sub-Saharan Africa is never diagnosed as needing a few thousand refugees from Iceland to round out its demographic and cultural deficiencies. Canada, the United States, and Western Europe are, however, constantly depicted as desperately in need of as many of the current denizens of Latin America, Sub-Saharan Africa, and the Islamic nations, and as many immigrants from other places, as possible, provided that *very* few of them are of European descent. Those nations that comprise the West simply *must* welcome, with open arms, as many migrants within their borders as they can—and those nations will, of course, have to rethink the whole idea of having borders *at all*. The West is forever being told that it has a moral responsibility to absorb as much of the non-Western world as it can possibly manage, and the justification for this claim is, invariably, one or another form of the assertion that the West has been a historically *unique* oppressor and abuser of other peoples and cultures. As startling as that bizarre and patently false rendering of world history may be, it is more startling still that so many citizens of the West are willing to swallow it whole, in what can only be described as some form of ethno-masochism unique to Westerners. Roughly half of the West currently cries, "Yes, we *deserve* to suffer!" No other culture, no other people, and no other society in world history, has *ever* been expected to embrace, with gratitude, its own demise. Perhaps this is the West's fatal flaw.

August 30

It is true that everyone, or *almost* everyone, lies. This may be indicative of corruption at the heart of the human condition, or it may be a result of the vast complexities of social interactions, or it may be that lying is sometimes legitimately preferable to speaking truths that are psychologically, financially, or militarily so detrimental and dangerous that society at large, and individuals in particular, simply *cannot* digest them. None of this excuses *you* for telling lies. You are obligated to tell the truth, even though you are probably, for practical purposes, incapable of telling the truth, the whole truth, and nothing but the truth, at *all* times and in *all* circumstances. If some lie is a "necessary evil," remember that it is still an *evil*. Like all fully functioning members of your species, you are, more or less, incapable of *never* telling a lie, and it is also true that you never *should* tell a lie. This is not quite the same thing as claiming that you should *never* tell a lie. The expressions "never *should*," and "should *never*," are not, strictly speaking, uniformly interchangeable across all contexts without the *slightest* alteration of the meaning conveyed. The long and the short of this matter are fairly straightforward. You and your fellow talking apes are liars, cannot *help* but be liars, and this is a vaguely tragic fact about the general psychosis of your big-brained species. So, you are *not* absolved of the sin of lying. You are, of course, still going to continue doing it. That is, perhaps, a shame. Then again, how much about you and your species cannot be described properly as something of a shame?

August 31

A statement is read in front of cameras and microphones, and the ideologues on across each section of the political spectrum, which seems to be largely *bipolar* these days, take that statement and sprint blindly in different directions, screaming at the top of their lungs, and towing with them their throngs of partisans. This is simply *pathetic*. Political discourse appears to be almost entirely impossible in this age of polarization, dishonesty, and craven vapidity. Politicians and their minions make statements that are as nearly devoid of content as is possible while speaking words, and the media spin the meaningless utterances into whatever form they believe will garner more viewers, while the nation and its culture degrade and decline ever further. The citizens are *very* poorly served by all of this disingenuous posturing, but the citizens also vote for these charlatans, support the corrupt media and their parent companies by thoughtlessly consuming their goods and services, and the public gets exactly what the public *causes itself* to get. In a democracy and free market economy, the public has no one to blame but itself. You can be forgiven for perceiving this as a form of collective karma. A largely corrupt, dishonest, and ignorant populace votes and spends money in a manner that virtually guarantees corruption and dishonesty from politicians, media, and the marketplace, and then the citizens are doomed to encounter the consequences of their own actions. This is not so much a "problem," as it is a form of justice. You get, ladies and gentlemen, what you *cause yourselves* to get. Get some! You *deserve* it.

September 1

The rise of "intersectionality" can only be understood as a form of societal mental illness, and if it remains undiagnosed as such, and untreated, your society will suffer this sickness unto its own demise. When individual persons are judged by reference to their race, ethnicity, sex, socioeconomic status, sexual orientation, and religious affiliations, and when the alleged grievances supposedly attaching to those properties are treated as if they automatically entitle some individuals to inherent victimhood, and others to inherent oppressor status, then some form of civil warfare has to be all but inevitable. It does not seem particularly likely, at this moment, that this sad state of affairs you observe will devolve into a literal *shooting* war (though this eventuality is *far* from impossible), but it appears to be *very* likely that unjust economic consequences, and irreparable damages to families, communities, and institutions, are now unavoidable. Your society is speeding toward either a cliff or a brick wall, and it is rapidly accelerating in the direction of the danger. At some level, nearly everyone *must* be aware of this. Not so long ago, you could only have witnessed what has happened and experienced this state of affairs as a tragedy. As things stand today, you can only regard the entire mess as a *farce*. It is a dark comedy of errors. Some form of collapse is on its way. Detachment seems the most rational attitude here. This is, of course, much easier to say or to write than it is to accomplish.

September 2

All talk about "toxic masculinity" is idiotic. There is *nothing* toxic about masculinity, and all of the toxic behaviors and other phenomena that are cited standardly as examples of toxic masculinity prove upon analysis to have *nothing* to doing with masculinity itself, but are just examples a flawed people who happen to be men and boys. The attempt, for example, to dominate other people is not a *uniquely* male characteristic, nor is it the case that all men, most men, or psychologically well-adjusted men are particularly given to this type of behavior. There is nothing surprising about the fact that psychologically and emotionally disastrous men tend to be toxic characters, but it is equally unsurprising that psychologically and emotionally disastrous women, children, and collectives are also toxic agents that cause damage, societal corrosion, and needless suffering. Rabid dogs are, in some sense, toxic creatures, but it is clearly not the fact that they are *dogs* that causes their toxicity, rather it is obviously the condition of being *rabid* that needs addressing. Of course, in the case of rabid dogs, the only viable manner of addressing their condition is euthanasia. You have no choice but to put a rabid dog *down*. If you euthanize a dog that is *not* rabid, on the misbegotten theory that being a dog warrants execution, then you are going to kill a *lot* of *good* dogs. *Good* men are going to be punished as a result of loose conceptions of *toxic masculinity*. This is worse than a shame. Your culture is in more desperate need of *real* men *now* than it has ever been before.

September 3

Going to a restaurant and eating a meal, in public, entirely on your own, and with no company or comradeship whatsoever, is actually a very valuable and useful exercise. Think of it as a bit of cognitive behavioral therapy. The first element of this practice is simply making the decision that you will publicly engage in a behavior that many people regard as a defective or pitiable experience. The next element of the practice is rousing the force of will necessary to execute and follow through on this decision, and to *will* this conduct irrespective of any public disapprobation or pity you may encounter. This is not, psychologically or emotionally, an *easy* thing to do. The eyes of others are weighty and disconcerting in conditions such as these. You will need fortitude for this deceptively simple-seeming task. The next element of the exercise is forcing yourself to notice that nothing terrible occurs as you sit alone in a restaurant eating a meal prepared by professional chefs. Indeed, it does not take a great deal of deep thinking to notice that you are experiencing an opportunity that much of the world's population will *never* enjoy. Many people will *never* go to a restaurant. As you sit eating delicious food that you are fortunate enough to be able to afford, you may notice that your solitude is *not* deficient. The moment that you experience while eating tasty restaurant food is nothing to be *avoided* merely because you do so alone, or because many people regard eating alone as a gloomy experience. The gloom exists *only* in their *minds*. It is *not* an objective feature of *eating good food. Bon Appetit!*

September 4

When you encounter someone who has the ability to do something that you either do not know how to do, or that you lack the physical or intellectual wherewithal to do, it behooves you to pay careful attention to that person, and to watch and listen carefully to the events unfolding before you. In doing so, you are nearly *guaranteed* to learn something valuable. Perhaps you will learn to do something that you currently do not know how to do. That is certainly an improvement. What you are more likely to learn more frequently, however, is that there is a great, *great* deal that you do *not* know, and it is a pettiness of spirit that causes anyone to begrudge the respect or the admiration that ought to attend witnessing competence, heightened abilities, or the manifestation of talents that are worthy of note. Watch a truly talented woodworker, and you will find yourself admiring the skill and the product that emerges from the process you are witnessing. See if you can find an electrician who will allow you to observe the wiring up of a kitchen or a living room. The complexities are bound to impress you. If you follow a plumber through the replacement of a collapsed sewage line, or a malfunctioning toilet, you are bound to develop a new respect for the scope of the project, and the varieties of skills that must be deployed to address the problem at issue. A good way to get back in touch with the feeling of humility is to observe, carefully, the deployment of skills and areas of knowledge that you *lack entirely*. Pay attention and learn something.

September 5

People who interrupt you simply demonstrate that they either have no interest in what you are attempting to say, or that they are *terrified* of allowing you to give voice to what you are attempting to say. Interrupting is not only rude and obnoxious, but it is also a manifestation of dishonesty or *cowardice*. Those who interrupt their interlocutor's attempted response to a question that they, themselves, have just asked also demonstrate an abject misunderstanding of the nature of conversation, or the purpose of an interview. These are the type of people that want to pretend that they are interested in an exchange of ideas when, in fact, they desire only a monologue, and they are either unwilling or unable to respond to any questions or challenges that may be directed at *them*. What kind of person is unable or unwilling to respond to questions *directly pertaining* to the topic at hand, or the subject about which the participants have *agreed* to debate? To say the very least, such a person is ill-equipped to participate intelligently in the conversation, or to engage in the debate about the topic at hand, and to say something *more* than the very least, persons of this stripe are unworthy of respect, poorly constructed for civil conversation, and utterly useless as interlocutors, debate partners or opponents, or even as fellow citizens occupying the same society as allegedly decent human beings. They are, in fact, useless across the board where intellectual inquiry is concerned. They *do not matter*. Treat them accordingly.

September 6

Consider the amount of money you have spent on items and experiences that you did not need, no longer use or enjoy, and that make no contribution to your well-being or the benefit of your family or friends. It is impossible to quantify these expenditures precisely, but that amount has got to be fairly *staggering*. Think of just *some* of the better uses of the money and other resources that you have frittered away. There is something at least vaguely shameful about this thoughtless frivolity, and you really should not excuse your wasteful behavior merely because it is generally common in your culture to waste time, money, and other resources. The fact that "everybody does it" is hardly an excuse. Think about some of the other things that "everybody does" that you would never contemplate with sincerity. Furthermore, it is, of course, not true that *everybody* does it. There are, in fact, responsible adults who marshal their resources rationally and use their time and money in ways that improve their lives, as well as the lives of their families, communities, etc. If some people can manage this feat, then you cannot produce any *honest* excuse for your failure to manage your affairs in similar fashion. It is long since time that you grew up, stopped mismanaging your life, and began thinking much more carefully about what you are doing with your limited time and energy. Are you working diligently to improve your character and your family's circumstances? If not, do not pretend to be a responsible adult.

September 7

Trends, fads, and various other socio-cultural tendencies come and they go, and you are always free to pay little or no heed to such goings-on. Indeed, were you to attempt to keep current on all of the latest types of cultural, economic, and social change, you would be incapable of accomplishing *anything* else. It is one thing to remain unperturbed by change, but it is something altogether different to be driven to distraction with the project of trying to keep your finger on the pulse of a dizzying array of phenomena that change *constantly*. It may well be that the best way to retain your equanimity across all of the changes that you see, hear, and otherwise experience, is to remain indifferent to as much of it as is humanly possible. Indeed, ignorance of this kind of thing may actually constitute a degree of bliss. Rational detachment from phenomena that lie beyond your control, and that lie beyond even your capacity to comprehend, before the constantly quickening pace of change turns the "brand new" into the "suddenly obsolete," and presents you with ever newer versions of the things that you once understood, is a form of cognitive *self-defense*. You remember when cable television was the "new big thing." You now see that cable television is being radically transformed and, quite possibly, turned into a thing of the past by the advent "on demand" viewing and listening options. The Internet seemed miraculous just two decades ago. Now, you take it more or less for granted, and you wonder when its mechanisms will be embedded in your skull. Be at ease with the pace of change, but remain indifferent to it. What, really, *is* the alternative?

September 8

Once again, you encounter the pathetic spectacle of masses of people clinging to beliefs that they find comforting, rather than accepting uncomfortable facts and overwhelming evidence that, if acknowledged, would compel them to admit that they have been *wrong* for a very long time. Once again, you find that this tendency is even stronger among academics and among the "intelligentsia" than it is among the general public at large. It seems that a certain degree of intellectual horsepower enables greater feats of wishful thinking, and entails a greater capacity to indulge in confirmation bias. How can there still be *Marxists* in the 21st Century? Surely, adherence to this ludicrous doctrine, even after the horrors it has visited upon humanity in the hundreds of millions, can only be the result of *extremely* selective assessments of the theory's predictions, the actual subsequent observations, and some fairly impressive theoretical gymnastics that are necessary to fail to perceive the obvious connections between Marxism, its implementation, the ensuing disasters, and the comparative success of free market capitalism. If Marxism is a *scientific* theory, as its proponents purported it to be, it must have the capacity to explain the observable phenomena without resort to the desperate equivalent of Ptolemaic epicycles upon epicycles upon poorly plotted orbits. For Marxist apologists, it can only be epicycles "all the way down." The mixed metaphor is not very troubling here. Surely, none of these people actually believe *anything* that they keep saying.

September 9

If a certain cohort of persons, circumscribed by whatever characteristics anyone might want to identify as an area of study, consistently underperforms in any area of endeavor, *might* it not be that the group thereby identified is simply *inferior* with regard to the area of endeavor in question? Why must ever more complex theories of bias, institutionalized disadvantage, and vast conspiracies of either the explicit or implicit type be forever marshaled and massaged to avoid the far simpler and more plausible hypothesis that some people are simply better than other people at this or that set of skills? There are, not so shockingly, *very* few Cambodians in the NBA. This has been the case for some time now. Why would anyone resort to manufacturing some bizarre theory of institutional discrimination to explain this phenomenon? As it turns out, *no one does*. For some reason, when it comes to disparities in performance on standardized tests, educational attainments, or the differences in economic achievements that are, to some degree, correlated with these disparities in performance, a certain brand of "intellectual," and a significant swathe of the general public, will *never*, under *any* circumstances, even *consider* the possibility that certain groups of people are simply intellectually more gifted than are other groups of people in the respects that produce these disparities. The *simplest* explanation is ruled out of bounds, no matter how much evidence might be brought to bear on these types of questions, from the outset of the investigation. Some indisputable facts are *prohibited*, and anyone who states these facts must be *destroyed*. Shameful.

September 10

Never say or write anything *about* another person that you would not be willing to say *to* that person's face in public as well as in private. Although this ought to go without saying, and although it is not the kind of thing about which you should need to remind yourself, it is nothing short of cowardice to speak ill of another person in any forum or, in any context, in a manner that you would be unwilling to engage in if you knew that you could face full and immediate consequences. Of course, one way to avoid violating this rule is simply to avoid speaking ill of anyone under any circumstances. There may be wisdom in the advice that "if you do not have something nice to say, do not say anything at all," as it applies to most people and most circumstances. There are, however, persons and behaviors that you are morally obligated to stand up and speak out against. It is not permissible to avoid speaking the truth about, for example, a child molester if you have compelling evidence of that miscreant's guilt. You will probably not "have something nice to say" about a being as repugnant as *that*, but you are not permitted to "say nothing at all" to the relevant authorities and to any family members that have, in your judgment, a right to be made aware of the crimes in question. The same may be said about a variety of forms of corruption concerning which you are not permitted to "look the other way," or to "say nothing at all" as innocent people are victimized. If you *must* speak of an evil, you must be willing to do so in public and *directly to* the evildoer. Do *not* allow your courage to flag here.

September 11

This is a date that you will always associate with the terrorist attacks on New York and Washington DC. Putting aside any considerations pertaining to your nation, any war on terror, or any socio-political entailments, the thing that springs to mind today is the Third Commandment. Scripture tells you that there is *one* sin that God will *not* forgive. There is no clemency for using God's name to *justify an evil act*, or *misusing* God's name as part of the perpetration of evil. For other sins, forgiveness is possible, but for violating the Third Commandment, at least as far as your understanding of scripture is concerned, there will be no absolution on offer to the malefactor. As for the terrorists who claim that they slaughter in the name of the Lord, you can only conclude that their behavior is not going to be forgiven if their God actually exists. Obviously, you do not wish to be presumptuous and assume that you know the mind of God, but if the slaughter of men, women, and children who are "guilty" of nothing other than going to work, going to school, or attending services at a church, synagogue, or mosque is *not* evil, you must confess a complete failure of comprehension in this arena. For this reason, you must be very cautious about *ever* claiming divine sanction for *anything* that you do or say. First, who are *you* to claim that the Lord endorses *anything* that you do? More importantly, you cannot be sufficiently confident about your words and deeds to risk associating them with God and, thereby, falling afoul of God's dictates in a way that He will not forgive. Of all types of hubris, this is the *most* dangerous.

September 12

Do not be too quick to dismiss criticism, and do not undervalue those who serve as your detractors. Of course, you know that you have *many* flaws, but you hope to reduce your defects over time, with considerable effort, and you must, therefore, pay attention when someone points out a shortcoming about which you may have otherwise remained ignorant. Resist the reflexive impulse to denounce the critic or to wave away insinuations about your peccadilloes. Surely, you are in no position to assume that all criticisms of your character or your behavior *must* be incorrect, or to insist that some form of malice or ignorance *must* motivate them. Indeed, even if a critic *is* malicious, it does not follow that the criticism is false, or that you *cannot* be guilty of precisely the charge at issue. If someone brings to your attention a previously unnoticed problem with your behavior, then you owe a debt of gratitude to the person, or persons, who offer you this opportunity to improve your character, or to alter your conduct in a manner that makes it more palatable. If, upon careful and honest consideration, you conclude that the criticism is inaccurate, or that it constitutes a misunderstanding of your motives or your beliefs, then you have no reason to be concerned about the false accusation in question. What do you care about another person's false beliefs about you? Everyone is free to believe what the available evidence indicates by that individual's lights. Be grateful for accurate criticism, and remain blissfully indifferent to misguided criticism. You need not trouble yourself in either case.

September 13

Any attempt to save a person who does not want to be saved is bound to be a waste of time and other resources as well as an enervating and frustrating experience. Even worse, the attempt to save a person who does not even recognize that there is a problem, or that devastating consequences are on the way, is likely to end tragically for *all* parties involved. The self-destructive character tends to entail a fair degree of self-*deception* as well. It is no surprise that corruption often masquerades as virtue for the purpose of fooling observers, or potential victims of the corrupt plot. What is far more pernicious is corruption that convinces the corrupt character of the agent *engaged* in corruption that virtue is the agent's true aim. That particular affliction may be *incurable*, and it is *very* common among the vicious. Politicians who claim that they are working to advance the common good, while they are, in fact, pursuing nothing more than their own interests, are legion. Indeed, it is almost certain that the vast majority of politicians fall into this corrupt category. Those politicians that actually *believe* that they are working to benefit the masses, and that are, all the while, lining their own pockets, padding their own bank accounts, and pursuing ever more power for their *own* purposes, these are the most dangerously corrupt sociopaths that can ever rise to positions of power. Those who manage to fool the public are just crooked. Those who manage to hoodwink *themselves* are the ones who perpetrate the most terrible and horrifying misdeeds.

September 14

You become convinced that the aging process afflicts you primarily when you are *asleep*. Yes, this *must* be the way of things. The vitality thieves set upon you as you slumber, and when you are least capable of defending yourself (the cowards!), and they siphon away your energy, your virility, and your mental acuity. The dastards have uncovered your weakness, and they sneak in through your pores, or through some orifice or other, and they chip away, slowly but relentlessly, at the very fiber of your physical, embodied being. It is, as yet, unclear what nefarious plans they have for the vitality of which they strip you. Is there, perhaps, some sort of black market where your energy can be purchased under cover of darkness? Have they erected a covert pipeline whereby others may "drink your milkshake," as it were? Surely, a malevolent force arrays its minions against you in this matter. What other explanation could suffice for the startling diminution of energy that you experience? Was it not only yesterday that you could snap out one hundred push-ups with ease? Was it not just the day before yesterday that you could run eight miles as easily as today you can run *one* (on a good day)? Were you not an Adonis just last week, and were you not showered with praise on account of your physique just within the most recent month? Yes, you remember all of this quite clearly. Look, however, at the shell of that former self in its current state. Look upon it and *despair*! If only you could lay your hands on these miscreants. Ah, but they *are* a clever lot. They control the way of all flesh, it seems. So it goes. The bastards never lose.

September 15

The Buddha used the term *dukkha* to refer to the central problem of the human condition as it is experienced by unenlightened beings. This is a term from the Indo-Aryan language spoken in the Buddha's day and region. The standard translation of *dukkha* is "suffering," but this is at least somewhat misleading. Westerners tend to associate suffering with physical pain, injury, or infirmity. The Buddha did not claim to have a cure for any of *that*. Birth, aging, sickness, and death were not phenomena for which the Buddha offered a panacea. He got old, and he died. This is an inevitable consequence of embodiment in a physical world. The Buddha *did* claim that he had a cure, or at least a system of management for *dissatisfaction, discontent,* and *distress*—all of which are the psychological and emotional conditions that he referred to as *dukkha*. You must die, but you are not obligated or compelled to fear death or to experience anxiety about your mortality or the mortality of your loved ones. An enlightened being understands that death is inevitable, and that resisting the inevitable is foolhardy. *Until* you die, you must age, but it is only the unenlightened condition that causes you to be distressed about the various correlates of the aging process. Gray hair is not, in and of itself, a problem. If you retain your equanimity irrespective of gray hair, wrinkles, age spots, etc., then the aging process will cause you no particular discontent. You need not convert to Buddhism in order to derive benefit from the wisdom the Buddha shared with the world. All you really need to do is pay attention and focus on what you *can* control. *That* is the trick.

September 16

As often as possible, take the time to pay careful attention to your experiences, and to learn the makeup of the various components of what you see, what you feel, what you hear, etc. In this way, you will inevitably come to understand a great deal about the immediate causes of your experiences and, over time, you will pick up on the more distant causes as well. Gradually, a much richer understanding of all that has led up to the current moment will become clear to you. Over time, you will begin to notice patterns and regularities. Certain types of events tend to precede others fairly consistently. Understanding this will aid you in *anticipating* events and preparing to address them. This skill will prove valuable. It is also very fruitful to observe the consequences that flow *from* your current experiences. First, you will find it easier to identify the immediate consequences of events in which you participate, as opposed to events that you merely witness. With practice, you will find that you can more readily, and more accurately, predict the longer-term consequences of your actions, and of states of affairs that tend to recur with some frequency. Again, you are likely to find this a useful skill, and you will be able to prepare for the consequences that you foresee. It is not enough merely to foresee coming events, but it will be necessary that you develop the ability to *act* in reasonable and appropriate fashion. Do as much thinking as you can *before* the cognitive dysfunction of duress descends upon you. Be prepared to act with *reason*.

September 17

The Amish live their lives mostly apart from the surrounding society and culture, they reject the prevailing values of communities other than their own, and it seems that this is *not* particularly troubling to anyone, and you can remember no effort to deploy government coercion to compel the Amish to integrate, or to force Amish communities to admit persons who reject their values. In other words, the Amish and their way of life appear to bother, more or less, *no one*. Certainly, they do not bother *you*. Indeed, for as long as you have been aware of them, you have admired the Amish and their way of being in the world. Why should other communitarian groups be prohibited from living a similarly separate existence from a surrounding culture that they find objectionable, or that they regard as merely alien? Suppose, for example, that an Orthodox Jewish community wishes to have as little as possible to do with communities other their own, engage in no form of violence against anyone, and decline to allow persons other than Orthodox Jews to settle on lands that they have purchased. Why should this be any more problematic than similar decisions on the part of the Amish? Indeed, as long as they do not disrupt the fairly smooth functioning of *any* surrounding society, why should *any* separatist group face coercive integration at the hands of the state? When a group of people want *nothing* to do with you that does *not* constitute a justification for interfering with their style of life. Leave them be. Mind your business. If only *governments* could heed this advice.

September 18

Another recurring dream thrust itself into your subconscious again last night, or perhaps a recurring *theme* worked its way into one of your dreams again. You find that you have been cast as a character in a play, without your consent, and you realize this just a few moments before you are to walk onstage and deliver lines that you have never read, and that you do not know how to deliver. You look everywhere you can think of to find a script, you ask passersby if they have seen one, or if they know your dialogue, and no one bothers even to respond. Somehow, you have the impression that your role is crucial to the play, but no one seems to care about what is going to happen, and many of the people you encounter appear not to understand that a play is being staged. Surely, this is an unconscious allegory for your experience of your conscious life in the real world of veridical experience. You *are*, in fact, performing a role in the grand, sprawling play that is the unfolding world all around you, no one has ever explained to you *how* you are supposed to play your part in the production and, as far as you can tell, there is *no script* or, if a script exists, no one has been able to find a copy or reveal one to you. You stand upon the stage, surrounded by people and props that seem to have been maliciously manipulated to make executing your role a needlessly difficult feat, and there is no way to distinguish between the audience and the cast! Really, is it any wonder that your attempts to sleep peacefully are afflicted with confusing dreams? The waking world is not really so much clearer, is it?

September 19

The next time you encounter an Overton Window, pull out a shotgun, blow it to smithereens, go find the jackasses responsible for erecting it, and make it clear that the shotgun is equally effective for other purposes as well. This is, perhaps, a little hyperbole, but only a *little*, and only *perhaps*. Anyone who dares to try to tell you what you can and cannot say is your enemy, whether either of you realize it or not, and he deserves to be treated as roughly as is necessary to dissuade any future attempt to deprive you of your freedom of expression. Where *do* these troglodytes come from, and *how* do they convince themselves that they are vested with the legitimate authority to shut you up simply because they do not agree with the sentiments you happen to be expressing. To be clear, there has *never* been *any* motivation for speech codes, or restrictions on free expression, other than suppressing dissident beliefs and departures from the prevailing orthodoxies that prop up the powerful. There is precisely *no concern* whatsoever regarding "giving offense," or "defending the sensibilities of the common person," behind *any* of this authoritarian nonsense, and there *never has been* any altruistic concern undergirding any conception of "political correctness," or speech policing. The rapidly narrowing Overton Window governing "acceptable" discourse is socio-cultural bullying by repressive cowards or Machiavellian schemers and *nothing* more. That you do not spit in their faces, or pound them to mash, is the biggest favor you will ever do these vermin.

September 20

Never allow your passions to tether you to idiocy, and do not act in accordance with the dictates of your spleen rather than the dictates of conscience and reason. When your mind is not, so to speak, your own, or when you are intellectually and emotionally out of sorts, try to refrain from acting on your impulses or "going with your gut." Remember that your "gut" is not terribly bright, and even your brain is not to be trusted when it is under the influence of drugs, alcohol, or intemperate passion. A passionate halfwit is a creature both dangerous and tedious, and you ought not to allow yourself to become one due to anger, fear, or disgust. It is worth reminding yourself that the most recent beating you gave, and the most recent beating you received, were *both* administered under the influence of rage. It has been more than a few years now, but the circumstances are still fairly clear in your memory. On a related note, you ought also to remember that the former of those experiences ended up being far more unpleasant over the long haul than did the latter. Thus, even when an irrational passion is momentarily quenched, the slaking of it often leads to suffering far weightier than the pleasure you derive from its satisfaction. The benefits of reason, wisdom, and virtue are stable and long lasting. The hedonic spikes corresponding to the pursuit and capture of the objects of passionate desire, by contrast, are brief, unstable, and not at all fruitful with respect to future consequences to which they are so frequently attached. Your passions are chains in waiting. Be on your guard against them.

September 21

It appears that this year's Victimhood Olympiad is well underway, and the competition is particularly intense this time around. What contingent will take home the *Most Pervasively Oppressed* trophy? Who will claim the *Most Historically Disadvantaged* gold medal? You might think that the Jews have an advantage insofar as over four thousand years of persecution is concerned, but it seems that the self-appointed assessors of grievance are, for the most part, *anti-Semitic* jackals. Surely, there is something like irony in this state of affairs. The gag could be continued indefinitely, but you just do not have the stomach for it. Why is it that so many of the power players in media, politics, and social networking seem so adamant about convincing individual persons to conceive of themselves, first and foremost, as members of intersectional groups with long-standing, intense, and unquenchable grievances against the designated "oppressors" of the day—including members of the identified groups who have never had the opportunity to oppress *anyone*? Is this all, at root, motivated by the effort to transfer power and money from the developed Western world to the developing world? Is it, instead, claiming injury as some perverse and inside-out method of garnering power? Are there just a lot of socio-cultural bullies with *far* too much time on their hands? Perhaps there is no point in such inquiries at all. Nothing that you find is particularly likely to change or improve the situation. The scoundrels in question are not susceptible to reason. This disease may very well prove to be the death of the West. Miserable.

September 22

You have investigated the matter sporadically over a period of a few decades, and you must confess that you simply have *no* idea what the vast majority of college and university administrators and their massive support staffs actually *do*. Not so long ago, colleges and universities managed, somehow, to function quite well without *any* of these newly created and absolutely "essential" positions, and with a fraction of the administrative personnel and corresponding costs. Is it a coincidence that the rise of the massive administration era has coincided with plummeting standardized test scores, abysmal performance compared with students in other nations, and increasingly hypersensitive and emotionally fragile students screeching at rallies about socio-political phenomena that they do not understand in the slightest? As academic standards and integrity become quaint remnants of a bygone era, these new cultural engineers posing as educators insist that the college experience is *improving*, and that access to this experience must be "inclusive" and ever more widely available. They wish to invite more and more young people to join in the pathetic spectacle that is "higher" education. Since when, you cannot help but wonder, is a college education supposed to be provided to "students" who lack the intellectual wherewithal to master a manual can opener, as well as the intellectual interest necessary to read even *one* book cover to cover? If your students are the future, then you had better stock up on guns, ammo, water purifiers, and long shelf-life food. The end begins to feel *nigh* indeed.

September 23

The not altogether serious theory of "resitentialism" maintains that inanimate features of the physical world vindictively manifest malicious intent toward persons and their interests. This theory is, of course, a bit of tongue-in-cheek tomfoolery on the part of one or more academics with a sardonic sense of humor and, perhaps, a bit of free time in which to allow this element of a witty soul to play. Although the theory is not presented in earnest, it can be, nonetheless, a useful tool or tactic for managing the tendency to become frustrated and angry when events occur in a manner that motivated the proponents of *resistentialism* to concoct the theory. There *are* occasions on which, if you did not know better, you could swear that your car, your computer, or your phone is actively engaged in some mischievous effort to thwart your intentions. When that kind of thing happens, instead of losing your cool, you might take a breath and tell yourself that the resistentialist scamps seem to be more active than usual today. Those rascals have hidden your keys, have they? Well, *that* kind of thing is their *raison d'etre*, is it not? Surely, you cannot expect the imps of the inanimate resistance to sit idly by while you go about your business unmolested! Would you have a trip to the grocery store go smoothly without a wheel on your shopping cart getting stuck in an infelicitous position that makes it needlessly difficult to move from one aisle to another? Do not be ridiculous. Just recognize that the inanimate gremlins are exercising their right to impede your progress out of sheer spite. You knew the risks, did you not?

September 24

The religion of Judaism, the Jewish people, and Jewish traditions have persisted through the ages, and a compelling case can be made that *no people* has been more historically persecuted than the Jews. You cannot help but be impressed by the lengthy continuity of Judaism and Jewish culture against the most thorough and most pernicious opposition you can readily imagine. Not only have the Jews outlasted the Egyptians, the Romans, and the Nazis, but throughout all of the trials and tribulations with which they have been beset, the Jewish people have made, by a *large* margin, the greatest contribution to the advancement of humanity and civilization, proportionally to their comparatively miniscule numbers, as can be claimed by *any* people. Consider what would be the current state of the sciences, the arts, literature, and entertainment, had the Jews been eradicated by Pharaoh in ancient Egypt. Your world, your nation, and your culture, simply *could not have been* what they have been without the contributions of the Jews. Is the persistence and the success of the Jewish people not at least an *insinuation* of the probability that there is a God, there is a plan, and that "the Chosen People" are a central element of that plan? This does not, of course, constitute anything like a *proof* of God's existence, but you can be excused for requesting a *better* explanation of the aforementioned phenomena. Read the Hebrew scriptures, see the foundations of civilization and objective moral values, and you cannot help but experience gratitude for the tribe that claims to have heard God speak at Sinai. That *may be* exactly what happened.

September 25

To the extent that Islam now encroaches on the West, it is to a significant degree a result of the fact that the West has made a moral disaster area of itself. This may not be a particularly pleasant fact to acknowledge, but it appears to you to be a *fact* nonetheless. How much cultural degradation can the West endure before an alternative that offers structure and, most crucially of all, a transcendent conception of an ultimate *meaning of life* becomes attractive? If human beings are inherently meaning-seeking primates, and if the increasingly secularized West increasingly denies the existence of any overarching or transcendent meaning, it simply is not terribly surprising that many of the primates will seek their meaning elsewhere. Observe contemporary Western culture, and the degree it is besotted with: drug abuse, divorce and devastated families, pornography, tribal divisiveness, rampant street crime, alcoholism and its deleterious effects, institutionally promulgated depravity and abomination, and the slaughter of nearly as many unborn human beings as the abortion mills can manage. Is it really so shocking that more and more denizens of the West look around them and long for something *sacred*, something holy, and something greater than the filthy machinations of humankind? The West has largely jettisoned decency, honor, and wholesomeness. The West has become largely degraded and corrupt. *Of course*, that condition is going to impel defections to some alternative culture and some alternative worldview. The West has lost its *faith*. Islam has *not*. *That* advantage may be insurmountable.

September 26

This morning, you woke from a dead, sound sleep because your cat jumped on your face with claws to your eyelid and nose, and this is, arguably, a less than optimal way to awaken on any morning. Your immediate impulse was to swat the cat away and curse, but you resisted both temptations. Perhaps you deserve kudos there, although a fairly compelling case could be made for the justifiability of that particular instance of kitty swatting. In any event, the day did not exactly get off to an ideal beginning. Things did not improve when you stubbed your toe on your way to the bathroom, and they got somewhat worse still when a back spasm struck as you were brushing your teeth. That is, of course, just another of the many manifestations of the rewards attending late middle age. Before you had your coffee, you had endured three fairly unpleasant episodes, and some small part of you wanted to climb back into bed and sleep until the back spasms had abated. Tempting though this course of action may have been, you recognized that you had an assortment of obligations and tasks that you needed to discharge and accomplish today, therefore, you "soldiered on" and set about the work of the day. A few ibuprofen help to mask the back pain, and getting your attention focused on the duties before you also seemed to have something of a palliative effect. Do not lose sight of the fact that these minor travails are as *nothing* compared to the difficulties that most people face regularly, and that they are *less* than nothing compared to those who face genuine suffering every day of their lives. Do *not* complain. Move forward with purpose.

September 27

As you were ripping weeds out of your front yard and making certain to extract the roots and all, so that the unwanted plant would not return, it occurred to you that the distinction between a weed and a desirable form of vegetation largely comes down to arbitrary human preferences. You found some of the weeds to be at least as aesthetically pleasing as the flowers that you were instructed to preserve and defend. Indeed, some of the flowers looked to you like they were in need of extirpation and replacement by some of the hardy, healthy "weeds" that you were extracting. Who determines what constitutes a "weed" as opposed to a desirable addition to the garden or the yard, and what are the criteria by reference to which these distinctions are "properly" made? You have no problem confessing ignorance about such matters, and you are aware that horticulture is not an area to which you have devoted *any* time or study. Perhaps experts could supply some closely reasoned rationale for preferring the presence of one form of plant, and the eradication of another. Perhaps there *is* such a thing as an *objectively* healthier lawn, or an *objectively* more fecund garden. Certainly, it is possible to quantify the total amount of *edible* product in any square foot of land. As far as aesthetics may be concerned, however, this strikes you as an area that is inherently tied to particular interests, and subjective preferences. If you like the way that a weed looks, and if *looking* at your garden is your foremost concern in tending it, why is it not permissible to cultivate weeds that please you?

September 28

There is a significant difference between being an intellectual or being well educated, and the condition of being *wise*. You have met hundreds, if not thousands, of highly educated intellectuals whom you do not regard as possessing even a modicum of wisdom. There is not exactly a shortage of educated imbeciles and wasted intellect. Wisdom is extremely difficult to define, and it is nearly impossible to enumerate necessary and sufficient conditions for someone to qualify as a wise person. Nonetheless, you have the sense that you know it when you see or hear it. Of course, you have never been foolish enough to regard *yourself* as a wise person, so it may be that you are mistaken on those occasions that you think you have encountered wisdom in others. Socrates, Epictetus, and the Buddha seem to be among the best historical examples of wise men that you have encountered through reading various accounts of their lives and their teaching. In each case, their wisdom seems to consist of a penetrating understanding of the fundamental human condition and, perhaps most importantly, the *limitations* upon the sphere of human understanding, and upon the human ability to control anything beyond the self-governance of one's own mind and behavior. Wisdom, then, seems to you to be largely a matter of understanding what you *cannot* control, and restricting your efforts to the few things that you *can* control. Intellectuals who espouse theories about how to "change the world" are, therefore, lacking in the most fundamental element of, the very *heart* of, wisdom. They lack intellectual humility.

September 29

It is fairly clear that, with the possible exception of some quantum phenomena, antecedent conditions and the governing laws of nature causally determine all events in the physical universe. Your body, including your brain, is a physical entity and is, therefore, subject to causal determinism. Even if there are quantum events in your brain that are, somehow, not subject to causal determinism (and you remain skeptical about quantum indeterminacy), there is no evidence that quantum indeterminism is amplified up to the macroscopic level. In other words, all available evidence indicates that your brain, the rest of your body, and the surrounding environment in which you find yourself embedded, are causally deterministic systems existing in dynamic equilibrium with each other. Changes in the environment are causally determined to alter your brain states through interactions between your sensory periphery and subsequent causal connections between your sensory apparatus and your brain. Thus, your brain does what your genetic inheritance, in conjunction with environmental stimuli, cause your brain to do, and the rest of your body, and your behaviors, are causally determined by your brain states. Where, in this analysis, is there any explanatory space for the concept of genuinely *free will*? It seems that the will can only be free, in any robust sense, if it is not subject to causally deterministic laws. Thus, the will can be free only if it is a non-physical phenomenon. Can you *govern* a non-physical phenomenon? Can the non-physical interact with your physical brain? Is free will an illusion? Perhaps it is. If so, so be it.

September 30

If you were to die right now, and if you were to find yourself called before a divine council for judgment, would you be able to defend the life that you have lived thus far to the satisfaction of the divine assembly, or would you expect your life as you have lived it to be found wanting and to incur proportionate punishment? Surely, you *cannot* believe that you would be found faultless. Even the *most* sympathetic would find flaws, sins, and transgressions aplenty in the account of your life. This is, of course, true for everyone, or nearly everyone, who has ever lived. Moral perfection is rarely found in humanity. A perfectly pristine life and character simply *cannot* be required for your life to be judged acceptable. It is equally certain, is it not, that full-scale moral dissolution cannot be permissible before the council of the divine, assuming for the sake of this thought experiment that such a congress exists. Even if such an assemblage is mere fiction, it can serve as a useful hypothetical posit by which to attempt an assessment of your various vices and virtues. If there were a God to judge you, would you qualify as a sufficiently decent human being by God's lights? The answer, not surprisingly, is not at all clear. You are reasonably confident that you are not one of history's greatest monsters, and you are equally confident that you do not qualify as a saint or moral exemplar either. Your imperfections are legion, but you try, at least some of the time, to improve and to practice honor and decency. Is *that* enough? A bit of a chill goes up your spine just now, does it not? You had better use what time remains to wash away such doubts as you can.

October 1

Why has exile largely disappeared as a *punishment* for citizens who have demonstrated that they are either unwilling or unable to make any positive contribution to society at large or even to those people with whom they are most closely associated? Of course, there are miscreants who belong in prison for many years or even the rest of their lives, but there are plenty of non-criminals who are, nonetheless, completely worthless, or even counterproductive, as citizens of the republic. Why can your nation not simply retract citizenship, after legal due process has been satisfied, for persons who are disinclined to do anything productive or useful with their lives? Able-bodied adults with minds functioning within standard parameters who, nonetheless, *choose* to be unemployed and permanently dependent upon social welfare programs, or other forms of collective largesse, are nothing more than socioeconomic parasites, and there is no good reason for taxpayers and their representatives to allow these free riders to continue bleeding the treasury so as to satisfy their dual vices of sloth and acquisitiveness. Adults who live their entire lives suckling at the societal teat are worse than worthless, and some federal or state agency ought to be empowered to eject them from the nation and prevent them from returning under any circumstances. Diogenes was exiled from Sinope for (allegedly) defacing the coinage. Are not those who siphon away coinage without *ever* having produced goods or services *far* worse than those who merely mishandle the currency? No one *needs* those people.

October 2

Surely, your body constitutes private property if the concept of private property is coherent, defensible, and applicable to *anything* else at all. If your home and your car are private property, and nearly everyone agrees that they are, then the flesh, bone, and blood of which your corpus is *composed* must be *your property* in the first instance. Thus, you ought to be afforded the legal authority to do anything with your body that does not encroach upon the rights, liberties, or legally defensible interests of other persons. Persons who are legally "of age" ought to be permitted to do with their bodies whatever they choose, given the aforementioned restrictions involving the rights of other persons. If adults want to drink alcohol, ingest narcotics, or fill themselves with poisons, and if they do so in a manner that does not place the lives or properties of their fellow citizens at risk, then what is the constitutional or moral justification for restricting or punishing such behavior? This is, clearly, not an endorsement of any form of self-destructive idiocy. You are entirely within your rights to point out the stupidity of sitting alone in an apartment and snorting cocaine that destroys the body, particularly the brain, and you are free to express your contempt for this behavior. Is it not hypocritical, however, to deny the imbeciles their right to self-destruction as you decry their stupidity? The rampant stupidity of other adults does not entitle *you* to take control of the lives that they lead. If they want to destroy themselves, it is not your business to prevent them from doing so. What have *you* got to lose?

October 3

When it is time for anything to end, whether that is leaving school, leaving home, retirement, or death, do everything that you can to move on with equanimity and a clear conscience. You should be able to do so *only* if you have given everything you have, and only if you have learned as much as you possibly could from the experience in question. Death should not terrify you, or even *trouble* you, so long as you have spent your life trying to improve your character and your understanding of the world around you, as well as comprehending your place within that world. What more can you do, what more can anyone do, than to live life with fierce determination to make the best of it, and to make the best of the person living it? Heraclitus told us all that one can never step twice into the same stream. This is true not only because new water is constantly flowing past, but it is also true because the person who steps first into the stream changes as constantly as does the stream, and the person who steps into the river at a later time is, like the river itself, not quite the same as before. Indeed, is not all the world like this, and is that not the real point of the metaphor that Heraclitus deployed? *Everything* is constantly changing. Some of these changes are subtle and gradual whereas others are abrupt and conspicuous, but no feature of the physical world remains constant and immutable. This state of affairs is neither good nor bad, but it is simply the way of things, and only a fool complains about change. Would you have the world other than it is? If so, just wait a bit, and it will accommodate you. Be careful what you wish for.

October 4

Imagine what could be accomplished if the "People of the Scripture" could put aside all differences, all historical and current grievances, and could work together toward a common goal. Consider a possible future, if it *is* possible, in which all Jews, Christians, and Muslims banded together in the name of their patriarch, Abraham, or better yet, in the name of the one that they worship as the Creator of the universe, and decided to set the world aright. Perhaps even *that* united force could not accomplish a goal of such magnitude, but it could certainly *approach* that goal more efficiently than any socio-political entity that has ever existed. There is something fascinating about the fact that a coalition of this nature would be so *obviously* and so *monumentally* beneficial to all of the practitioners of those faiths, juxtaposed with the fact that it is so *obviously* and monumentally *unlikely* to happen. When the closest thing to a solution to *all* of your worldly problems stares you in the face, and you spurn this solution, can this be understood as anything other than a kind of masochism or self-destructiveness? Do the Abrahamic legions value their mutual hatred, enmity, and conflict more than they value putting an end to all of that needless discord and moving forward to create a world after the fashion of God's intentions? It would, unfortunately, appear so. Surely, this must be *worse* than a shame. Is it, perhaps, God's *intention* that there should be this enmity between and among those who most fervently believe in Him? You have heard the claim that the Lord "moves in mysterious ways," but *this* is all too baffling.

October 5

It is a good idea for you to cultivate pessimism governed by rational analysis of your circumstances, probable future events, and an honest assessment of your limitations and flaws. The value of pessimism lies in its nearly universal applicability to any circumstance that may arise. If the *worst* actually occurs, a pessimistic approach will prepare you emotionally and psychologically for that eventuality. You will be prepared because you will have anticipated the worst transpiring, and you will have done all you could have done to ready yourself. If *anything* other than the worst transpires, you will have anticipated and expected a *worse* possibility, and you will be pleasantly taken aback by the fact that the worst did *not* occur. As a pessimist, you will be equipped when the dark times befall you, and you will be able to breathe a sigh of relief when skies are clear and sunny. Furthermore, there is simply no denying that all lives are afflicted with various forms of suffering, and any number of sources that are all but guaranteed to instigate suffering. There are *very* few, if any, human lives that are not stricken with unpleasant experiences and these will prove sufficient to break the average person who is not adequately prepared to absorb punishment. One form of preparation, one method of cognitive training, is what the Greco-Roman Stoic philosophers referred to as *premeditatio malorum,* or imagining the various ways that things could go wrong or prove psychologically, emotionally, physically, financially, or otherwise challenging. This is not exactly an *expectation* of the worst, but it is a cognitive exercise designed and intended to prepare you for the worst, should it occur. Remember, thou art mortal.

October 6

Never be concerned about telling anyone what you genuinely believe, what you value, whom you do and do not respect, or what you intend to do. It is, obviously, much easier to remain unconcerned about such matters if your beliefs are admirable, your values are virtuous, your heroes are worthy of admiration, and your actions reveal a noble and commendable character. Thus, in order to share who you *really* are with others, and to do so without hesitation or compunction, you will need to be a decent human being, and you will need to live the kind of life that you can hold up to the world as a flourishing example of humanity. If your *entire* life were laid bare to anyone who cared to observe it, and if the whole thing were available for vigilant inspection, would this *not* horrify you? Imagine all of your thoughts, intentions, and *every* action you have ever performed in private, made available for observation and scrutiny. Unless you believe that you are the moral equivalent of the Buddha or Jesus, even a modicum of honesty should compel you to admit you are *very* fortunate that the world does *not* genuinely know you. Just consider the number of times that you have been disgusted with yourself, the occasions on which you have been disappointed by your failures, and all of those things you have done for which you are very grateful that no one was watching. Is your life not a mass of accumulated human wreckage? On second thought, you probably ought to reconsider that bit regarding not being concerned about telling others what you believe, what you value, and what you have done. Maybe just *keep quiet* instead.

October 7

It is worth remembering that your relationship to the entire world is best characterized as "passing through," and wondering how you ought to go about doing so. Consider the innumerable many ways of passing through the world from your birth until your death, and think about how many of them would be little more than pointless wastes of time. Just look around you a bit and, even if only briefly, pay sufficient attention to get a sense of how the lives being lived out in *your general vicinity* are going. Would you want to trade places with *anyone* that you have ever met? You have encountered lots of people who are richer than you, smarter than you, better looking than you, and blessed with all sorts of other advantages that you lack. You have never encountered a single person that you would rather *be* than yourself, nor have you encountered a "way of being in the world" that you can imagine yourself engaging in without significant discomfort. This is *not* because your life is *superior* to the others you have encountered. It is because you cannot imagine being *comfortable* living your life as you perceive others living theirs. There is something about the world as conditions stand that does not allow you to be quite comfortable in general, but it is even more difficult to imagine living psychologically at ease as anyone or anything other than yourself. The business of just "passing through" vaguely restricts the degree to which you can feel at home in a place that you seem not to belong. Surely, lots of other people feel this way also. Are you, and all the others who feel this way, just "doing it wrong," or are you actually *in* the wrong place? This is getting kind of *whiny*, is it not? So, just stop.

October 8

This afternoon, you received news that you were going to incur a substantial and unexpected financial expenditure. The amount of money involved is not a *crushing* burden, it will not require a loan or taking on another paying job, but it does constitute an unanticipated payment that may require some alteration of other expenditures. In short, you might have to cancel a bit of travel that you had been planning. All things considered, the whole affair amounts to, at most, a fairly minor inconvenience. Your initial impulse upon hearing the news was a moment of frustration, tinged with a bit of anger, but that lasted no more than a few seconds altogether. Had this same sort of event transpired just a few years ago, you would have remained angry and frustrated *much* longer, and there is a good chance that you might have said and done some regrettable things. This *is* progress. It is not vanity or hubris to note the progress you have made, and to regard it as an improvement to your character. Any self-congratulatory thoughts or words beyond *that* would probably amount to an unhealthy arrogance. It is one thing to *notice* an improvement, and another thing entirely to puff your self-esteem up with undue pride because of it. Do your best to continue moving in the direction of self-rectification, self-control, and self-improvement, but do so with humility, and never forget the many flaws you lug about with you. Remember, you *still* got frustrated and angry, even if only briefly, over a fairly trivial inconvenience. Do not, in this (or any) case, convince yourself that you have become a sage.

October 9

Last night, just a little before bedtime, you heard about another impending divorce involving a friend of a friend. You have met the couple in question no more than three times, and you are not particularly well acquainted with either of the individuals involved. Strangely, you found it a bit more difficult than usual to fall asleep, and you are fairly confident that the news of this divorce was the primary event keeping you preoccupied and awake. Untold numbers of marriages dissolve every day, and you hardly spend a thought on *any* of them. It may be advisable to ask yourself why *this one* has any particular purchase on your imagination. Perhaps it is primarily a matter of social proximity. A member of your extended family regards one of the members of this couple as a close friend. This lends a little bit of emotional immediacy to the situation. If a divorce can happen to a friend of the family, then the same kind of thing can happen *within* the family, it would seem. Of course, you have known this since you were a child, and there has been no new revelation about marriages falling apart. It is, however, not unlike a *death* among the circle of family friends. You have been well aware that all people are mortal for at least as long as you have been aware that divorces happen, but the actual instantiation of an unpleasantness often provides a metaphorical slap in the face to remind you that everything falls apart sooner or later. Perhaps you are old-fashioned in this respect, but you always regard divorce as a grave misfortune for the family. You are reminded of our susceptibility to grave misfortune. Sleep did not come easily. This does not bode well, does it?

October 10

The stories that the media *refuse* to tell are almost always more important, and almost always have greater impact on cultural developments than do the stories that they tell, and sometimes *invent*, relentlessly. Sensationalism rarely provides any genuine insight into events in the real world, or into probable directions in which the future may unfold. The media *lie* at least as often as they tell the truth, and they *elide* the truth any time it does not suit their preferred narratives. Anyone who *still* believes that it is necessary to read a newspaper in order to be properly informed, or that watching network news broadcasts is an effective method for learning about events of the day, has clearly *not been paying* attention to the avalanche of demonstrably false "news" stories that have been debunked and discredited over the last few decades. The ideological bias, and the suppression of investigations that the media find uncomfortable, have long since ceased to be surprising. You have not believed anything that you have read in a newspaper, merely *because* it appears there in print, since you were a teenager, and you *should not* have believed the "news" even then. Journalists have demonstrated as clearly as possible that their profession is afflicted by more pervasive dishonesty than any other, with the possible exceptions of practitioners of the law and the sale of used cars. The "mainstream" media is, at this point, nothing more than an appendage of one political faction, and is complicit in the corruption originating there. This is just one more instance of the cultural degeneracy that seems limitless.

October 11

Your culture has largely *lost its faith*, not only in God, but also in its own traditions, values, and world historical significance. It has, somehow, become fashionable among the citizens of your nation to blame their ancestors for nearly all the world's ills and suffering over the last few centuries. This contention is, of course, patently ludicrous, and it holds your nation and its culture to a standard that, if applied to *any other* nation or culture, would render *far* worse judgment against them than could be borne by its citizens. It is interesting that *no* other nation or culture *ever is* held to the same preposterous standard as the one to which citizens of your nation, and citizens of much of the rest of the world, hold your ancestors and your current populace. This type of ethno-masochism or cultural self-flagellation is both *entirely* unjustifiable and also extraordinarily detrimental not only to your nation, but also to most of the rest of the nations on the planet. If your nation fails, and there are very good reasons to suspect that it will do so, and that its collapse will occur far sooner than most of its citizens would predict, then the "free world" will either be left defenseless, or it will have to find a new protector, and that new guardian will, without question, exact a tremendous price for its services. It is ironic that your nation's most virulent enemies will begin their assault upon your fellow citizens by slaughtering precisely those people who most vocally denounce your culture and its ancestry. The people who most despise their own nation will be the *first to go* when that nation is subsumed under the control of its enemies.

October 12

The injunction to "love your enemies" is a bit of abject stupidity, and anyone who genuinely heeds that advice is not long for this world. It is all well and good to respect the fact that even your enemies are *persons*, and that you are obligated to recognize that even *they* are entitled to acknowledgement of certain basic human rights and liberties, but *that* is *not* love. If a man pulls a knife and advances menacingly in your direction, love is hardly the appropriate response at that particular moment. If you are carrying a firearm, draw it out, draw down on that man, and let him know that his alternatives are *stop or die*. If you are *not* carrying a weapon, and if you do not have your wife and children with you, then turning tail and running is a perfectly reasonable alternative. It is even more foolish to bring *nothing* to a knife fight than it is to bring a knife to a gunfight. What, however, is love supposed to do for you in this situation, or in *any* situation in which an enemy seeks to destroy you, or seeks to harm your family, or seeks to destroy your society? The Buddhist and mostly pacifist nation of Tibet no longer exists as an independent nation. It is just another part of China now. Perhaps they managed to love their enemy, but what good did it do them? Several million Tibetans were summarily slaughtered, and their culture has been all but obliterated. It simply cannot be surprising that these sorts of consequences follow very frequently in the wake of the foolishness of loving one's enemy. It is imprudent enough to ignore your enemy, but the prospect of managing love for your enemy is not conducive to flourishing. What did *Jesus* do to the moneychangers in the temple?

October 13

There is a great difference between the experience of shame and the experience of embarrassment. You can be embarrassed because you become aware that other people are watching you fail, or because other people are laughing at one of your many inadequacies. Those kinds of experience should not cause you to feel *ashamed* of yourself. Shame is a psychological and emotional reaction to *moral* failure or a failure of *character* on *your* part. Behaviors that can cause embarrassment, but that are not inherently shameful, are nothing to fear. You have not degraded yourself if you have simply failed at some task, or stumbled, or performed poorly due to something beyond your control, or because of some condition about which you could not have been aware. Nearly all lives are replete with experiences of this type, and these do not constitute failures of *moral* magnitude. Shame attaches to behaviors that you know to be evil, or vicious, or cowardly, or other acts that you know to be inherently corrupting of your central sense of self. A boxer who, for example, gets knocked out by an underdog opponent may be embarrassed by his performance, but there is nothing shameful about this. A boxer who, on the other hand, throws a fight or "takes a dive" to an underdog opponent for the sake of enriching himself at the expense of his dignity and honesty has, thereby, *shamed* himself. Shame is an injury to your character that only *you* can inflict. You probably should not be embarrassed very often, but if it happens, that should be no great concern. You should *never* shame yourself, and if *that* happens, it should be a *very* great moment of distress.

October 14

Certain places on the planet seem to produce a disproportionate number of exceptional combat athletes. The same kind of thing appears to apply to certain areas producing exceptional sprinters, or exceptional long-distance runners. Of course, great fighters *can* come from, and *have* come from, just about everywhere on the planet, but certain areas seem to be particularly fecund places for making superior warriors in the cage, the ring, and the wrestling mats. What is it, for example, about Dagestan that generates fighters of such exemplary skill, stamina, and toughness? Moreover, what is it about that region that causes its fighters to be nearly impossible to knock out? Perhaps living there is so difficult insofar as warfare and the general absence of creature comforts are concerned that it makes for people who are naturally inclined to work extremely hard in training, and people who are unwilling to give up under circumstances that would discourage even most athletes who are accustomed to fighting and battle sports. It is possible that environmental factors also play some role in this particular phenomenon. Perhaps a specific gene pool in conjunction with a certain set of factors pertaining to altitude and topography tends to give rise to a natural warrior class. It may be that the culture associated with certain regions is conducive to a fighting spirit that is absent from other areas, or is maybe just present elsewhere in lesser quantities. Combat has been an absolutely essential element of the evolution and history of your species, and the nature of contemporary, wealthy, Western civilization may be something of an anomaly. The human race *needs* tough people.

October 15

Where does anyone get the idea that a life of greater material ease and comfort constitutes a *better* life? Clearly, a life of grinding and stifling poverty is not a reasonable object of your pursuits, nor is it an object of pursuit for the vast majority of the human race, but many of the people you most admire were not only poor, but they actively avoided accumulating wealth and comfort. Socrates exhibited no interest in acquiring wealth, even though he probably could have become wealthy quite easily. The Buddha owned virtually nothing, never advocated to his acolytes that they ought to concern themselves with money or the material things it can buy, and taught that attachments to pecuniary concerns would only generate suffering and discontent. Diogenes of Sinope, the great Cynic philosopher, chose to live a virtually homeless existence, and he ridiculed people who lived acquisitive lives rather than focusing their efforts on being mentally disciplined and liberated from the most pervasive materialistic desires and pursuits. Jesus may or may not have been an incarnation of God, as many Christians believe, but he was surely a man of admirable character and a crucial world-historical figure. Did Jesus not declare that a wealthy man would have a more difficult time getting into heaven than a camel would have trying to pass through the eye of a needle? That is hardly an endorsement of wealth accumulation or conspicuous consumption. Nearly all the world admires at least one of the figures just mentioned, and much of the world *still* pursues money and the things that it can buy as if a life without them is, somehow, not worth living. This is, to say the least, a little peculiar.

October 16

Tyranny will enter your society through incremental changes to the law and, more importantly, through an increasingly pervasive inclination toward self-censorship due to fear of the consequences of speaking truths that persons in positions of power and influence do not want spoken. The process is already well underway, and you are, by now, accustomed to watching and listening as your friends, family, and colleagues do *not* say what they believe, and *do* say what they *know* to be untrue. There is not one human being on the face of the planet who sincerely believes, for example, that an adult human being with testicles, a penis, and Y-chromosomes in every bodily cell, with the wonderfully ironic exception of some *sperm* cells, can simply *decide* to be literally a *woman*. Obviously, there is not a single minimally rational adult who believes patent nonsense such as this, and yet there are adults who are willing to *pretend* to believe it on television, in online social networks, and even a handful in your workplace. These are sad, pathetic, wretched creatures, and you are better off living the rest of your life alone in a cave than spending so much as ten minutes indulging in any form of communication with *any* of them. There is *nothing* to be gained, and a great deal to be *lost*, by associating with liars, charlatans, and professional purveyors of idiocy. The culture dies when its denizens cease to care more about the truth than they do about maintaining a putrid and cowardly *status quo*. Deceit and indecency are now the "coin of the realm," the emperor has no clothes, and no one seems able to "rouse the rabble" anymore. Time is short.

October 17

When you encounter ridicule, it is incumbent upon you to consider whether it is or is not justified and, to whatever extent is possible, consider the motivations from which the ridicule flows. Do not pretend to believe that your behavior and utterances have *never* deserved mockery. You *have* had occasion to make an ass of yourself, have you not? If the ridicule is deserved, then you owe a debt of gratitude to those who mock you, as this will cause you to attend to a character flaw and set about the business of eradicating the defect in question. If your feelings get hurt along the way, that is *your* fault, and it is also a small price to pay for the sake of improving your rectitude. If, on the other hand, the ridicule is undeserved or based on some form of misunderstanding or misinterpretation, then the entire matter is of no significance to you. The person who misunderstands you has a defective set of beliefs or perceptions. What is that to *you*? The contents of another person's consciousness are not proper objects of concern or interest on your part. Let other persons be mistaken and do not trouble yourself about things that are simply none of your business. As for the *motivation* for ridicule or criticism, this also should be nothing to you. Perhaps the critic intends to tell the truth and has virtuous motives, or perhaps the critic wishes to tarnish you with lies and slander. Your detractors are free to speak about you honestly, dishonestly, and to do so for any reason or no reason. Who are you to attempt to govern the speech or the attitudes of any person other than yourself? Do *not* attempt to enlist in the Speech Police.

October 18

It is inevitable that some frauds, charlatans, and incompetents will succeed, and will fool enough of the public to prosper, to become famous, and to garner unearned and undeserved respect. You were *never* issued any guarantee that honors would be doled out in a manner that is fair or justifiable. When, in human history, has pristine justice governed the distribution of honors, attention, remuneration, or the admiration of the masses? Functioning as an effective swindler has, for a very, *very* long time, been a lucrative business, and an excellent method for rising to positions of power and influence. The Roman Caesars were not always the noblest, wisest, or most virtuous citizens of the empire. Caligula and Nero were not exactly the moral and intellectual equals of Marcus Aurelius. As you read through contemporary literature in philosophy, science, religion, and self-help, you encounter a lot of very valuable work, produced by honest intellectuals doing their level best to construct arguments, explain recondite concepts, and provide edification to their readers. Unfortunately, you also encounter a lot of nonsense and disingenuous posturing, produced by liars, frauds, and impostors who seek to enrich themselves by preying upon the sloth and ignorance of their readership. For this state of affairs, some considerable blame *must* be laid at the feet of the credulous readers. A great deal of the blame attaches to the charlatans and poseurs, of course. None of the business of assigning blame, however, is *your* responsibility or any proper concern about which it is wise or virtuous for you to trouble yourself. Let the liars and the gullible have each other. What is this to you? Just do not *become* what you behold.

October 19

If you find yourself in an echo chamber or a monoculture, it is advisable to get out of that environment immediately, and to avoid returning to it. There are certainly challenges that attend associating with persons and groups with whom you disagree. The experience can be frustrating, it is likely that someone is going to willfully misrepresent your beliefs and statements, you may get shouted down and interrupted at every opportunity, and it is not particularly likely that your efforts will change anyone's mind. It is not, therefore, ridiculous or indefensible to try to avoid that kind of situation. It *is*, however, inadvisable to go out of your way to associate *only* with persons and groups with whom you generally agree across the board. You are not likely to learn a great deal from those who say the same kinds of things that you say, think thoughts like your own, and live, more or less, the same style of life that you live. It is also unwise to insulate yourself from all of the sources of information other than the ones that you find agreeable, or from the sources that could provide you with *new* information that simply is not available through the media with which you are most comfortable. Finally, you virtually assure your own intellectual stagnation if you decide that you will not allow yourself to encounter challenges to your beliefs, values, and worldview. Do you aspire to *remain* wrong about everything that you are currently getting incorrect, or to assure your continuing ignorance about every area concerning which you currently know nothing? That is hardly a goal that will prove conducive to attaining wisdom.

October 20

Very few people are capable of telling nothing but the truth over the course of one full day, much less to do so over the course of a full lifetime. If you encounter anyone who claims never to have told a lie, do not turn your back on that individual, do not let that person hold your wallet, and do not ever even *consider* allowing that person to associate with your children. Not only do you have good reason to suspect that this is a person of questionable character, but you can also be reasonably confident that active efforts to conceal that character are reflexively common to this human being. Each of us ought to make our best attempts to be honest as often as we can manage, and *you*, as often as you mention the subject of *dishonesty*, really ought to do everything within your power to speak the truth as often as is, in your case, possible. Although you recognize and frequently extol the virtue of honesty, you are not so foolish as to believe that it is possible, for anyone other than a full-blooded sage, to embody this virtue consistently over the course of a full, and fully-lived, human life. There are simply too many circumstances, and too many different personalities, and too many varieties of reaction to hearing or reading the truth, for you to believe that honesty is *always* the best policy. The bride is properly described as "beautiful" irrespective of how she actually looks, and even the stupidest child is not properly described as "stupid" in public, and certainly not in conversation with that child's parents. It is not *always*, for practical purposes, possible to *evade* the question that simply cannot be answered with an honesty that can only cause *needless* harm.

October 21

The plumbing seems to have gone partially inoperative today. You are not much of a plumber, so this is going to be both inconvenient and a fairly expensive malfunction that will need to be rectified. Not so long ago, this kind of thing might have sent you into conniptions of anger and frustration, but these days you are fairly content to just make a few calls, pay the inevitable bills, and go on about the business of living your life. In some sense, this indicates that a certain degree of passion has gone out of your life, but it certainly seems not to be the type of passion that was, all things considered, worth keeping. Indeed, you increasingly find it strange that so many people seem to *value* passion as if it is great virtue, or even the primary thing that makes life worth living. Consider all of the needless damage that has been done, and all of the lives that have been lost or destroyed without just cause, simply because someone allowed the passions to drive them to words and deeds that could only be described as indefensible. Passion is *not* to be trusted. It seems to arise, primarily, from a portion of the brain that has fairly little connection to the areas most intimately involved in the reasoning process. Anger, fear, hatred, lust, and anxiety seldom lead to admirable behaviors, and frequently lead to utterances that you would prefer to have avoided. How many times have you said and done things under the influence of one or more of the passions that you later had cause to regret? How many times has the regret set in almost instantly upon hearing the words come out of your mouth or witnessing the behavior in which you just engaged? *Beware* the passions. They are *dangerous* indulgences.

October 22

There is something about a country singer on stage with nothing more than a guitar, a microphone, and perhaps a kick drum, that evokes a powerful feeling of admiration for the pure *simplicity* of the performance. A troubadour in a cowboy hat stands before a crowd with no band behind him, no theatrics or pyrotechnics, no backup singers, and holds forth with wonderfully sad stories set to music that sounds as if it emanates from a coal mine, a cornfield, or the dank recesses of a dive bar in Appalachia somewhere. There is something beautiful and intimate that passes between the artist and those members of the audience who are tuned in and sincerely attentive to the experience at hand. This type of country music, to be contrasted with the pop music that masquerades as country behind a few references to whiskey, trucks, trains, and hard times delivered with a counterfeit twang, is a form of storytelling that appeals, evidently, only to a certain kind of listener, but resonates with you *so* deeply that you feel your entire body vibrating concomitance with it. The stories are mostly about loss, dark nights of the soul, self-inflicted suffering, failure, and heartbreak, and that is a central element of their appeal. *Real* country music is a yearning for something that you seldom experience, and something that you long to hold onto, though you know that it always slips away. The world damages everyone in it, and ultimately kills everyone who ever gets to live. Good country music will not allow you to avert your eyes or stop up your ears and pretend that the whole thing is all grins and giggles. People *die* in country songs. It is like life in that way.

October 23

Evil does not always allow you the opportunity to move out of its path before it can destroy you or the things about which you care the most. If you *can* get out of its way without sacrificing anything that you value more than your own life, then it is probably advisable to do so. If, on the other hand, this option is simply not available to you, then you have no alternative but to confront the evil before you. Do you believe that you are *prepared* to do so? In their fantasies, most men probably imagine themselves acting in heroic and successful fashion, facing down the threat, and saving the people they love from the danger at hand, but these are, presumably, *mere* fantasies in most cases. You have seen *far* too many men fold, cower, and flee in the face of menace to believe that courage and fortitude are anything like the norm. Are *your own* heroic fantasies nothing more than projections of virtues that you *wish* to possess, or would you rise to the occasion should one of the more terrifying circumstances come to fruition? There is, as far as you can tell, no way of knowing for certain unless and until you are faced with the kinds of danger that you sometimes imagine. On the one hand, you hope never to be compelled to engage with a threat to life, limb, and family but, on the other hand, your *curiosity* about how you would fare has always been fairly captivating. Neither warfare nor an encounter with armed miscreants has yet befallen you. For this, you are grateful, and yet, there is a vague, and perhaps adolescent, yearning to know if you have the mettle to do what must be done in such a case. There is also the fear that you would fail. It makes for an interesting mixture, does it not?

October 24

Your dog is, on occasion, the most wonderfully lovable goof, and the most purely joyful creature that you have ever encountered. Though it may be something of a shame to admit this, you have *envied* your dog more than once. Every time that you open the door to the backyard and watch your pet sprint and bound toward some bird or squirrel that he clearly has *no* chance of ever catching, and every time you have witnessed his absolute delight in this type of quixotic romp, a little piece of you longs to be so easily thrilled by such simple experience as this. From your dog's perspective, it seems that the moment is lacking *nothing*. The chase is on, the opportunity for play is right in front of him, and he dives in with all four feet and not a care in the world. Would he actually kill a squirrel if he *could* get his paws and teeth on it? Your suspicion is that he would do so only by accident or as a bit of collateral damage from the enterprise of playing with the world. He does not seem to have any meanness or malice in him. The dog is not, as far as you are aware, capable of cruelty for its own sake, and though he *has* had occasion to bare his fangs and growl viciously when he believed the family to be threatened, he has always instantaneously reverted to his usual silly, happy self the instant that you let him know that there was no real danger. He loves his family, and you believe he would fight to the death anything that endangered you or your loved ones, but apart from that instinctual or evolutionary drive, he appears to have *no* interest in violence or conflict. For him, the world is a playground filled with toys and curiosities. Yes, you envy him. Why would you not?

October 25

Where is it written that you are *obligated* to get along in convivial fashion with *every* member of your extended family? Of course, it is both wise and virtuous to avoid needless friction or enmity within the immediate family, provided that you can do so without endangering anyone, and without stultifying all meaningful discourse among the people with whom you are closest. A family that fears and avoids honest communication cannot be described as "happy" or "healthy" in any profound sense. When it comes to cousins, nephews, nieces, aunts, uncles, and even more distant relatives, you should not expect to like and respect *all* of those people, nor should you anticipate that all of them would admire you or take much of an interest in your life at all. At some point, the value of congeniality with more distant relations provides something like a declining utility. Add in all of those who have married into the extended family, and all of those in dating relationships with nephews, nieces, cousins and the like, and the idea of trying to embrace all of that humanity with cordiality begins to border on the absurd. Any group containing that many people, spanning all of the available generations, is simply *bound* to include a few assholes that do not deserve a welcoming embrace. Of course, you can be fairly confident that *you* are the asshole for whom some of the distant relatives have no use and no patience. Do not begrudge them this attitude toward you. We cannot, as it happens, "all get along," and the effort to do so really is not worth the intestinal damage and grinding teeth. Keep peace, as best you can, with the family that matter most. As for the rest, keep a healthy distance where it is advisable to do so.

October 26

When you act in haste, you invite errors and you also leave yourself susceptible to needless bouts of frustration and anxiety. Like a beast of prey, you *are* dangerous when you are in a hurry. You have an unfortunate tendency to treat anyone and anything in your way like an obstacle to be dispatched or cleared as quickly as possible and as brusquely as necessary. As far as inanimate objects are concerned, this attitude is, at least in most cases, not particularly problematic. Where other *persons* are concerned, however, your tendency to shunt them roughly to one side and pass quickly by their field of influence can be interpreted as, and is often *correctly* interpreted as, indifference to their well-being, or even an active desire to do them just enough harm to let them know that you are capable of doing serious damage if you decide to do so. Not everyone is going to yield gracefully in these types of conditions. Not everyone is going to be sufficiently intimidated to move out of your way and accept the abrupt treatment. Sooner or later, someone is going to take umbrage and demand a reckoning. This presents at least two problems. First, the ensuing conflict is only going to cause you to lose more time, become more anxious about getting to where you are going, and potentially prevent you from accomplishing the task at hand. Secondly, and more importantly, if the conflict escalates into physicality, then you are virtually assured to incur a host of new difficulties that are not justified by a trivial inconvenience. Consider the possibility of prison, lawsuits, and jeopardy regarding your continued employment. If haste causes you to risk all of that, then *avoid* haste.

October 27

Most contemporary television programs seem to be designed and intended to corrode any remaining decency to which the viewership may cling. There are few forms of licentiousness that are *not* embodied in characters with whom the audience is supposed to identify and sympathize. Being a serial adulterer is, evidently, insufficient reason to regard the character as a villain, or even as a deeply flawed cautionary example. It is no longer uncommon that a murderer, indeed even a serial murderer, serves as the beloved protagonist in a series or a televised movie. Nearly all wealthy characters are depicted as attaining their wealth through corruption, connections to organized crime figures (themselves often lionized on television), or sloth conjoined to a propitious inheritance that is squandered in profligate fashion. Impoverished characters nearly always have problems with excessive gambling, substance abuse, prostitution, or some other character flaw that the audience is expected to overlook as merely a product of unfortunate circumstance. Clerical figures are usually either child molesters, or abusive to spouse and children, or engaged in dirty dealing for pecuniary gain. Children are generally disobedient, lazy, precociously obnoxious, addicted to video games, or they are casually sexualized at earlier and earlier stages of development. Every deviant imaginable is presented in the most sympathetic light possible, and any character that questions or rejects the debauched party is portrayed as a moral monster. The moral universe of the television world is upside down, inside out, and utterly degenerate. This is *not* an accident.

October 28

It is increasingly difficult to guide your children to a wholesome life and a noble path through a society that is increasingly noxious and from which it is nearly impossible to separate. Apart from going to live as hermits in the deep woods, or atop some remote mountain range, there is little hope of sheltering your children from the deleterious influences of television, the Internet, and their peers who have been corrupted by television, the Internet, and terrible parenting. On a nearly daily basis, you encounter children cursing at their parents and teachers in the most vitriolic fashion imaginable, and violent crime is reaching epidemic proportions as it involves younger perpetrators and more defenseless victims. Gangs are a more pervasive influence today than at any time during your formative years and adolescence, and it is difficult to find a public school or neighborhood that is not touched by their unsavory influence. You can, of course, *advise* your children about the many dangers awaiting them, and you can do your best to model appropriate adult behavior, but you *cannot* follow them through every moment of every day, or usher them through every potential cultural minefield. The society with which they must contend is a degraded and moribund version of the social order in which you were raised. Today, it seems that *disorder* is the norm, and moral decay saturates nearly every institution and every collective that your children will encounter. Imagine what might have become of *you* if the culture in which you are embedded today had been the world in which you grew up. Would you have made it *this* far?

October 29

Avoid bitterness as much as possible as you consider persons and events from your past, and as you contemplate the distance you have traveled from the cradle to this moment. You sometimes have the inclination to experience resentment as you remember the occasions on which you did not receive appropriate credit for your efforts, and the occasions on which you were blamed for conditions that transpired due to no fault of your own. This cast of mind is both unhealthy and irrational. You have no business being concerned about getting credit, being blamed, or about the motives or character of the persons affixing praise or blame. Your job is to do your best, improve yourself as best you are able, and make what meager contributions you can to the people around you. If your contributions are noticed, or if they are ignored, this type of thing is simply none of your business, and these types of conditions lie beyond your control. It is childish to insist upon being perceived accurately by other persons, it is petulant to complain about anything that is, or is not, said about you, and it is ignoble to allow your attitude to depend upon the thoughts, utterances, and behaviors of persons other than *you*. A bitter attitude toward other people is a bad habit into which you are inclined to slip all too easily and all too frequently. This is a manifestation of psychological weakness on your part, and what it may indicate about those other persons and their character is not worthy of your attention. Mind your own business and remain *indifferent* to the things that you cannot control. This *cannot* be repeated enough.

October 30

Reading the *Bible* is an excellent method of gaining insight into the fundamentals of the human condition, and the persistence of those conditions over time and cultural change, and this is true whether God does or does not exist. The story of Abel and Cain reveals the dangers of envy and ingratitude at least as well as does Shakespeare's *Othello*, and neither work depends upon historical accuracy for communicating the relevant messages and lessons. Atheists and agnostics make a mistake if they regard the *Bible* as a useless text or as mere superstitious fantasy and, therefore, unworthy of serious study or deployment in public educational institutions. Educators do their students *no favors* by declining to introduce them to scripture because of questions concerning its historicity. The same can be said of the canonical texts of Hinduism, Buddhism, Taoism, and Islam. You need not believe every jot and tittle of the myths, legends, and allegories contained therein, if you are to derive benefit from studying various wisdom traditions, and you need not concern yourself with the distinction between religion and history if you want to extract the most important lessons from scripture. It is fairly clear that the *Book of Job* is intended as allegorical, and *not* historical, but this does not detract from its lessons regarding human suffering, fidelity and persistence through the worst of times, and the unreasonable demand that mere human beings ought to be able to uncover and understand everything that transpires and every reason or cause underpinning every event they encounter. Why suffering? God only knows.

October 31

When you were a child, like most children in your culture, you loved Halloween because of the costumes and the candy. As an adult, your attitude toward this holiday has changed somewhat. You still enjoy a vicarious excitement when you see how much fun little kids are having dressing up as their favorite characters, going door to door, sometimes with their parents and sometimes on their own, getting their bags filled with candy and chirping, "Trick or treat!" It takes a pretty hard heart to fail to derive enjoyment from watching little children having fun and laughing along with each other. That part of the holiday is still all well and good. What you find vaguely distressing, however, is the behavior of some *adults* on the final day of October. Is it just your imagination, or do a lot of adult women use Halloween as an excuse to dress like dirty whores, all the while pretending that they are just participating in a holiday tradition? Worse still is that this phenomenon appears to be "trickling down" to younger "women" each year. It is no longer particularly shocking to see a fourteen-year-old girl dressed up in a costume that a Vegas showgirl would regard as a little too revealing. Who are these parents that allow their adolescent, and in some cases, *pre-adolescent* children to leave the house as scantily clad as the law allows, and far *less* well covered than even a minimal degree of modesty or decency ought to allow? If the sexualizing of children is *not* a sign of cultural degeneracy, and if it is *not* an indication of slouching toward the normalization of pedophilia, then you must confess ignorance of a more plausible explanation. Soon, *nothing* in this arena will be impermissible.

November 1

On this day in history, an earthquake hit Lisbon in 1755 killing more than 50,000 people in the capital city of Portugal. That is more than fifteen times the number of people who died in the United States on September 11th, 2001. Your general emotional response to these two tragedies is, perhaps not surprisingly, quite parochial and nationalistic. It is not surprising that the latter event has much greater psychological purchase for you because you lived through the occurrence, watched the news coverage almost ceaselessly on television for days afterward, and you *went to college* with a person who escaped from one of the Twin Towers before it collapsed. In addition to all of that, however, is the inescapable fact that this event constituted an attack on *your* nation and *your* culture. The Lisbon earthquake was not a morally culpable agent, and it had no malicious intentions or desires to kill anyone. It was, presumably, a matter of plate tectonics, fault lines, or some other elements of geologic physics, and it would be nonsensical to describe the event as morally *evil*. That tragedy is a product of human frailty conjoined to environmental facts that periodically illustrate just how easily people can die *en masse* if they are simply in the wrong place at the wrong time. The attacks on September 11th illustrate a very different facet of the human condition. It was yet another reminder, this one a bit closer to home than most, that there are people who actually enjoy slaughtering other people, or that some people actually regard slaughtering *certain* others as something like a moral or ideological *duty*. The world *is* going to kill you, and one of your fellow humans may be its instrument.

November 2

The expression "practice makes perfect" is a bit of an exaggeration, presumably for the sake of alliteration, but the hyperbole does not undercut the value of the message or the efficacy of assiduous practice. When you first began wrestling, for example, you were utterly incompetent and you had only come to the sport during your first year in high school. Many other members of the team had been wrestling since they were small children. For several months, you found that you could not beat *anyone* you matched up against, and you got pinned repeatedly. When you finally won your first match in the practice room, your opponent was another newcomer to the discipline, he was every bit as unskilled as you, and you beat him by one point that was, in all honesty, more a matter of luck than proficiency. By the time you graduated from high school, you were still mediocre at best, and you watched many of your teammates surpass your meager success by wide margins. Four years of practice did *not* make you perfect. Indeed, all of that practice did not even make you a *good* wrestler. Nonetheless, you made *progress*, and *that* really is the point, and ought to be the *goal* of practice in any endeavor. You will never attain *perfection* in anything that you do. Even *undefeated* boxers get punched in the face repeatedly. Rocky Marciano's *record* was perfect insofar as he never suffered a defeat as a professional boxer. He did, however, get *knocked down* on several occasions. Perfectionism is irrational for imperfect members of your imperfect species. Progress is the goal. Try to become a little better than you are now. *That* is *not* failure.

November 3

Why should intentionally false accusations not carry the same potential penalties as do the crimes and misdeeds alleged? If it were up to you, all persons convicted of first degree, premeditated murder would be either executed or sentenced to life in prison with no possibility of parole. If a person attempts to *frame* another person for a murder that the accuser knows that the accused did *not* commit, and if it can be demonstrated beyond a reasonable doubt that the accuser issued a knowingly fabricated charge, then, were it up to you, the *false accuser* would spend a life term in prison with no possibility of parole as well. If someone levels an intentionally false accusation against a colleague at work that, if believed, would result in the termination of the accused from employment at the institution in question, then the accuser should also face termination as a *lying* and *malicious* informer. The phenomenon of unsupported allegations destroying lives and careers has become so pervasive and so common that nearly *anyone* is susceptible to ruination because of mere accusation. Your culture is filled with more than its share of genuine malefactors, and there is certainly no need to *invent* misbehavior or conjure *phony* crimes out of thin air. If the presumption of innocence is abrogated, then any vague facsimile of justice or fairness will disappear entirely. As far as you can tell, this is the direction that your culture is going. You have seen careers destroyed by utterly implausible accusations supported by precisely *no* evidence whatsoever. Concern for victims must extend to victims of *false allegations* as well as it is properly extended to victims of *actual* crimes and misdeeds.

November 4

Time spent with family is rarely wasted, and if it *is* wasted, that is always the result of fatigue, sloth, or indifference on the part of the family members involved. When you find yourself with family members of an older generation, there is always an opportunity to learn from them. Do not waste opportunities to find out about life and events as they occurred before you were born or when you were too young to remember any events. Older people are also a potential treasure trove of information about parenting, about finances, and about simple pleasures that are far more rare today. If you find yourself keeping company with family members of a younger generation, then you have an opportunity to be better informed about contemporary developments in music and entertainment, although you should expect at least some of what you hear to be either disappointing or vaguely horrifying. Younger family members are also likely to have greater alacrity with developments in technology and sources of information that you would be less likely to encounter otherwise. Again, remember the caveat concerning the likelihood that some of what you find with the assistance of younger family members is probably going to be disturbing on some level or another. Finally, family members of your own generation are quite likely to have experience in fields and occupations other than your own, and there will always be something worth learning from at least one or two siblings, cousins, or spouses that comprise your generation of the family. *Listen* more than you speak in these cases. Pay close attention.

November 5

It seems that nearly everyone regards being a good teammate as a virtue, and there are certainly good reasons for that attitude among persons who voluntarily and happily participate in team sports and collectivist enterprises. Not everyone, however, is felicitously made for teamwork and collectivism. There are plenty of natural "lone wolves" out there, and many of them are neither inclined to be good teammates, nor are they disposed to enjoy participating in enterprises requiring large numbers of people working together. You have no obligation to adopt any mindset that is either unnatural for you or that you regard as anathema. If you do not like to be surrounded by lots of people, and you *never have* enjoyed that condition, then you are entirely within your rights to steer clear of crowds and all endeavors that require the involvement of many hands to get the work done. In your case, it is almost always better for you to get as much of the necessary work done on your own as is possible, and to submit to group efforts only sparingly, and only if or when it is absolutely necessary. Time spent among large groups of others is very draining to you, and it has never led to positive psychological or emotional outcomes. Indeed, you have nearly always suffered the most unpleasant consequences of trying to "work and play well with others," and anger, frustration, and misery have been your reward. This is, of course, entirely your own fault and nothing more than a result of inadequate mental discipline, but for now you would do well to avoid crowds and "teams" as much as possible. Do not burden yourself unnecessarily.

November 6

Confidence is, to say the least, a double-edged sword, and it can be your best friend or your worst enemy depending upon the endeavor in question, the skill set that you bring to that endeavor, the opponent or the challenge that you need to overcome, and a host of circumstances that are largely, if not entirely, beyond your control. *Overconfidence* is almost always fatal or, at the very least, extremely deleterious to your interests and to accomplishing any goals. Underestimating your opponent or the challenge that lies before you is tantamount to *inviting* defeat. A complete *absence* of confidence is, however, just as injurious to your prospects as is an undeserved abundance of confidence. If you enter into any competition, any enterprise, or any pursuit that requires significant effort on your part, and that entails substantial consequences should you fail, then you had better maintain a genuine conviction in your ability to get the job done. Never *defeat yourself* by entering into any competition assuming that you are going to lose, or entering into any venture presupposing that you cannot accomplish the task at hand. Not only is a lack of self-confidence damaging to your interests, but it is also an incipient excuse in the making, which makes it a close relative of cowardice. There is, therefore, a delicate balance when it comes to this particular mental state. It is imperative that you manage a degree of confidence, but it is equally essential that you avoid an excess of *unjustifiable* certainty that you will succeed. In this way, it is a bit like cooking a *filet mignon*. There are not many options apart from *just right* and *ruined*.

November 7

Every man must find something to which he is duty-bound if he wants his life to be meaningful and if he wants to experience his life as if it is something worth living. Women also need to find meaning and purpose in their lives, but obligations present themselves to women much more readily and naturally than is the case for men, or perhaps it is more accurate to say that life unfolds for women in a manner that makes the answer to this question *easier to find* than it is for most men. If you find yourself asking, "What is it that I absolutely *must* do?" you are on the trail of the meaning of life as it manifests in your case. For *far* too long now, men have been told that they are expendable, that they are "toxic," and that they are responsible for every oppressive system in history. Why would any man *choose* to participate actively in trying to find his life's purpose if he believes these ludicrous lies, or if he is convinced that the rest of the world is going to believe this nonsense no matter what he does or does not accomplish. Obligations, or potential obligations, present themselves to men in a manner that is sometimes a bit oblique, and those men who are willing to grasp onto a passing potential obligation are much more likely to experience their lives as fulfilling. *You* have certainly benefitted immeasurably from the obligations that go along with the family that you have acquired later in life than is usual, and purpose is available to you in abundance now, whereas you sought it but failed to find it all too often in the past. Find a "cross" that suits you, pick it up, bear it without complaint, and know that you have found a purpose. Without a purpose, what *is* the point?

November 8

Knowing when you are done with some facet of your life, and understanding why it is necessary to make a transition and move on to new challenges is essential to your long-term development. The danger of getting stuck in a particular vocation, or a specific area of comfort, carries with it the risk of intellectual stagnation. The body changes, circumstances change, and your peripheral interests tend to alter over time. As long as your core values are the attainment of wisdom, virtue, and self-rectification, there is nothing wrong with exploring new areas in which to enact your pursuit of those core values. There would be something sad about having all and only the same interests you pursue at the age of *eighteen* and still at the age of *eighty*. Imagine the eighty-year-old version of yourself still competing in wrestling and football. *That* would be more than a little absurd, would it not? Imagine the eighteen-year-old version of yourself putting final affairs in order in anticipation of death in the not-too-distant future. What was the sum total of your "estate" when you were eighteen? Had you been diagnosed with a terminal illness at that age, then considerations of your death would have been appropriate. As your past actually stands, however, such preparations would have been macabre to say the least. Try to be attentive to changing circumstances and changes in your own makeup over time, so that you can adapt in a rational fashion rather than insisting that change *must not* overtake you. There is a dynamic equilibrium between the stability of your core values and the inevitable changes that you must encounter. This is nothing to fear.

November 9

The number of utterly silly propositions that are commonly brandished by charlatans, lunatics, and ideologues in the same way that one might brandish a club is, as far as you can tell, on the increase. The absolute ideological monoculture in academia has rendered most disciplines outside of the hard sciences *worse* than useless, and this condition threatens penetration even into sciences such as physics and biology. In the traditional media, the same sort of monoculture has caused the broadcasting of "news" to transform into nothing more than propaganda disseminated for the benefit of the same monoculture that now dominates the academy. When the conventional outlets whereby information is gathered and subsequently circulated to the public cease to be even moderately reliable, and when the purveyors of information lie and dissemble as casually as they inhale and exhale, it is not surprising that distrust among the general public will become more pervasive in proportion to the pervasiveness of disinformation. Indeed, it would be a shame if the public were to prove sufficiently gullible to believe, *en masse*, the ludicrous nonsense that is foisted off on them as orthodoxy that they *must* embrace if they are to be accepted as intellectually and morally well-developed. Already, there are far too many people who reflexively believe what their teachers and professors tell them, and also embrace various forms of twaddle that is broadcast by dimwits who enjoy posing as regnant priests deciding what counts as culturally appropriate dogma. It seems that intellectual autonomy is slipping away from a significant proportion of the public. Do *not* join their ranks.

November 10

Hypersensitivity is never a virtue, and people who are easily insulted are never to be taken seriously, and you are certainly *never* obligated to do *anything* to appease pathetic emotional weaklings. Unfortunately, whining and complaining have become standard modes of communication for far, *far* too many people who lack either the capacity or the inclination to construct and defend arguments to support propositions that they wish to assert. If you are going to speak what you believe to be the truth, it is inevitable that other people are going to disagree with you, and some of them are going to direct criticism at you. They are entirely free to do so, and you should not be the least bit concerned about what they say. The primary thing to remember is that *you* must *never* descend to their level of whining and griping about criticism, whether it is fair or unfair, whether it is accurate or inaccurate, and whether it is motivated by malice or sincerity. If you are going to criticize hypersensitive people, and you *are* going to do so, then you must never indulge in hypocrisy by allowing yourself to become insulted by *any* response to the criticism. Your contempt for hypersensitivity is justified not only by the fact that it is a character flaw, but also by the fact that your culture is laboring under the burden of the increasingly common insistence that we must all *avoid offending* the pathetic, useless jellyfish posing as persons. There can hardly be a clearer sign that a culture is dying than a general injunction prohibiting disparagement of the most ignoble and least admirable members of the society in question. Whining weaklings are *not* exempt from criticism.

November 11

To what extent, and how often, do your actions depart from your stated beliefs and values? This is a crucial question if you wish to be honest about your integrity and the development of your character. Any time you observe *anyone*, including *yourself*, behaving in a manner that is not consonant with that person's alleged worldview, you have to be suspicious about that person's commitment to the principles he or she espouses. You claim that you are deeply interested in developing your character, enhancing your wisdom, and steadily increasing in virtue, but you waste an awful lot of time on inconsequential pursuits, and you frequently behave in ways that cannot be described as particularly virtuous or wise. Thus, you can only conclude that you are not especially serious about your pursuit of virtue, or that your mental discipline is woefully insufficient to make much headway in that pursuit. You have encountered plenty of people who claim to be concerned about the plight of the poor while they reside in mansions with enough unused bedrooms to house twenty homeless people. Do you believe that such people are actually concerned about the poor, or do you believe that they are concerned about *appearing* to care about poverty? Some might say it is cynicism, but you believe what you *see* them doing, and what you see them *not* doing, as opposed to the precious claims that they make about themselves. When it comes to your assessment of your own character, do you believe what you *see* yourself doing, or what you *hear* yourself saying? The two do not coincide perfectly, do they?

November 12

Yesterday was Veterans Day and, according to the United States Department of Veterans Affairs, the appropriate reference to this holiday does not include an apostrophe because the day does not "belong" to veterans, but its purpose is to *honor* veterans. It is not clear why that day cannot be used for honoring or celebrating veterans while also, in some sense, belonging to them, but that is hardly the most important thing to be said about this day. You are acutely aware of the fact that, were it not for the United States military, throughout the nation's history and certainly carrying through to today, neither you nor any other American citizens would have the opportunity to enjoy the lives of comparative peace and prosperity that we actually do, or should, appreciate. It is, for all practical purposes, impossible for any foreign military to invade the continental United States, precisely because this nation's military poses an insurmountable obstacle to any such undertaking. There have been, and will continue to be, periodic terrorist attacks, but as tragic as these events are, they do not constitute the kind of threat that is likely to cause the nation to collapse, and your relatively stable existence to evaporate. For this, and for much more as well, you owe all veterans a debt of gratitude. Oddly, the potency of the military does not strike you as sufficient to forestall the collapse, or severe and precipitous decay, that you see coming. You do not expect your nation to fall prey to any collection of foreign powers. You do, unfortunately, expect very dark days to befall your nation and such "culture" as remains attached to it, because you perceive the whole thing to be rotting from the inside out. What can *you* do?

November 13

You never cease to be amazed at the sheer quantity and pervasiveness of obviously irrational desires. There are many cravings that, if satisfied, will clearly cause far *more* trouble for the agent in question than would be the case if those desires were to be left unfulfilled. How many people long for fame, and how many of those people would be emotionally decimated by the scrutiny and excess attention that typically attend fame or notoriety? It is, of course, impossible to know in advance what the actual consequences of fame would be for any individual before the longing for fame is realized, but just look at the number of famous persons who end up addicted to drugs and alcohol, divorced many times over, tortured by unwanted media attention and, oddly enough, bankrupted by either their own stupidity or by unscrupulous parasitic lawyers and money managers. The lives of formerly famous athletes seem to go awry about as often as not, and elderly pop and rock music stars generally look as if they spent decades intentionally destroying their bodies and minds. You assume that this form of self-flagellation is typically *unintentional*, but this is not a proposition on which you would be willing to wager a great deal of money. As for the topic of wealth, and the seemingly unquenchable desire for it that dominates so many lives, you really cannot help but wonder if what so many people are willing to trade away in pursuit of wealth is not generally, properly regarded as more valuable than the money for which it is traded. Time, energy, and decency often seem to be frittered away in the desperate quest to acquire more money. Those who *succeed* in this quest get to drop dead like everyone else. Bully for them.

November 14

You have begun to suspect that toddlers often cry because they have realized that their parents are imbeciles and they have no viable alternative to being raised by incompetents who are virtually guaranteed to ruin them in more ways than their youthful minds can imagine. You also wish that you could say, honestly, that you are just kidding about this. Unfortunately, you have had too many conversations with adolescents who have revealed that they have no respect for their parents, and that they would have been much better off having been raised by someone else. Though you have never asked them to recount the specifics of their upbringing, they have frequently volunteered an enormous amount of unsolicited information about their lives and the various forms that their parents' incompetence has taken. There is no way, of course, to verify or refute the content of these various claims, nor would you be inclined to do so if you had the opportunity, but it seems as unlikely that *all* of the stories are fabrications, as it does that *none* of the accounts are fabrications. What is to be done about bungled parenting, especially when the bungling has been going on for nearly two decades and any attempt to address the incompetence is likely to incur unpleasant consequences for all or most of the parties involved, and it is extremely unlikely that any benefit is to be derived? There are, after all, no legal consequences for mere stupidity and ineptitude in the process of raising children. Were there *criminal* conduct involved, you would have no hesitancy about reporting the matter. To *whom*, however, do you report parental idiocy? Morons *are* permitted to procreate. They really seem to enjoy doing so as well. So, here we are.

November 15

At the risk of recounting your experience of a banal and seemingly uninteresting phenomenon, the liars are lying again today. Today, you encountered one of the more stunningly, *obviously* false allegations against a public figure that you have ever heard. The person issuing the accusation is clearly concocting the story out of some form of malice or mental illness, the individuals and media corporations spreading the "news" of the allegation demonstrably do *not* believe a *word* of this ludicrous tale, and approximately half of the people consuming this information and commenting about it on social media are unmistakably *pretending* to be persuaded by the allegedly compelling nature of the account. This strikes you as a manifestation of something akin to a cultural mental illness, a mass delusion, or an indication of societal decay that is well beyond treatment. If the only plausible explanations for an assertion are abject stupidity or pervasive dishonesty, and if otherwise rational adults proffer the proposition, then it is reasonable to infer that moral corruption is probably the motive behind the behaviors that you behold. The culture into which you were born is, at this point, largely gone, or so utterly degraded and depraved that the society in which you find yourself now is, at best, a fairly disgusting specter of what it once was. Liars and charlatans occupy the *vast* majority of the available positions of power in politics, the media, and academia. Perhaps it has always been thus. Perhaps this is a more recent development. In either event, it is just another facet of your "civilization" about which you can do no more than take note, and sigh.

November 16

It really should not be so very difficult, especially in *your* case, to remember that you are nothing special, and that even the slightest *hint* of self-aggrandizement reveals you to be at least vaguely delusional. Your life is more than halfway over and your greatest accomplishment, apart from convincing your wife to marry you (which actually *is* something of a miracle, but clearly depends upon *her* more than it does upon you), is mastering the art of *appearing* to know more than you actually *do* know. Hurrah! You have, on the odd occasion at least, managed the feat of serving as a passable impostor before people who really could not care much less whether you are or are not what you pretend to be. You have picked up a few polysyllabic words and have learned, more or less, where to drop them into a conversation or a bit of composition that very few people will ever read. You are also fairly adept, when you wish to be, at nodding in a fashion that is sometimes felicitous to conversation, or to *avoiding* conversation. Clearly, those extra years in graduate school were not wasted on *you*! If someone describes a politician as "Machiavellian," you have a general sense of what that person intends to convey, or you can at least make most speakers *believe* that you do. You are fairly adept at convincing a room full of people, who know even *less* than you know, to believe that you know more than does the average person. In other words, you are a reasonable facsimile of what a stupid person *thinks* a smart person sounds like. Unfortunately, you have spent enough time in the company of persons who are genuinely smart to know better than to try and fool any of *them*. You could use a new hobby.

November 17

If you want to be free, or to be as close to free as humans are capable of being, you had better learn self-discipline and moral restraint. Though this may, initially, seem paradoxical, careful consideration should reveal that mere licentiousness, or merely doing whatever you happen to feel like doing, is not freedom, but is a form of *enslavement* to the passions, the bestial drives, the whims, and the winds of chance or circumstance. Do you regard *your dog* as "more free" than you? Surely, your dog is far less constrained by intellectual or moral considerations, and if left outside and out of your sight, the dog will do, more or less, what he feels like doing, but from this it does not follow that your dog is *free*. The animal does not have an innate capacity or inclination to *resist* its innate urges. Thus, the feral dog is bound to behave in accordance with the dictates of its evolutionary inheritance conjoined to the dictates imposed by its environment. Perhaps the same rules apply to *your* thoughts and behavior. It is entirely possible, and not terribly implausible, that heredity and environment (broadly construed) causally determine all of your cognition and actions. Even if this *is* the case, you can learn to improve your capacity for self-control by encountering propitious environmental phenomena such as wise teaching conveyed to you through literature, interpersonal interaction, and careful attention to your responses to various forms of stimuli. In this way, you can increase your ability to determine your conduct through the gradual development of intellectual autonomy. Whether this constitutes full-fledged *free will* is, ultimately, beside the point. Govern yourself. *That* is enough.

November 18

Once again, you slept poorly last night. Somehow, you have not mastered the art, or the skill, of turning your mind off, or even coaxing it to *slow* its impulsive "churning" enough to enable a sleep state to set in. In this case, you fell asleep in a reasonable period of time after lying down, but you were jolted awake around three o'clock in the morning, and you stayed awake until the sun rose and your cat started whining for his breakfast. You infer that his caterwauling is about food, as it seems to subside after he is fed. Perhaps this is presumptuous of you, but he is just a cat, and an educated guess is probably the best that you can manage. In any event, you did not get enough sleep to feel like you are "firing on all cylinders" in either the physiological or cognitive "departments." Nonetheless, you have obligations to discharge, and you have reasonable desires to satisfy, and doing those things will require both physical and intellectual effort on your part. Feeling sorry for yourself, or allowing lethargy to take control of you, or using the vaguely "foggy" feeling in your head, behind your eyes, as an excuse for doing nothing, or for doing less than you are capable of doing, is simply *not* a viable option. Losing a decent night's sleep is as *nothing* by comparison with the kinds of challenges that other people face, and that others have faced, throughout human history. Get up, rouse yourself as best you can, get some coffee into your body if that seems likely to help, and set about doing your duty. You are, for example, scheduled to do an upper body workout today. You are not *inclined* to do that. You will, nonetheless, force yourself to exercise anyway, because you refuse to give in to weakness. Get to work. No complaints.

November 19

As much as you love and enjoy your family, you must admit, in moments of candor, that you also like having the house to yourself when everyone else is at work, school, or just *out*. Being alone at home affords you the opportunity to indulge in writing and research, as well as the opportunity to watch and listen to podcasts, debates, and other materials that would bore the rest of your family to tears. Just as you have no interest in the kinds of programming that fascinate your kids, they could not care less about a debate regarding the strengths and weaknesses of the fine-tuning argument. When the family is all home, and when they are all in the mood to spend time together, which does *not* have to be *every* moment that they are all at home, you have the opportunity to play family games, watch movies that everyone can enjoy, and hold conversations in which the kids and the "old folk" can all participate freely, and all the parties concerned can learn a little more about each other. That is genuinely *valuable* time for the family as a unit. Do not, however, undervalue time alone to contemplate matters that do not easily lend themselves to group discussion. Yesterday, you found that you had the urge to go back and reread an article about the Buddhist conception of "right mindfulness," and you had the opportunity to do so without the need to drag anyone else into the enterprise. You would actually enjoy the prospect of discussing Buddhism with the kids, but they show no interest, and you have no interest in trying to *force* them to be fascinated by such matters. Time by yourself provides you the chance to indulge *your own* interests.

November 20

On some days, your schedule requires you to wake up and prepare for work a bit earlier than your wife needs to get up. On other days, these roles are reversed. When you wake up earlier than she does, try to cause as little disturbance as possible, and offer your wife the opportunity to get a little extra sleep. She faces a day of work, and meetings, and dealing with various potential annoyances. The more rest and restorative sleep she is able to enjoy, the better equipped she will be to do all the things that need to be done, and the more likely she will be to do so without sustaining any more psychological or emotional irritation than is absolutely necessary. You are well aware that *you* tend to be more irritable, and more easily given to expressions of anger or frustration when you have not had a good night's sleep, so be mindful of affording your family members their chance to maximize their "sack time," so as to help them maintain their mental stability. Brush your teeth, shower, get dressed, and slip out of the house as quietly as you are able, and make sure that the car stereo is not turned up loud enough to wake your family or the neighbors. Ideally, when your wife wakes up, you will have gone to work without disturbing her in the slightest. Consider how grateful you are on those mornings when her schedule requires her to get up first, and you wake to find that she has managed to do everything she needed to do without waking you for even a moment. This is no trivial matter. Respecting your spouse entails doing what you can to help your life together pass by as smoothly as circumstances will allow. Be *considerate*.

November 21

When the horns sounded, and Joshua's army shouted, the walls of Jericho came tumbling down and Joshua conquered the city. What happened next, however, has always left you a little baffled. Joshua's legions killed *every living thing* in Jericho, with the exception of those who were ensconced with Rahab the prostitute. Rahab had hidden Joshua's spies, so you can understand why those in her house would *not* be slaughtered. What, however, necessitated killing all the men, all the women, the *young* and the old, and even the *cattle* and the *donkeys*? Presumably, the mass carnage must have had something to do with defilement and "cleansing" the city, and it is worth noting that this was accomplished by burning it to the ground, but *why* kill children, cattle, and donkeys? Surely, the donkeys cannot be held responsible for the various depravities of the inhabitants of Jericho. It is not, after all, as if the city was some type of ancient democracy governed by the "one *mammal*, one vote" principle. What did the sheep and the donkeys do to warrant "putting them to the sword" and then burning their carcasses? You are aware of the claim that "the Lord moves in mysterious ways," but slaughtering the *children* seems a little draconian, does it not? What had those little kids been up to in Jericho? Joshua also issued an injunction against rebuilding the city and declared that anyone attempting to do so would be *cursed* and would have to *sacrifice his children* to the project. Whatever the evil donkeys had been involved in, it is clear that those beasts of burden must have been very *bad*-asses indeed.

November 22

You watched a news report last night about tyranny, mass incarceration, and government-sponsored murder in a distant, underdeveloped nation. Perhaps it is unwise to report this kind of thing about yourself, but you were unable to rouse anything more than a *very* slight feeling of pity for the oppressed in this case. Were you to find yourself and your family in a similar condition, that would surely be terrifying to you, and you cannot easily imagine the toll it would take on you emotionally and physically. As it happens, however, you are about as distant from the people facing these terrors as is possible for denizens of the same planet. Not only geographically, but also culturally, you have as little in common with those on the receiving end of the tyrannical despotism as can be the case for members of the same species. Perhaps there are persons for whom the distance and the unfamiliarity are no obstacle to empathy in such cases. As it happens, you appear not to be one of those persons. Though you experienced pity as you watched video footage of some of the horrors inflicted on the populace of the region in question, those feelings evaporated almost immediately when a commercial for a fast food chain popped onto the television screen right after the news segment ended. There may be some part of you that would *like* to be moved in a more profound fashion when you encounter stories like this one but, in all honesty, no greater emotional reaction ever seems to arise when you learn of distant injustice. This is probably a character flaw. You do not, however, *want* to care any more intensely than you *do* care about such things. You *embrace* the distance.

November 23

Do *not* concern yourself with how well other people are doing their jobs, or with how well other people are functioning within their families or communities. The temptation to engage in such assessments arises with you fairly frequently, but it is advisable that you resist the urge to pay too much attention to the utterances and behaviors of friends, neighbors, or colleagues. No one charged you with the obligation to govern any of those people or to sit in judgment of the manner in which they conduct their lives. You became aware today that one of your colleagues is, according to another of your colleagues, engaged in an adulterous affair. You do not *know* whether this accusation is true, it is *none of your* business whether this accusation is true, and you informed the latter colleague that you have no interest in hearing any further reports about the matter. Indeed, you find that you are now suspicious of the colleague who felt the need to report to you the alleged inappropriate conduct. *Why* did this person tell you about a third party's supposed misconduct? Actually, even *that* question is unworthy of your consideration. There is no good reason for you to care about the motives or the conduct of either of your colleagues in this matter. Let this incident serve as a reminder that *you* will never commit adultery, and that *you* will refrain from engaging in the type of gossip and salacious calumny that your colleague appears to find fascinating. Rather than condemning either of the other parties involved, you are better served to use this incident as a prompt to refocus on *your own* conduct. Mind *your* business.

November 24

At what point did everyone agree to use the term "phobia," or to apply it as a suffix in reference to phenomena that some people dislike, distrust, or just have no interest in discussing or debating? There are traditionalists within the Jewish, Christian, and Islamic traditions who believe that scripture indicates that God has prohibited homosexual conduct, and they regard homosexuality as a sin. This view may be incorrect, it may be a defensible bit of scriptural exegesis, or it may be a controversy that continues for many years to come. It is not at all clear how regarding any particular type of behavior as sinful or prohibited constitutes a *phobia*, given that the term "phobia" has typically been used by psychologists to designate an extreme or irrational fear of something or other, and have generally associated phobias with *anxiety* disorders. There may well be persons who are subject to some type of extreme or irrational fear of homosexuality or homosexuals, but merely regarding the behavior as *forbidden* does not seem to constitute any such psychological condition. Nearly every religious Jew, Christian, and Muslim presumably regards stealing as prohibited by God's command, but you have never heard anyone refer to *theft-o-phobia* as a character flaw or psychological dysfunction. There may or may not be a legitimate debate worth having about the morality of homosexuality, or about its alleged prohibition within the aforementioned religious traditions. The attempt to label everyone on one side of the issue as subject to some type of cognitive malfunction is simply a disingenuous ploy to *avoid* honest debate and analysis, or so it seems to you.

November 25

Are you better off visiting a physician on a regular basis, or are you better off treating a visit to the doctor's office as a last resort? This question may not have quite the obvious answer that many are inclined to presume. Consider the cases of unnecessary surgery and other superfluous invasive procedures that you have heard and read about over the years. It seems that the vast majority of prostate removal surgeries, at least according to a number of sources, are needless as prostate cancer tends to be so sufficiently slow-developing that most men diagnosed with prostate cancer are more likely to die of other causes than of the prostate malady. There are also, according to a variety of sources, reasons to suspect that a significant proportion of surgical procedures to certain ligaments and tendons can be safely forgone, and the relevant injuries can be managed through rest and physical rehabilitation. Even in the case of correct diagnoses of terminal illnesses, the attempts to cure these conditions often cause enormous suffering, the treatments are typically exorbitantly expensive, and the success rates are not exactly cause for sanguine optimism for those diagnosed. Might it not be the case that you are, at least in a significant number of potential instances, better off allowing "nature to take its course," rather than subjecting yourself to invasive, often ineffective, and always inconvenient, attempts to extend your life in a condition of dependence upon other persons to whom you will become either a burden or a source of revenue? If you break your leg, go and get treatment. If you are diagnosed with cancer, maybe palliative care will suffice.

November 26

Anyone who uses a *child* as a mere *prop* to advance a socio-political contention, or to manipulate the emotions of the more tenderhearted members of the voting public, is, by virtue of *that* very act, a con artist. It makes no difference what side of the debate the charlatan defends, even if the con artist happens to *agree with you* in this instance, such behavior is always illegitimate use of the innocent in service of the nefarious interest of exploitation. If the general public were both rational and decent, which it mostly is *not*, then all attempts to use children for any exploitative purposes would incur swift and severe consequences for the adult (or adults) involved. These frauds who force their children to hold up signs that the children cannot even *read*, and clearly could not have written, are taking advantage of the fact that the children are in no position to object to this mistreatment, and are also taking advantage of the fact that small children are generally predisposed to defer to Mommy or Daddy's authority and presume their good will. This behavior is, to be blunt, not so terribly far removed from pimping out children and devoting the proceeds of their prostitution to an allegedly beneficent endeavor. You are entirely within your rights to feel *nothing but contempt* for parents who use their children as Kantian "mere means," and do so, not for the benefit of the youngsters (as when, for example, they vaccinate them against their will), but in order to advance some political agenda that the child cannot understand. Children are *not* to be *used* for emotionally manipulative purposes. A two-year-old holding a sign that says, "Stop climate change for me," is being *abused*.

November 27

You have heard the injunction, "Do not judge a book by its cover," more times than you can count and, the fact is, you have *never* taken this ridiculous bit of advice seriously. Even when you were a fairly young child, you noticed that you often had *no alternative* when encountering strangers. If the aforementioned expression merely indicates that persons can have virtuous traits of character though they appear frightening or otherwise problematic to you, then it is pretty clearly correct. If, on the other hand, it is actually a command to form *no judgment* about a person unless and until you have had sufficient experience with that individual to gather compelling evidence regarding that individual's character, then it is simply awful advice that is likely to get you robbed, beaten, or killed if you adhere to it. If you are alone in a parking lot at night, and three young men with whom you are not acquainted fan out and approach you from divergent angles, then you have all the information you need to be justifiably suspicious of their intentions. If a small or elderly woman sees a large, apparently homeless man, shambling toward her in a manner that appears to indicate that he is under the influence of drugs or alcohol, then that woman *had better* respond as if that man represents a danger to her. If it turns out that she is mistaken, then she may have an opportunity to apologize. If, however, it turns out that the man *does* intend to harm her, then she is going to suffer dire consequences for failing to "judge" that "book" by "its cover." *False negatives* are much more dangerous than are *false positives* when it comes to identifying dangerous, malevolent people.

November 28

It is advisable to avoid crowds, especially very *large* crowds, as much as is consistent with practical concerns. Large crowds are far more likely to give rise to riots and other violent skirmishes than are comparatively dispersed small groups of people. Airborne illnesses and unpleasant physiological conditions communicated through skin contact are bound to find you if you spend a lot of time embedded in closely crowded environments. Terrorists armed with guns or bombs seldom attack far-flung, tiny villages across broad swathes of thinly populated countryside, foothills, or isolated mountainous regions. Stadiums, concert halls, and other arenas are most susceptible to structural failure and collapse when they are filled to the rafters with foot-stomping, dancing, screaming fans. Crowds and densely populated places are flat-out dangerous to your physical well-being. Additionally, there are good reasons to suspect that, for many people, and even more good reasons to suspect that, for *you* in particular, any extended experience of the "huddled masses" is *very* likely to exacerbate your predispositions to anxiety, irritation, frustration, anger, and all of the unfortunate consequences that tend to ensue. The last time you went to a concert, you found the urge to get up from your seat and move to the back of the venue, where there was more open space and fewer people, nearly impossible to resist. Furthermore, you judged that you and all persons with whom you came into contact would be better off and have a more enjoyable evening if you sought periodic respite from the close quarters of the mezzanine. The heightened potential of ending up in prison for assault is *another* reason to avoid crowds.

November 29

Because you were not being mindful and not paying careful attention to the task at hand, you managed to slice your hand badly while using a *can opener* last night. In addition to the pain, the blood that probably ruined the shirt you were wearing, and the difficulty that you are now experiencing while trying to write these words, you must also endure family and friends snickering as you explain why you are wearing the bandage wound around two fingers. Though some small part of you might be tempted toward slight exasperation over people laughing at your injury, the fact is that you really cannot blame them. What kind of an idiot opens a can, gets distracted by a buzzing insect, and takes a swipe at the insect in the hopes of killing it, only to slash his hand across the top of the can that is now sticking straight up in the air because the idiot has *just* opened it? Well, look in the mirror. You will find precisely that kind of imbecile staring back at you with a sardonic expression and bandages on his somewhat mangled fingers. The first lesson from this incident is that you really ought to pay attention to sharp objects in your immediate environment, especially when they are sharp precisely because *you just caused them* to become sharp. The second lesson is that you may as well learn to laugh at yourself, along with everyone else, when you do something *that* stupid. The third lesson is that you should not be quite so cavalier about swatting the life out of flying insects, even when they are near the food in your kitchen. Finally, the fourth lesson is that you might want to consider investing in one of those new can openers that does not leave sharp edges around the top of the container.

November 30

It might be just about time for you and your wife to prepare another big batch of *Sunday Gravy* for the whole local clan. This will require enough food to make certain that twelve to fifteen grown adults can get good and *stuffed* on fusilli, meatballs, braciole, sausages, and the gravy (pasta sauce to the average American) derived from the "secret recipe" your mother has handed down to you from untold prior generations. The entire enterprise of producing the meal will take the two of you, working with nearly no rest breaks, about six hours to complete. Thus, timing and teamwork are both of the essence here. Before the real work even begins, you will need to acquire the ingredients, make sure that you have an ample supply of all the various herbs and spices involved, an adequate supply of the necessary measuring devices, and enough clean bowls, pots, pans, and kitchen utensils to pull off a *major* culinary undertaking. This will involve a lot of work, and you cannot recall ever managing a similar feat without burning yourself, or getting covered with grease, sauce, wet meat, and shredded Parmesan cheese. Oh, but the food, the family, and the sated gustatory contentment when it is all over will be worth the pain and the effort. A meal that takes this long to make and to consume virtually guarantees that embarrassing stories will be told, hilarity will ensue, and the family will bond a bit through the intimacy of eating delicious food together. Perhaps you will go the extra mile and provide some cannoli for dessert. Those are going to have to come from the store. You do not enjoy the family's company enough to make cannoli *from scratch*.

December 1

Does it not seem to you that the dissolution of modernity continues both briskly and smoothly across the entirety of the Western World? For this, you can thank God, or perhaps the death of God, if you find yourself in a derisive mood. Apart from such moods, you can only look on and wonder what the people of the West can possibly be thinking or hoping. The sky actually *is* falling, metaphorically *for now*, but the order of the day seems to demand that everyone pretends not to notice. Does a civilization like this *deserve* to survive? This is, admittedly, a theme to which you return almost obsessively, but how are you to *avoid* doing so when the impending downfall of the West is so blindingly obvious and so pervasively unspoken? The lemmings are strolling casually toward the abyss, and the abyss edges also toward them. You cannot be the only one who perceives this. Indeed, others have *written epitaphs* for the Occident. Apart from a bit of occasional talk here and there, however, no one seems to be *doing* anything to forestall the implosion. Perhaps the rescue project is simply too large and too forbidding, and the average citizen feels paralyzed by the enormity of the task at hand. Then again, it may be that the average person is simply terrified of acknowledging the problem, because everyone knows about the epithets, shibboleths, and genuine dangers to life, limb, and livelihood that will rain down upon anyone who gives voice to concerns about the direction we are all headed. Finally, you cannot help but wonder just how many Western citizens actually welcome the destruction of their culture. A *people* that desire to be eradicated almost certainly *will* be.

December 2

Why would *anyone* expect white, heterosexual males to support, gleefully and *en masse*, the agenda that the Left designates with terms such as "multiculturalism" and "diversity"? Even those who sincerely value this agenda and long for the society that they hope it will produce, even *they* should recognize that there is precisely *no* upside in *any* of their designs for white, heterosexual males. How does one increase "diversity" within any institution without a commensurate decrease in the percentage of white, heterosexual males within that institution? Clearly, doing so is mathematically *impossible*. There is something perverse and masochistic about anyone embracing a worldview, or a value system, that aims at reducing the relative number, the relative power, and the relative influence of the very group with which the individual in question is guaranteed to be most closely identified by those who seek to ascend to *greater* relative numbers, power, and influence. White, heterosexual males in the West are being marginalized and displaced and, for some reason, they are expected to hop voluntarily aboard the very bandwagon that is intended to whisk them away to minority status. There are *never* going to be equity programs designed to make sure that future generations of white, heterosexual males do not face institutionalized discrimination. Whites will *not* be treated fairly in a multicultural future. Like lambs to the slaughter, you watch the dimwitted white liberals trudging toward a future for which their descendants will, quite rightfully, *despise* them. It is *very* odd to watch this unfold as you listen to the sheep bleating.

December 3

At the very beginning of *Ecclesiastes* we are told that, "everything is meaningless," however, you cannot help but suspect that this message is not to be taken literally or ingested in isolation from the rest of the text or without careful exegetical efforts directed at the remainder of the book of *Ecclesiastes* itself. When you ask, as does the author of *Ecclesiastes*, what people get from their various efforts, your first instinct is to turn inside and look for the answer to that question within your own consciousness, within your own understanding, and, if the term is tolerable, within your own *soul*. Of course, all kingdoms will ultimately fall. Of course, all persons will ultimately die. Of course, all human endeavors will, in the longest of long runs, come to *nothing* as far as the external world is concerned. The universe is very old, its future is, at least potentially, infinite, and the law of entropy guarantees that all life will be extinguished from the entirety of the cosmos. The distant future *will be* devoid of life, meaning, or purpose. From this, it does *not* follow that everything you do *now* is pointless or that you have no legitimate reasons to pursue such goals as are available to you and your extremely limited capacities. You are here for now, and you have no way of knowing how much longer you have to participate in the ongoing enterprise that is human life on this planet and in this cosmos. You *will* choose, whether you want to do so or not, a method of living the unique human life with which you have been entrusted by either God or chance, and you will live your life in a manner that either is or is not worth living. This is a *forced* option. There is no *third* alternative. Now, get to it.

December 4

Lunatics and liars are free to speak as much and as foolishly as they see fit to speak, but you are under no obligation to pretend that you take persons fitting that description seriously, and you need not feign respect for the human detritus that clamors most loudly and relentlessly. No member of the Flat Earth Society should be deprived of the right to freedom of speech or freedom of expression. Let each and every one of them say whatever they want to say about the topography of this planet, the relationship between it and the heavens, and any other topic that urges itself upon them. Do not, however, *degrade* yourself by pretending that you offer any of these quacks a "fair hearing," or by suggesting that anyone else ought to do so either. If the Communist Party of America wants to hold a convention or a conclave in your town, you are duty-bound to do nothing to attempt to prevent them from gathering, or to try to shut down the venue at which they plan to meet. They are absolutely free to make fools of themselves to their hearts' content, and other fools are free to join them, indulge in moronic chants, and wave flags bearing hammers, sickles, and pictures of their dimwitted heroes from dusk until dawn if that is what they wish to do. You are, however, as much of a fool as Marx ever was if you make believe that the "dictatorship of the proletariat" is a cause worthy of struggle and bloodshed, and you are as dishonest as Stalin if you profess not to have noticed that communism tends to culminate in totalitarian despotism, the eradication of individual rights and liberties, and that the entirety of this repugnant ideology is marinated in the blood of innocents. Freedom goes both ways.

December 5

All authoritarians, no matter where they claim to lie across the political or ideological spectrum, are corrupt, dishonest, and devoted to tyrannizing the public at any and all costs to everyone and everything other than their own interests. Authoritarianism *is* despotism. Those who wish to *boss* you, unless you have voluntarily contracted to allow them to do so under explicitly *limited* parameters, are your *enemies*, and it is foolish for you to treat them otherwise. Any person other than a police officer, a judge, or some other figure that you recognize as lawfully endowed with certain limited authority, or a person who is functioning within the legitimate confines of an assigned role that you voluntarily recognize as rightful, might just need the beating that is justly due to *all* bullies. At the very least, scoundrels who bark commands at you without justification have earned your contempt and scorn. Let all such sons of bitches suffer the well-deserved consequences of their domineering behavior. Those who wish to treat you as if you are a child had better be able to wield the power to *compel* you to conform to their directives, or they had better be prepared to encounter the "sweet reason of the mailed fist," or realize the crushing humiliation of the insistent aggressor who gets a brutal comeuppance handed to him in public. Those who appropriate the authority to dish out directives or commands to persons who have not agreed to obey, should probably recognize the danger of the enterprise in which they are engaged. You need not trouble yourself about bringing those hazards into *clear* focus for these villains.

December 6

Autumn and winter speak the truth. They are indicative of the way of things, and of the future of humanity. In autumn, all of those elements of the natural world that exhibit a life cycle begin to show signs of change and hints of the downhill slide toward their demise. There is a kind of beauty in this process of dying or slipping into hibernation, and the colors of the foliage draw tourists and ecstatic observers from all over the world. As the transition to winter occurs, natural things begin to fall away, and they begin to recede from view. Is this not a crude allegory for the culmination of every individual experience of the human condition? You are, at this point, at least in the beginning of the autumn phase of your life, and you have long had the sense that, for you, winter is not as far off in the distance as some might presume from looking at you. Noticing this, you cannot help but wonder what the current "season" of the *human race* might be. Some have suggested, though not in so many words, that humanity is still enjoying the acme of its springtime. From your perspective, this appears to be *very* unlikely. This may be a manifestation of narcissism or self-centeredness on your part, but you have the sense that the human race is at something like the same stage of its life cycle as you are. You have no desire to be *correct* in this assessment. You certainly do not crave the extinction of your species. Indeed, insofar as you care about the matter at all, you would prefer a long future for humanity. If you are brutally honest with yourself, however, you will find it difficult to deny that you perceive hints and suggestions of the autumn of the human race. Time will tell.

December 7

As the power of government expands, the autonomy of individual citizens contracts, and this is nearly a law of nature. No government in history has ever provided more opportunities for liberty and fewer restrictions on human behavior than would have been provided by the *absence of government*. Unfortunately, the evil that is government also appears to be necessary if any large collection of persons sharing a geographic region is to coexist in moderately peaceful and stable fashion. Of course, it might be worth asking whether peace and stability are worth the trade-off required by the persistent miasma that is government, but it is extremely unlikely that government shall be abolished from the face of the earth any time soon. Given that you reside in a place that is dominated by a governing class, and seeing as there are few, if any, places on the planet that are not dominated by some government or other, you need to consider the most rational and practical way to respond to this state of affairs. It might be worth your while to consider the option of simply *ignoring* the lying imbeciles who run your municipality, state, and nation. Unless and until some agent of the state kicks in your door, or stops your car, or confronts you as you walk down the street, you are free to pay them and their asinine pronouncements precisely *no* mind whatsoever. If legislation is passed prohibiting some activity that you enjoy, just keep engaging in that activity until some official tells you to stop or issues you a citation. If this happens you can either pay the penalty, fight it through the legal system, or continue ignoring the "powers" of the state until you are *forced* to acknowledge them. At *that* point, the real fun begins.

December 8

You are not convinced that you have the capacity to be as disingenuous as is apparently required to function successfully as a politician. You have, at long last, *ceased* to be amazed at the lies that politicians are willing to tell at the drop of a hat, and the brazenness with which they reflexively flout expectations of minimal decency in open, public discourse. As it happens, most of the citizens seem content to keep voting for these pathetic hucksters and, therefore, they get precisely what they deserve, and precisely what they cause themselves to get. When you imagine yourself running for public office, the rumination lasts about two seconds before you begin to get that nauseous feeling that you get when you see someone eating soggy eggplant. You cannot be quite certain what you will do if you live long enough to retire, but you can be very certain that running for office is *not* part of your future. Posturing is not a skill you have developed, nor is it an activity in which you enjoy engaging. The political sphere has degenerated into a mud pit, if not a cesspool, and those who voluntarily wade into it, knowing full well that they are going to be covered in filth immediately, thereby reveal their true character. Politicians are willing to cover themselves in filth and fling feces at everyone in their vicinity if they believe that doing so will enable them to ascend to a position of power. What kind of person values political position, and the power that comes with it, more than he or she values decency, integrity, and the ability to tell the truth without massaging "the message" to make it palatable to a largely ill-informed public? Evidently, politicians are such persons. Thus, *you* are no politician.

December 9

When you were young, you had the desire to be accepted by your peers and even maintained hopes of being one of the "cool kids." In retrospect, you realize that this was absurd on multiple levels. Your peer group was always composed overwhelmingly of tedious dullards with nothing to say, and mindless conformists who are willing to say and to do just about *anything* that the rest of the group expected or demanded of them. Why in the world would you want to be embraced by such a motley crew aboard a sprawling ship of fools? As for your youthful aspiration to be cool, you now recognize that this condition is utterly incompatible with your nature, and also that the condition of "being cool" is about as pathetic an ambition as you can imagine. It is a bit like striving to become a parasite or a malignancy that will trouble its host until both host and bloodsucker *die*. At this stage of life, you shun and spurn the company of the general public, and especially avoid association with "cool people" as if they are all infected with some form of the plague and are bent on transmitting the disease to you at all costs. Indeed, it seems that the mob of humankind *does* carry something like the moral, intellectual, and emotional equivalent of an *infection*, not to mention various *literal* diseases, and you cannot help but suspect that those who suffer from the most acute forms of maladies of character *are*, in fact, desperate to metastasize and spread their afflictions as far and as wide as they are able. Society is not so very different from a sprawling leper colony within which the phenomenon of leprosy is still a secret.

December 10

If you ever find that you are beset with the feeling of helplessness, remind yourself that you are being irrational and that your mental discipline is inadequate to the task of governing your cognitive states properly. Are you unable to desire only those conditions that you are able to produce simply by deciding that it is to be so? Are you, for example, incapable of deciding that you will not lie and then acting in accordance with that decision? If you *are* able to reason, and conduct yourself in conformity with the dictates of reason, where does your experience of helplessness come from? If, on the other hand, you are *not* able to govern your thoughts and your subsequent conduct in a manner that accords with the prescriptions of reason, then either your psychological or moral discipline is deficient, and you are in need of more rigorous and more careful training in these areas. Perhaps your feelings of helplessness attach to conditions of the external world, and you are frustrated that events "out there" do not transpire as you wish them to. What sort of childish, irrational nonsense is any wish of this nature? Are you not aware that you have no control over events beyond the direction of your will? The proposition that you cannot control events that lie beyond your control is a fairly simple tautology. What kind of imbecile insists that events beyond his control *must*, nonetheless, unfold in a manner that is pleasing to his whims and desires? This is a failure of rationality, and an embarrassing lapse of the simplest application of basic mental discipline. Do *not* allow yourself to become emotionally dependent upon any condition that does not conform to your will. Thus, the feeling of helplessness is dispelled.

December 11

Introversion is not a character defect, it is not a behavioral flaw, and it is not a condition standing in need of extirpation. When you feel the need to be reclusive for a little while, or even a longer while, you need not become concerned that there is something wrong with you, or anything deficient about the time spent alone and apart from others. Your life is not a movie or a staged production that has value only insofar as some audience or other finds it interesting or entertaining. If all other persons on the planet disappeared five seconds from now, you would be shocked and baffled, but your life would not lose all meaning or purpose, you would not be inclined to commit suicide for lack of company, and you are fairly confident that you would adapt, over time, to this new circumstance. The ability to associate with others is, at least in most cases, overrated. Aristotle claimed that human beings are inherently social, or "political," beings, and he may well have been correct about humanity at large, and he may have had a point about the characteristics that separate your species from many others, or he may not, but this does not mean that *all* persons are, at *all* times, inclined to socialize with others, or even that *all* persons have a general psychological and emotional need for human contact. There have been hermits throughout human history, they have existed in nearly every culture and every inhabited area of the globe, and there is no particular reason to believe that their lives have been miserable or unworthy of living. You are not a hermit (yet), but you have no difficulty understanding why one might *choose* a life of solitude.

December 12

All of the attempts to constrain you or compel you to behave as others would have you behave, or to influence you to believe what others would have you believe, or to cause you to value what others would have you value, should prove to be of no avail to those who wish to command you. If you are concerned about such attempts, then you reveal weakness of character on *your* part. Who is possessed of the paranormal ability to reach directly into your mind and alter your beliefs through sheer fiat of the clairvoyant's will? If such powers are not mere fiction, then you might want to consider developing your mystical abilities. If, on the other hand, no one possesses that ability to seize control of your mind, or the capacity to insert beliefs and values into your consciousness without your consent and complicity, then what is the source of your worry about those who wish to influence you through their words, deeds, implied threats, or their manipulations of the mob? You have nothing to fear from those who fancy themselves commanders of the culture, or those who deem themselves manipulators of media. At what point did you come to believe that you are compelled to follow along with cultural evolution that does not accord with your values? Let the culture adopt every form of depravity that captures its imagination. What do you care for that? Let the media spew their lies and their imaginary narratives to the gullible public. As long as *you* are *not* part of the credulous masses, then you should not be taken in by their propaganda. If others are fooled, and some *will* be fooled, then you are free to pity them if you wish. Remain untroubled by nonsense.

December 13

About two thousand years ago, Seneca complained that philosophers too often concerned themselves with teaching students how to win debates, and exhibited too little concern with teaching and, perhaps more importantly, *showing* their pupils how to go about living a noble and flourishing life. In this regard, not a great deal has changed over the last couple of millennia. Indeed, if anything, the situation is worse today than it was during Seneca's era. Philosophers in the 21st Century exhibit *far* more concern with tenure, remuneration, and ideological indoctrination of their students than they ever display in the pursuit of virtue or the exhortation to noble conduct. Do not pretend that you have not been guilty of the same type of inversion of values that you point out among your contemporaries, either. It is not as if you insisted on a "virtuous conduct clause" during the most recent contract negotiations, and you certainly pay attention to the direct deposit notifications from your bank at the end of each month. Even Seneca can be suspected of a bit of hypocrisy where such matters are concerned. He enjoyed significant material wealth and political power, up until that minor "misunderstanding" between he and Nero that culminated in his compulsory suicide, and there is no record of him donating all of his riches to charity over the course of his adult life. There are, it would seem, *very* few moral exemplars in the history of your profession. Perhaps this is somewhat less troubling given the general dearth of saints across the history of humanity. Most of the *literal* saints were, truth be told, not terribly exemplary. That, however, is no excuse.

December 14

Does the author conjure the words into being and express them in accordance with the author's will, or do the words assert themselves and express themselves through the author as a medium? Are those two possibilities mutually exclusive, or are those just two descriptions of the same process? Not so long ago, you would have regarded questions of this type as hopelessly pretentious, and you would have laughed at anyone posing such inquiries. In all candor, you are not certain that you do not still regard these as laughably pretentious questions. It is, nonetheless, true that you have written many pages filled with words over the years and, upon reading what you had written, found that you were more than just a little surprised by the thoughts you found expressed on the page. Indeed, it is not at all uncommon for you to have *no recollection* of having written the words on a page that you pick up and look at just a few days after the writing occurred. You have actually had the somewhat unnerving experience of listening to a reader quote your words back to you and not recognizing those words or even experiencing them as "ringing a bell" for you. As you have never been diagnosed with multiple personality disorder, or any other dissociative condition, this phenomenon is at least a little bit peculiar. You have written pages of text while also holding a conversation or listening to music, and found that you had to go back and read the page to find out what you had been writing about. *Where* are the words coming from if you are not conscious of producing them? Perhaps there is a homunculus in your head that does the real writing on your behalf. If so, he still gets none of the royalty checks.

December 15

Bodyweight exercises provide benefits to your health, physical well-being, and cardiovascular functionality, but they also provide the additional advantage of understanding your body's strengths, limitations, and various subtleties of proprioceptive experience. In other words, you get to understand the intricacies of the feeling of *inhabiting* your body that you have not noticed when you engaged in other forms of strength and cardiovascular conditioning. Performing many different variations of push-ups, for example, and adding in isometric holds, or manipulations of your shoulders, back, legs, and neck at different stages of the push-up process, gives you insight into the delicate relationships between these various joints, ligaments, tendons, and the enchainment of motions involving these related parts of yourself. As you engage in a variety of lower body exercises, you learn a great deal about the manner in which engaging your quadriceps tends to affect the gluteus, the hamstrings, the abdominals, and the calf muscles. It is interesting how infrequently you are fully aware of the many intricate connections between the various parts of your body, and the surprising connections that exist between the parts that are not adjacent to each other. You have, for example, noticed activation occurring within the muscles of your neck and upper back while you are engaged in lunges and pistol squats that, to the untrained eye and the untutored brain, would appear to be exertions having about as little to do with your neck and back as could be the case with *any* exercise. This is *not* a trivial observation. You must understand how a tool works if you are to deploy it properly.

December 16

Loudmouthed men who like to talk about how dangerous they are, and like to play peacock when they believe that there is an opportunity to intimidate someone or impress a stranger, these men are generally insecure and desperate for attention. It may be that every man carries a bit of that kind of baggage with him, and it may be that some are immune to those failings, but those who *constantly* resort to shows of bravado and machismo are genuinely defective creatures. If you hope to identify the most dangerous man in the room, or to determine the presence or absence of a threat in your environment, it is not particularly advisable to focus on the men making the most noise or going furthest out of their way to appear to be menacing or to pose as hooligans. It is probably a better use of your attention to look for signs of men carrying weapons, indications of *groups* of men attempting to surround you or flank you, and evidence of special training in the military or in other combative vocations. Unless it is absolutely unavoidable, you do not want to find yourself engaged against a man armed with a gun, knife, or bludgeon. Even if you are similarly armed, nothing good will come of that altercation. As for members of the military, you ought to respect them enough that you would never intentionally behave in a disrespectful manner toward any of the warriors who provide the umbrella of safety and security that you enjoy, and if there should be a misunderstanding between yourself and a member of the military, you would be well served to offer to buy him a drink rather than offering to fight him. If you *must*, then fight to win, but try to avoid this eventuality altogether.

December 17

Pandering is an ignoble endeavor, and those who engage in it are *never* to be trusted with power or political office. Thus, it follows that *all* politicians are never to be trusted with power or political office. On the surface, this might appear to produce something of a quandary, and perhaps a situation bordering upon paradox, but none of that is of any special concern given that your nation and its culture are, at this point, nothing more than ongoing exercises in absurdity. A society that is best understood as a cautionary example, or a specimen of a civilization in its death throes, should not quiver or cower at the prospect of merely continuing to elect untrustworthy charlatans to continue the corruption that is campaigning and governing this moribund enterprise. Anyone who enters the arena of democratic politics is tacitly admitting willingness to say just about anything that the befuddled masses insist upon hearing during the election cycle in question, and that same politician will *always* prove willing to assert an utterly contrary proposition or completely incompatible platform in the very next election cycle. Any politician taking a principled, immutable stand on unyielding moral ground will be separated from office the moment that the fickle, depraved public changes its mind and decides that yesterday's virtues are today's vices, or that the absolute foundations of their moral beliefs are, in fact, nothing more than passing fads that they are willing to trade away like baseball cards or obsolete appliances. In a democracy, the people always get what they deserve. For this reason, democracy is a hopeless system for governing a nation.

December 18

You encountered a wheelchair-bound man struggling to exit a coffee shop this morning, and your first impulse was to open the door for him and help lift his chair over the ridge across the base of the doorframe so that he would be clear of the obstacle and able to proceed with his day. Not so many years ago, there would have been *no* problem and no complaint even considered if you had simply walked up, surveyed the situation, and said, "Hey, let me give you a hand," as you proceeded to open the door, tilt the chair slightly, and push it an inch or two so as to assist the man in exiting the building that he was clearly attempting to leave. As things currently stand, however, in a cultural climate that has become so besotted with the disease that some misguided people refer to as "political correctness" or as "sensitivity," you stood dumbly watching this man struggle needlessly and, only after nearly thirty seconds of witnessing this futile exertion, you finally asked, "Sir, would it be okay if I helped you with this?" As the wheelchair-bound gentleman was a generation older than yourself, he replied, "Yeah, what took you so long?" and you both laughed at the absurdity of the question. Of course he wanted you to help him! The poor bastard was stuck partway through a door, and he was unable to dislodge himself. What the hell else would any minimally decent, able-bodied human being do but offer the guy a slight lift and nudge to help him out? You freed him from his predicament in approximately two seconds. The fact that you hesitated to do so is an unbecoming comment on you, or on the culture at large, or both. There is perversion in this.

December 19

When you play Scrabble®, it is generally inadvisable to hold the "U" tile for more than a few turns in the anticipation that you will acquire the "Q" tile. Beginners and casual players of the game often commit this error, and it is usually attributable to the fact that they are unaware that "QI" qualifies as an officially legitimate word, according to the explicitly stated rules of the game. It is also unwise to retain the "Q" tile into the latter stages of the game because, as the board fills up, there will be fewer and fewer opportunities to form a word containing the "Q" tile that is any longer than two or three spaces. If the tiles are running low, and you are holding the "Q," just form the word "QI" or "QUA" if the opportunity presents itself, and be done with it. If you hold out in the hope of getting your "Q" onto a "triple letter" square, or into a word that crosses a "double word" square, you risk having to "eat" the "Q" at the end of play, which incurs a penalty of twenty points for your failure to play the "Q" sitting on your rack. This is an embarrassing, annoying, and unsightly state of affairs. Somewhere in *Leviticus* there must be an injunction citing this condition as "an abomination before the Lord," or threatening punishment that will be meted out to seven generations of the sinner's descendants. Well, there *should* be something like that *somewhere* in scripture or, at the very least, in the stated policies of some online forum devoted to aficionados of the game. In any event, if your understanding of this issue does not surpass that of the average novice or casual player, you probably ought to limit yourself to crossword puzzles. Amen.

December 20

Always leave *at least* a twenty percent tip any time you dine at a restaurant or get drinks at a bar. If you cannot afford to leave a tip that large, you probably have no business going out to dinner. Anyone who has not waited tables is likely to underappreciate how difficult, frustrating, and injurious that job tends to be. Many customers are, frankly, obnoxious, imperious jackasses trying to show off for their friends or family, and utterly absurd complaints about the food and the service are *far* more common than many people realize. A *lot* of people who should *never* be permitted to eat at a restaurant insist, nonetheless, on eating at restaurants, diners, and related establishments. Waiting tables *sucks*. Furthermore, labor is often simply underappreciated in contemporary Western society. It may be underappreciated elsewhere as well, as you have witnessed some incidents in Guatemala and Peru that constituted egregious displays of poor form on the part of the customer, but you cannot claim to have sufficient experience in those places to render broad generalizations with any confidence. It is also worth noting that wait staff tend to remember good tippers, and they are likely to offer better service and special perks to customers who are reliably generous tippers. That is *not* the morally justifiable reason to tip well, unless you subscribe to some form of ethical egoism, but it is worth recognizing the additional, but morally unnecessary, benefit of leaving a tip that demonstrates an appreciation of the labors devoted to making your experience an enjoyable meal. Remember that having the opportunity to eat at a restaurant is not available to everyone. Spread the wealth a little.

December 21

The next time you find that you are in the grip of some unpleasant psychological or emotional state, you might try a bit of fairly simple *cognitive restructuring*. Although this is a bit of an oversimplification, this practice, or process, involves considering the circumstances that you are experiencing from a perspective that will leave you less susceptible to the emotional states that you wish to avoid or dispel. It is crucial to note that this practice does not involve, or *should* not involve, lying to yourself or ignoring any salient portion of the experience at hand. You will do yourself no favors if you insist that your house has *not* burned to the ground as you stand looking at the smoldering rubble that used to be your home. *Lying* does not help. What you can do, however, is to note that your initial, reflexive response to the circumstances with which you are confronted need not be *determinative* of your assessment of those conditions upon careful, rationally-guided reflection on the matter. Suppose you *are* looking at the smoldering rubble of your house. One thing to note is that *you* are *still alive*, and the world has many materials for replacing the destroyed home with a new structure. Whatever you may have lost, it is worth remembering that you were eventually going to lose all material belongings sooner or later anyway. You cannot take it with you when you *die*, after all. This challenge offers you an opportunity to learn a bit about which persons genuinely care about your welfare and which ones are merely fair-weather friends. What appears to be a "disaster" can often become an opportunity. Do not be *delusional*, but do not be a *wimp* either.

December 22

Is there something that you need to get off your chest? If so, the way you are feeling is *your* fault entirely and *you* must either suffer this condition or you must do something to rid yourself of the unpleasantness that confronts you. If you have something to say that is worth saying, then open your mouth, or put pen to paper, or get your fingertips on a keyboard, and unburden yourself of whatever it is that seems to be troubling you. On the other hand, if the thing that you need to "get off your chest" is still *on* your chest because you are unable or unwilling to give voice to it, then stop feeling sorry for yourself and start pursuing some new goal worthy of your time and effort. You simply have *no* excuse for complaining, even within the confines of your own consciousness, about *anything* that you are currently experiencing. What constrains you apart from *yourself*? What compels your silence apart from some kind of reticence that originates within *you*? Surely, you are not going to attribute your actions, or inactions, to parties or powers beyond the control of your will, your faculty of deliberation and choice, or your capacity to direct your own utterances and actions. If you have something that you wish to say, something that you need to say, or something that you believe you are obligated to say, then you are able to say it and you can attribute your silence to nothing other than *your own* weakness. Not to belabor the point, but what exactly is your problem, pal? Stop the internal bellyaching and say your piece, or swallow hard and accept the fact that you lack the requisite wherewithal to lay yourself bare before the world.

December 23

Why did it take Pharaoh so long to recognize the power and indomitability of the Hebrew God? The story from *Exodus* may or may not be historically accurate, and the events recounted therein can be disputed and debated by persons who have religious commitments and those who lack such commitments, but as the narrative is concerned, and as an opportunity to indulge in character analysis is concerned, the question of Pharaoh's reticence is worthy of consideration. *How many* miraculous assaults upon his people, his kingdom, and his authority does this guy need to experience before he realizes that he is overmatched and it is in his interests to acknowledge his helplessness before this unprecedented power. Would you not have given in and let Moses' people go after the sixth or seventh plague? Of course, in Pharaoh's defense, God kept "hardening his heart," and telling Moses that was why Pharaoh would not let the people go, so it is not entirely clear where the blame is to be laid for the extended captivity of Israel, but between the frogs, and the locusts, and the hail, you would think that Pharaoh would let the people go to worship their God as Moses had requested. Perhaps the moral of the story is that any government official who tries to use the power of the state to prevent people from worshipping God in their own way thereby runs the risk of elevating *himself* to a position rivaling God, and that tends to lead to unfortunate consequences for everyone concerned. There may or may not be a God, but it is fairly clear that a *mere man*, even a Pharaoh, King, or Emperor, does *not* qualify as a deity.

December 24

Going to the shopping mall today can be explained by masochism, insanity, or perhaps just by poor planning. Not only are the shopping malls going to be packed today and tonight, but they are going to be filled with people who are either insane or desperate because they have forgotten about Christmas until now, or they have been too busy to get their shopping done until today. Persons meeting any of those descriptions are going to function as beasts of prey, and if you voluntarily go to the place that they are going *en masse*, you must be either a masochist or someone who has planned so poorly for Christmas that you are willing to subject yourself to the indignities and the chaos that you know will attend this trip to the purchasing complex. If you allow yourself to be relegated to this circumstance, you are less than a hop, skip, and a jump removed from the lunatics who camp out overnight, in some cases they do this for *several* nights, just to be among the first consumers to purchase the newest technological doohickey, or just to be among the first to acquire tickets to the latest superhero movie, or just to be among the first to enter the shopping mall on "Black Friday" after Thanksgiving, knowing full well that people die and get beaten to pulverized mash at shopping malls on Black Friday every year in large cities around the United States. What is it about the holiday season that triggers both the most acute acquisitive urges among some people, and the basest impulses to both do violence and subject one's body to arenas in which violence is most likely to occur? Clearly, this can only be explained by reference to the old dictum that God moves in mysterious ways. Maybe that fails here.

December 25

This is the day that all of Christendom celebrates the birth of Jesus Christ, the Savior and Messiah. There is no particular reason to believe that this character from the *Bible* was actually born on this day of the year, but there *is* something pleasing about snow on Christmas, so you need not harp on the arbitrary selection of this day as opposed to any other. You will readily admit that you do not know whether God exists or not, and you will even more readily admit that, if God *does* exist, you do not know which, if any, of the Abrahamic traditions has come closest to describing the nature of the Almighty, or revealing the proper way to understand His commands, or why it is so important for God's true acolytes to wear funny hats, but you certainly *hope* that there is a God, and admire faith that exhibits itself in noble and admirable works. Of course, there is *some* disagreement about what noble, admirable, and pious behavior looks like, and there have been a handful of minor conflicts about such matters throughout history. For this reason, you cannot condemn unbelievers, or even declare that they are wrong to reject religious belief, to distrust "people of faith," or to dismiss all religious traditions as superstitions that engender violence, oppression, and irrational hatred. As it happens, your best guess is that the Jews are probably closest to telling the grand narrative correctly, but you were not born a Jew, and you have not converted because you figure that God would have *made* you Jewish if he had wanted you to be a member of *The Chosen People*. Perhaps your lot is to be one of the "righteous among the nations." Perhaps it is all just made up. You really do not know. Merry Christmas!

December 26

You are told that the *Gospel of Mark* has had an ending appended to it that was not part of the original text and probably was not written by the author of the rest of the book. Were you considering any other composition, whether a book, a play, a movie script, or whatever, would you not assume that someone, for some reason or other, thought that the original ending did not *work*? What might it be about the original ending that might have been regarded as problematic by the first people to read the original text? In Hollywood, it seems that producers and studio heads are drawn, disproportionately, to happy endings. If the ending is not "up," the audience will be disappointed, word will get around, and the movie will be a flop. That, in any event, appears to be a reasonable synopsis of the concern that leads to most Hollywood films culminating in happy endings. Considering this particular Gospel, what about the original text might have engendered concern about the ending causing disappointment among those comprising the early "audience" for the book? It is not as if you are referring to a romantic comedy in which the lovers do not end up living happily ever after. The "problem" in *Mark* appears to be that, although Jesus has risen from the dead, the women who receive this news from the "angelic figure" at His tomb respond by *fleeing in terror*. The angel told them to go and spread the word of the resurrection, but they "told no one" because they were scared to death. *Where* is the story supposed to go from there? Jesus has conquered death, but the first people to find out about it responded by succumbing to terror, and they, therefore, "told no one." That is *not* an "up" ending.

December 27

You woke up this morning because you heard your dog barking and snarling in a manner that indicated some type of acute concern on the dog's part. Shortly after waking, you became aware of the experience of having heard a loud sound while you were still asleep. There had been a crashing sound in the dream you were experiencing and, although you cannot remember much about the content of the dream, it seemed to you, after hearing the dog's barking, that the crashing sound was probably caused by an event in the real world outside of your dream state. This chain of inferences occurred, from *your* perspective at least, in something like the space of a heartbeat. Before your conscious mind caught up with your bodily response to all of this, you were already on your feet, and in your peripheral vision, you could tell that your wife was sitting up in bed. At about this point in the affair, you became aware that you were clutching something in your right hand, and you also experienced, almost simultaneously with this awareness, a collision of your left shoulder with the door to your bedroom. You realized that you were moving toward the front door of your house, and you surmised that you were doing so either because the crashing sound came from that direction, or because that is the most likely place that an intruder might try to exploit for entry into the house. Your trip down the hallway is nothing more than a blur in your memory, but the experience of opening the front door and looking through the external metal barrier is a bit clearer. You looked down because you perceived something moving. It was a cat.

December 28

Once again, a stranger asked you *where you served*. This has become a fairly common occurrence since you started shaving your head, and you suspect that your tattoos might have something to do with the apparent presumption underpinning this question. In the past, you found some jollity in responding, "Pizza Hut," but that gag became stale many years ago. Although you were never able to serve in the military because you destroyed your knee on your eighteenth birthday and, evidently, the military powers that be are disinclined to offer a commission to some guy with a weight-bearing joint that is severely compromised. You really cannot blame them, but you like to believe that you would have made a passable military man. There *are* reasons to be suspicious about this, however. The anxiety and depression disorder might not have been the kind of mental illness to comport conveniently with the battlefield or with other arenas of military responsibility. Since you are *both* slightly crazy and vaguely disabled, your sense that you might have made a career in the military is, probably, not supportable by any evidence you might try to point to in the actual world. Nonetheless, you derive a bit of satisfaction from the fact that strangers periodically assume that you served your country in one or another branch of the armed forces. A number of them have leapt to the conclusion that you were in the Marines. That is an even *more* satisfying compliment. *Could* you have made a go of it as a United States Marine? What is the harm in allowing your ego to believe that it is *possible*? A boy *can* dream.

December 29

There is something ineffable about love, and about your experience of it, is there not? You know that Aristotle defined love as "willing the good of the other," and there is certainly wisdom in that but, as a *definition*, that quip simply will not do. You are aware that you love people who have long since passed away, but it is unclear how you are supposed to go about *willing the good* of dead people. You are also aware of loving ideas, theories, music, and art, but it is less than clear to you what it means to *will the good* of inanimate objects or of entities that are neither conscious nor sentient. The *ineffable* element of your experience of love may be the most salient and most satisfying part of the entire phenomenon. Indeed, the attempt to offer a set of necessary and sufficient conditions for an experience to qualify as *love* probably constitutes an effort in futility, if not an outright bit of travesty. Imagine the attempt to *define* what you feel for your wife. Why should anyone expect mere words to be adequate to the task? It is unwise to presume that language, which has evolved in rough, scattershot, slapdash fashion, and has been used throughout *most* of human history primarily for purposes such as alerting others to predators, distinguishing between edible plants and others that are deadly, and indicating some tasty animal's trail to other men carrying spears, will be adequate to meet the challenge of communicating what *love* is. Perhaps there is a bit too much talk about what love is, and a bit too little of its proper enactment. In any event, although you may struggle to *define* it, you have learned to know it when you *feel* it. Understanding *that* is *more* than enough for you.

December 30

Be certain that you do not trade away your decency or your honor in the pursuit of anything for which you have witnessed all too many politicians, celebrities, attorneys, salespersons, academics, and media members exchange theirs (if they ever *had* anything to trade). No amount of money, fame, or power will ever purchase you a *scintilla* of virtue. At his trial, Socrates mentioned his practice of challenging his fellow Athenians, and asking them to defend their obsessive pursuit of wealth and power, though they exhibited *no* concern for acquiring wisdom or embodying virtue. He found no one who could provide a rational justification for living human lives in this manner. These were the lives that Socrates described as "unexamined" and "not worth living" for rational beings. It is one thing for a pig to pursue pleasure as an end in itself. What more, after all, is a swine to do? If *you*, however, aim to make your life an endeavor that amounts to something more, something with higher and nobler goals than those to which a *boar* attains, then do not wallow in filth or search for trifles and truffles. In other words, do not make a pig of yourself. If you admire the example set by Socrates, then you are obligated to do your level best to emulate his pursuit of wisdom. Socrates was willing to *die* rather than give up this quest. What are *you* willing to sacrifice to the endeavor of ennobling your character and accumulating such wisdom as your limitations can manage? If you do *not* value material things more than you do the pursuit of wisdom, then one quick glance around your home should be sufficient to convince you that you have a *lot* of explaining to do. An expensive sty is still a pigpen.

December 31

Have you come full circle on this New Year's Eve, or are you merely back where you started? In the former case, you should be able to make the sincere claim that you have learned valuable lessons over the course of this year, and that you have improved your life, your character, and your relationships with various elements of the world around you. *Can* you make this claim with a straight face? In the event that you are just back where you started, it is incumbent upon you to investigate what went wrong, how you failed to improve, and what you intend to do about it in the coming year. Do *not* declare some New Year's "resolution," as this practice has become no more admirable since you started your current project. What, if anything, have you learned? How, if at all, have you improved your character or your understanding? What *have* you been doing with this year? Whatever your answers to those questions, the conclusion draws near. The hour is almost upon you, and *nothing* will forestall its advance. Time has never waited patiently for you to learn your lessons, and as the years pass you by, they wear away your future, and they erode your hopes that you might make something admirable of your life. It is not only *this year* that fades away, is it? You are older now than you have ever been, and death is closer now than ever before. You do not know *how* closely your death approaches, but you know that you come nearer to dying with each passing moment. It is, indeed, getting close to midnight, is it not? While others prepare for midnight kisses, you stand wondering what this "celebration" *really* means. It is *all* slipping away from you. The countdown continues. Happy New Year?

Other Books by this Author

Meditations on Self-Discipline and Failure: Stoic Exercise for
Mental Fitness (O-Books, ISBN 978 1 78535 587 5)
A Life Worth Living: Meditations on God, Death and Stoicism
(O-Books, ISBN 978 1 78904 304 4)
You Die at the End: Meditations on Mortality and the Human
Condition (O-Books, ISBN 978 1 78904 393 8)

BOOKS

SPIRITUALITY

O is a symbol of the world, of oneness and unity; this eye represents knowledge and insight. We publish titles on general spirituality and living a spiritual life. We aim to inform and help you on your own journey in this life.
If you have enjoyed this book, why not tell other readers by posting a review on your preferred book site?

The Holy Spirit's Interpretation of the New Testament
A Course in Understanding and Acceptance
Regina Dawn Akers
Following on from the strength of *A Course In Miracles*, NTI
teaches us how to experience the love and oneness of God.
Paperback: 978-1-84694-085-9 ebook: 978-1-78099-083-5

The Message of A Course In Miracles
A translation of the Text in plain language
Elizabeth A. Cronkhite
A translation of *A Course in Miracles* into plain, everyday
language for anyone seeking inner peace. The companion
volume, *Practicing A Course In Miracles*, offers practical lessons
and mentoring.
Paperback: 978-1-84694-319-5 ebook: 978-1-84694-642-4

Your Simple Path
Find Happiness in every step
Ian Tucker
A guide to helping us reconnect with what is really important in
our lives.
Paperback: 978-1-78279-349-6 ebook: 978-1-78279-348-9

365 Days of Wisdom
Daily Messages To Inspire You Through The Year
Dadi Janki
Daily messages which cool the mind, warm the heart and guide
you along your journey.
Paperback: 978-1-84694-863-3 ebook: 978-1-84694-864-0

Body of Wisdom
Women's Spiritual Power and How it Serves
Hilary Hart
Bringing together the dreams and experiences of women across
the world with today's most visionary spiritual teachers.
Paperback: 978-1-78099-696-7 ebook: 978-1-78099-695-0

Dying to Be Free
From Enforced Secrecy to Near Death to True Transformation
Hannah Robinson
After an unexpected accident and near-death experience, Hannah
Robinson found herself radically transforming her life, while a
remarkable new insight altered her relationship with her father, a
practising Catholic priest.
Paperback: 978-1-78535-254-6 ebook: 978-1-78535-255-3

The Ecology of the Soul
A Manual of Peace, Power and Personal Growth for Real People
in the Real World
Aidan Walker
Balance your own inner Ecology of the Soul to regain your
natural state of peace, power and wellbeing.
Paperback: 978-1-78279-850-7 ebook: 978-1-78279-849-1

Not I, Not other than I
The Life and Teachings of Russel Williams
Steve Taylor, Russel Williams
The miraculous life and inspiring teachings of one of the World's
greatest living Sages.
Paperback: 978-1-78279-729-6 ebook: 978-1-78279-728-9

On the Other Side of Love
A woman's unconventional journey towards wisdom
Muriel Maufroy
When life has lost all meaning, what do you do?   .
Paperback: 978-1-78535-281-2 ebook: 978-1-78535-282-9

Practicing A Course In Miracles
A translation of the Workbook in plain language, with mentor's
notes
Elizabeth A. Cronkhite
The practical second and third volumes of The Plain-Language
A Course In Miracles.
Paperback: 978-1-84694-403-1 ebook: 978-1-78099-072-9

Quantum Bliss
The Quantum Mechanics of Happiness, Abundance, and Health
George S. Mentz
Quantum Bliss is the breakthrough summary of success and
spirituality secrets that customers have been waiting for.
Paperback: 978-1-78535-203-4 ebook: 978-1-78535-204-1

The Upside Down Mountain
Mags MacKean
A must-read for anyone weary of chasing success and happiness
– one woman's inspirational journey swapping the uphill slog for
the downhill slope.
Paperback: 978-1-78535-171-6 ebook: 978-1-78535-172-3

Your Personal Tuning Fork
The Endocrine System
Deborah Bates
Discover your body's health secret, the endocrine system, and
'twang' your way to sustainable health!
Paperback: 978-1-84694-503-8 ebook: 978-1-78099-697-4

※

Readers of ebooks can buy or view any of these bestsellers by
clicking on the live link in the title. Most titles are published
in paperback and as an ebook. Paperbacks are available in
traditional bookshops. Both print and ebook formats are
available online.

Find more titles and sign up to our readers' newsletter at
http://www.johnhuntpublishing.com/mind-body-spirit

Follow us on Facebook at https://www.facebook.com/OBooks/
and Twitter at https://twitter.com/obooks